Murderous

Marxism

William Johnson

Copyright © 2025 by William Johnson

All rights reserved. No part of this publication may be reproduced, distributed, or transmitted in any form or by any means, including photocopying, recording, or other electronic or mechanical methods, without the prior written permission of the publisher, except in the case of brief quotations embodied in critical reviews and certain other noncommercial uses permitted by copyright law.

Library of Congress Control Number: 2025923498

Published by Hemingway Publishers

Cover design by Hemingway Publishers

ISBN: Printed in the United States

Dedication

To my loving wife, Cathy, who encouraged me to take the steps to write this book.

FOREWORD

The foreword explains why I am writing this book. The second chapter explains Marxism and the brutality committed in the name of this political philosophy. I also look at Marxism, the death tolls of Communism, and make comparisons to other acts of mass murder throughout the ages. I will cover the Soviet Union and Eastern Europe. Communist comparisons will cover aspects of Afghanistan, China, North Korea, Cambodia, Cuba, Sendero de Luminoso, and Ethiopia.

Table of Contents

Dedication iii

Forward iv

Chapter 1: The black hole of history! 11

Chapter 2: Overview of the Soviet Union 1918-1991 30

Chapter 3: Post War WWII: Communist actions in Eastern Europe. 190

Chapter 4: If Communism is not that frightening, why did so many people flee Marxist regimes? 256

Chapter 5: Fake News: Bias reporting, and censorship of communist brutality and famines. 262

Chapter 6: Communist countries wage war against each other 275

Chapter 7: Conclusions 284

Bibliography 287

Printed Newspaper and magazines. 295

Videos 296

Online editions 297

Online News sources and articles. 300

Online Articles, without an author's name. 314

Foreword: Why this book?

Marxist history: Communism's brutal past is being suppressed.

There have been many books written on the history of Communism, but these texts tend to be long and tedious to read. This work is more of a straightforward, quick read, written to inform the average person about the crimes of Communism. (For sources, please read the notes at the end of the Foreword.)

The Soviet Union will be the focus of this book, but I have also included Eastern Europe, which fell under the control of the Soviet Union after World War II. The book also contains Communist Comparisons and Points to Ponder. Communist Comparisons draw upon the similarities between Marxist totalitarian regimes. For instance, communists claim to be the guardians of the worker class, yet they have set into motion the most devastating famines in world history. Their deliberate actions starved to death tens of millions of people. There are numerous fiendish similarities between these ruling systems: mass terror, promoting hatred, the destruction of faith, secret police, and concentration camps.

Additionally, some of the communist comparisons are connected to contemporary subject matter: WOKE controversies, Vladimir Putin, and the Communist Party USA (CPUSA). Furthermore, most do not realize that the Nazis copied Soviet methods of repression. Points to ponder are small nuggets of history that offer a unique take on a certain aspect of the historical subject matter.

Skeptics might challenge the facts, but footnotes and sources tend to stop them cold in their tracks. I frequently identify my source in the text. Yet, hardcore supporters of Communism will adamantly insist that the facts in this book are false or misleading. This book does not intend to persuade them. They will never lose faith in this terrible political creed.

Another reason for writing this book is that the history of Communism has been suppressed in the educational community and the media. Communist brutality is glossed over, and their atrocities are tossed into a figurative historical black hole. These inconvenient facts run contrary to the liberal narrative that extols the supposed virtues of Marxist theory. Many people still express admiration for the former Soviet Union and other communist states. On the other side of the coin, they have total contempt for the United States and other Western democracies. They have unlimited capacity to block out every diabolical facet of the history of Communism, while fixating on the flaws of the United States. Communist brutality is minimized, and the shortcomings of democracies are greatly magnified.

Universities, liberal bastions for Communism.

American and Western universities tend to have departments dominated by liberal professors who are open admirers of Marxism. Academics, at times, purposely mislead gullible students about the true nature of Communism. Case in point, the United States Senator from Vermont, Bernie Sanders, was a former professor who lavished praise on the Soviet system.

When I was in graduate School at North Carolina State University in the 1990s, I witnessed this craziness. One professor tried to defend the Soviet Union by proclaiming that the USSR suffered from a "bum rap," a euphemism for a false allegation[s]. Another professor at N.C. State University admitted that he and other like-minded academics "were singing the blues" after the fall of the Soviet Union in 1991. I was stunned that a scholar could be so willfully blind to Soviet history. This same individual openly advocated censoring information. When I questioned the murderous nature of Communism, he just smirked and shrugged it off. To him, the brutal nature of Communism was necessary to ensure the glorious victory of Marxism. This type of attitude pervades academia and makes writing this book more important.

Marxism is rising from the ashes.

In the United States and other countries, Marxism has once again gained in popularity. The reasons are many for the resurgence of this "cult of resentment," which was kept on life support by pro-Communist groups and academia after the fall of the USSR in 1991. Like a cancer that returns, Marxist propaganda has found a new conduit into mainstream society through the Internet and social media, much in the same way syringes facilitated heroin usage.

The new 2.0 version of Marxism: Woke and Cultural Marxism.

Since 2020, we have seen the rise of the radical "woke" political movement, which stems from the same Marxist political tree. "Woke" is part of "Cultural Marxism," which is an offshoot of Marxism. Instead of fanning the flames of class warfare, "Cultural Marxism" is a century-old political philosophy that heaps scorn on the institutions of a society: religious belief, law enforcement, civic groups, business, and the history of a country. Woke supporters denigrate these institutions and a country's history on social media, through universities, the news media, and the American public school system. They want to eliminate or radically alter these institutions in the image of the "Woke" belief system. Furthermore, they want to cancel US history and replace it with a Marxist revisionist version, which blames the United States for all the woes in the world.

Followers of "Woke" also champion "critical race theory" (CRT), which casts minorities as perpetual victims and whites as racist villains, incapable of change. CRT is being blasted across social media and used to indoctrinate impressionable school children and college students. Unfortunately, universities, government and corporations have embraced the notion of "diversity, equality, and inclusion" policies (DEI), which gives them license to discriminate against others who are not part of their chosen list of victims. "Woke" also includes a radical climate change agenda, along with a bizarre reinterpretation of gender identification, which are also part of their radical plan for changing the United States and other parts of the West. The Communist Party USA's (CPUSA) website emphatically supports all "Woke" policies. When critics point out that corporations that adopt CRT and DEI risk "Go Woke, Go Broke," a CPUSA writer ridiculed the idea, declaring that "Woke ain't broke …"

Twenty years before "Woke" burst onto the scene, the historian Jean Revel eerily described the methods used by communist rabble-rousers to diminish democracy; in an attempt to assert control within a country. His description of how communists operated in the past fits all too well with the present Woke insurgency.

"Communism's stroke of genius was to authorize the destruction of liberty in the name of liberty. It allowed liberty's enemies to carry out their work of annihilation… under a 'progressive' rational… [for]… defending the oppressed… " The writer also noted that, "Communism has nothing whatsoever to do with 'the history of social liberation': in practice it has been liberation's worst enemy."

Tearing down statues.

In 2020, tearing down American statues became a barometer of how far liberals and Woke supporters would go to cancel American history. What started as a movement to remove Confederate statues morphed into taking down the statues of Christopher Columbus, Abraham Lincoln, and Teddy Roosevelt. A frenzied group of Woke warriors even tore down the statue of a nineteenth-century African American civil rights advocate, Fredrick Douglass. It is incomprehensible that woke mobs would tear down the very civil rights icon they supposedly revere, which clearly illustrates the irrational nature of this movement. In contrast, none of these social elitists have tried to tear down the statue of Soviet mass-murderer, Vladimir Lenin, which is in the progressive city of Seattle. If pain or suffering committed by past historical figures were the litmus test for removing statues, surely the blood-drenched deeds of Lenin would warrant this monument being ripped down. Liberal hypocrisy and "Woke" double standards are the hallmark of this "movement."

Woke corporations.

Corporations have embraced this new agenda to placate the legions of "Woke" warriors and increase their market share. After the 2020 elections, some American corporations actively suppressed opposing viewpoints. Twitter, Facebook, PayPal, and YouTube all censored or suspended the accounts of individuals and organizations that questioned the 2020 election results or the government's handling of the COVID-19 crisis. Instead of the state censoring, "Woke" corporations are doing the dirty work of suppressing public opinion.

The most troubling example of potential corporate censorship has been directed at the internet search engine company, Google, a subsidiary of Alphabet Inc. The implications are disturbing. In George Orwell's novel, *1984*, the totalitarian regime employed censorship to manipulate and eliminate information, thereby swaying public opinion. In that same vein, Google has been accused of writing mathematical formulas (algorithms) that steer users away from content they deem undermines WOKE ideology.

The most egregious example of censorship at Google occurred after the assassination attempt on Donald Trump on July 13th, 2024. The widely used search engines tried to steer people away from looking up information on the attack on the former president. Members of Congress became so alarmed that they confronted the corporation about this form of censorship. In a letter to Senator Rodger Marshall, Google executives only admitted to technical glitches that suppressed information retrieval on the assassination attempt of Donald Trump.

Even more alarming, in February 2024, Google introduced a new artificial intelligence search engine, Gemini AI. Not only was the search a complete failure, but it also showcased the liberal bias that is endemic at Google. Gemini made absurd assertions about Stalin and failed to condemn pedophilia. Furthermore, the artificial animator created inaccurate historical illustrations. George Washington became an African American, as did almost all historical figures.

In contrast, the animator was incapable of creating Caucasians, which led some experts to surmise that bias was built into the system. If left unchecked, imagine what AI will be generating in several decades? This type of censorship could potentially include the suppression of facts about Communism. Modern corporations, especially social media, should be looked at with a suspicious eye.

Black Lives Matter and ANTIFA.

In 2020, Black Lives Matter burst onto the American political scene with their radical CRT ideas and their proposals for eliminating law enforcement and implementing DEI across the country. At one time, the Black Lives Matter organization acknowledged on its website that its members were Marxist-trained, but since then, they have scrubbed that fact from their website. One writer noted that, "Like the Soviets, Black Lives Matter Purges Its History." Marxist organizations adhere to secrecy.

ANTIFA is another semi-Marxist organization, dedicated to looting, rioting, and overturning US political institutions in the name of social justice. ANTIFA is "short for 'anti-fascist,'" and some group members display the hammer and sickle, the symbol of communist countries, on their shields and helmets. Andy Ngo, an independent journalist, has written about the dangers of ANTIFA in his book, *ANTIFA Unmasked: Inside ANTIFA's Radical Plan to Destroy Democracy*. Since then, Ngo has also become a target of ANTIFA. Besides being vilified and threatened online, Ngo was videotaped being beaten up by these thugs, while the police stood by and did nothing. Ngo is Asian and gay, but this brutal attack was never considered a hate crime. As Jean Revel pointed out, some communists consider a wicked act to be justified if it brings revolutionaries closer to their version of social liberation. Andy Ngo's articles shone an unflattering light on ANTIFA, so beating him up was justified.

Many Americans seem unable able to grasp the potential threat that these groups pose. Furthermore, social media and other groups on the internet glorify and boast of the allure of Marxism. When you go to the website of the Communist Party USA, there is no mention of their history of misery, just scathing critiques of the United States, Israel, and capitalism.

William Johnson

The American public school system, which has been in decline for years, rarely denounces this toxic philosophy, and in some cases, teachers even encourage students to embrace this ideology. If we apply the liberal WOKE litmus test of zero tolerance for any wrongdoing, then Marxism should be cancelled. Furthermore, if you know the awful history of Communism, then you are less apt to be suckered into believing WOKE propaganda. All too often, people only hear of negative things about the USA and very little critical analysis about Marxist-communist states. No context, no balance, and unlimited bias. This is what I mean about history going into a black hole (Please read the notes below for details and reference materials.) [1]

---

[1] In the book, *In Denial: Historians, Communism & Espionage*, John Earl Haynes, and Harvey Klehr, outline how Marxist historians and professors openly admire the former Soviet Union. Paul Hollander's book, *The End of Commitment: Intellectual, Revolutionaries and Political Morality*, has summarized the biographies of dozens of individuals that were devoted Marxists, until the brutal reality of this political philosophy snapped them out of their delusional mindset. Yet, other individuals in Hollander's book remain unrepentant. No matter how much brutal information is presented to them, they remained steadfast in their beliefs. This was not the case with Vasili Mitrokhin, a former KGB agent, that worked in the secret police security force of the Soviet Union. He worked in the Soviet Archives and was shocked by the secret documents he discovered. For several years he copied notes. Mitrokhin literally had a couple suitcases of material covering the terrible deeds committed by the Soviet Union. He defected to the West, and collaborated with the historian, Christopher Andrew, to write, *The Sword and the Shield*, and *The World Was Going Our Way*. Both books detail Soviet skullduggery not known in the west, and I will refer to the material in these books as the Mitrokhin Files, throughout this book. *The Black Book of Communism* was written by former communist sympathizers, and is a comprehensive text, which chronicles the gory history of all the communist states. The list of books outlining the misery caused by the Soviet Union goes on and on.

-These are two examples of persons that have been thrown into a metaphorical black hole, by academia and intellectual elites that have suppressed inconvenient information about communism. Victor Kravchenko was probably one of the most famous high-ranking defectors from the Soviet Union. Victor was an engineer, who witnessed all the brutal acts perpetrated by Stalin. He defected in 1944, and later wrote, *I Chose Freedom,* but academia and the media have ignored him. Hollander, Paul. The End of Commitment. Pp. 47-48. Harry Dextor White was the Assistant Secretary to the US Treasury under the administration of Franklin Delano Roosevelt presidential administration. He was also a spy, who passed information to the Soviet Union. He was discovered and identified through the US military Venona Project; a top-secret decryption group that operated

Murderous Marxism

during WWII. Venona discovered hundreds Soviet spies and collaborators during the war; yet few have heard of Venona, Harry Dextor White, or the massive Soviet spy ring in the US. Hayes, J. & Klehr, H. <u>Venona: Decoding Soviet Espionage in America</u>. Pp. 17, 18, 125-126, 139-143.

-Marcus, David. "Google's Gemini AI has a White People Problem." Fox News. Feb. 26, 2024. ONLINE

- Sims, Joe. <u>Communist Party USA</u> (CPUSA) web site article. "Resist Trump 2.0." Nov. 19, 2024. ONLINE

-Parks, Kristine. "Arizona Republican whose family fled communist regime says some Americans ignore ideology's atrocities." <u>Fox News</u>. Feb. 5th, 2024. In the state of Arizona, two Republican state legislators sponsored a state law requiring public school students to study Communist atrocities. Ben Toma, the House speaker of Arizona, fled Romania, and the bill's other supporter, Republican Rep. Quang Nguyen escaped from Vietnam. Both men experienced totalitarian regimes in their former countries, and they have become alarmed at the lack of knowledge by US school children of communism's bloody legacy.

-Yeonmi Park escaped from North Korea as a child and eventually made it to the United States. Years later when she was attending Columbia University, she was shocked to hear professors praising communism. She was dismayed at the pure propaganda preached by these "Woke professors. Hill, Bailee. "North Korean defector shocked at what she learned at 'woke' Ivy League school: Brainwashing'" <u>Fox News</u>. Feb. 13, 2023.

-Ngo, Andy. <u>Unmasked: Inside Antifa's Radical Plan to Destroy Democracy</u>. Pp. 1-4, 8, 9, destroying statues 55, Marxist roots of Antifa, and BLM pp.131-137, Andy Ngo assaulted 2019, 145-153.

-This article documents a Marxist teacher, Tim Hernandez, an unabashed communist, who posts his opinions on multiple online forums, and he has called for a "Cultural Revolution" in the United States. The Cultural Revolution occurred in communist China during the 1960s. Mao unleashed a fanatical youth-oriented movement, to radically change all cultural aspects of an already communist country. Historians have described this event as being traumatic for China, and it nearly ripped the societal fabric of this ancient civilization. Grossman, Hannah. "Colorado teacher calls for 'FORCEFUL cultural revolution' targeted at 'whiteness': 'This is sacred'" <u>Fox News</u>. May 18, 2023."

- This same teacher is now a local politician in Colorado. Grossman, Hannah. Marxist teacher who called for 'forceful cultural revolution' lands seat on state legislature" <u>Fox News</u>. August 28, 2023.

-Xi Van Fleet immigrated to the United States from communist China. Xi had witnessed the destructiveness of Mao's "Cultural Revolution," and she was horrified with the rise of "Woke," and CRT. She recognized the direct parallels between CRT, cultural Marxism and the "Cultural Revolution" of communist China. She wrote, *Mao's America: A -Survivor's Warning*, about the threat of Cultural Marxism. Please see her You Tube video: Race vs Class: The Same Ideology That Erased Freedom in China Is Taking Over America.

William Johnson

- Buck, Daniel. "Woke Education Is Going Strong, Even in Middle America." <u>Wall Street Journal</u>. May 23, 2025.

-Lynn, Andrew. "Cultural Marxism." <u>The Hedgehog Review</u>. ONLINE Fall 2018.

- Johnson, Julia. "Google execs pressed to testify after admitting Trump assassination attempt search omissions were by design" <u>Fox Business</u>. Aug. 14, 2024.

-Isakowitz, Mark. VP, Government Affairs & Public Policy, US., & Canada Google LLC. Letter to Senator Rodger Marshall. Aug. 12, 2024.

-Herlihy, Brianna. "Oklahoma schools chief to announce plan to ban DEI in Sooner State's public school." <u>Fox News</u>. Dec. 21, 2023.

-"Friedrichs, Rebecca. "Why America's kids are hip to BLM and LGBT but are failing ABC and 123."

-Olivastro, Andrew, Gonzales, Mike. "Like the Soviets, Black Lives Matter Purges Its History" <u>The American Heritage</u>. Sept. 23, 2020. Retrieved Jan. 1st, 2023.

-Flood, Brian. Parents Defending Education leader says Chinese Communist influence on American schools is deeply troubling" <u>Fox News</u>. Sept. 12, 2023.

-Revel, Jean-Francois. <u>Last Exit To Utopia</u>. Pp. x, xviii, 10, 11, 86, 88, 208.

- "Cult of Resentment" Praeger University.

-MacKinnon, Douglas. "Woke bullies rewrite 'Willie Wonka' book and will censor every bit of history and literature…if we let them" <u>Fox News</u>. Feb. 21, 2023.

-Kole, William. "Statue of Slave kneeling before Lincoln is removed in Boston. <u>Associated Press</u>. Dec. 29, 2020.

-Johnson, Julia. "Google execs pressed to testify after admitting Trump assassination attempt search omissions were by design." <u>Fox Business News</u>. August 14, 2024.

-Hauser, Christine. "Christopher Columbus Statues Removed From 2 Chicago Parks." <u>The New York Times</u>. July 24, 2020. Online.

-Pengelly, Martin. "Frederick Douglass statue torn down on anniversary of the great speech." <u>The Guardian</u>. July 6th, 2020.

-Pogrebin, Robin. "Roosevelt Statue to Be Removed from Museum of Natural History." <u>The New York Times</u>. Jan. 19, 2022.

-Volodzko, David. "Dear Fremont: We need to talk about Lenin and your statue of the genocidal tyrant." <u>The Seattle Times</u>. July 7, 2023.

Chapter 1
The Black Hole of History!

Communism is the greatest man-made disaster of the modern world, and Marxism is its North Star. Communists have ruined economies, destroyed the environment, and brought misery to billions of people; yet this terrible history is not well known. For Communism to thrive, unscrupulous supporters of Marxism push "unrelenting class warfare," of the rich versus the poor. Over time, Marxism and its advocates have created a "cult of resentment," which started as an intellectual appeal to workers in the nineteenth century who were mistreated by industrialization. It would be the chaos of the First World War, which gave the communists their chance to seize power in Russia. Warfare, poverty, and corruption made fertile grounds for radical groups. Various socialist groups, including the Bolsheviks, and legions of desperate soldiers and civilians, became unwitting followers of this "cult of resentment." The destruction wrought by the world wars of the twentieth century provided the perfect opportunity for communists to foment a worldwide Marxist revolution. The number of wasted lives, money, and resources can scarcely be calculated. These terrible deeds have gone down a figurative "black hole,' of historical suppression.

The Bolsheviks established the first totalitarian country, and in several years, they used a variety of terror techniques and brutality to gain control and retain power over the former Russian Empire. A few of their terrible tactics included impalement, gassing, mass shootings, boiling people alive, hangings, roasting victims in a blast furnace, or confining individuals to cages with rats that gnawed them to death.

These are a few of the diabolical tactics utilized by communists. In reality, man-made famines made up the bulk of those who died in communist regimes. It has been estimated that Communist regimes might have killed over 100 million people in a century.

To be clear, the actions of communist regimes in no way resemble Marxism, which liberal professors babble on about in a classroom. Communists bent on instigating revolution and overthrowing a government used terms like "national liberation" and "class consciousness," but what they really meant was something entirely different. Instead of national liberation, they used mind-numbing terror and violence to take over a nation and control it.

What is Marxism?

Marxism is the political/philosophical theory of Karl Marx, a 19th-century German philosopher. Working with Friedrich Engels, they wrote the Communist Manifesto and Das Kapital (also known as "the Capital"), which criticized capitalism for enslaving and impoverishing the industrialized workers of the world. They asserted that "history is determined by economics," rich versus poor. Both seemed to have a gift for recognizing the painfully obvious; even worse, their supposed solutions were ludicrous and never worked. Poverty has been around since ancient times, well before the advent of capitalism.

To summarize, Marx and his collaborator, Engels, theorized that capitalism would cycle through one economic crisis after another until the working class revolted and seized power, ushering in a classless society, and the people would decide how resources would be utilized. Marxists use the term economic cooperation. All their theories failed miserably. Modern-day communist nations claimed to follow the Marxist banner but have never actually implemented his political philosophy. Class-consciousness really meant class warfare and whipping up hated against those deemed to be enemies of the workers and the peasants. Instead of the masses determining how resources would be used, centralized planning ministries implemented communist command economies. The actual path to power for these communist elites was based on mass murder and terror. Hardly an honorable system.

What did Marx want to abolish?

These are a few of the dictates of Karl Marx, as outlined in the "Manifesto of the Communist Party."

- **"Abolition of individuality and freedom. And rightly so!"** One can only surmise that Marx wanted people to become mindless drones and join the cult of Communism.

- **"Abolition of the family!"** He predicted that, **"The... family will vanish as a matter of course..."** The philosopher blamed the family for being in league with the industrialists to exploit child labor, which is an absurd notion. Marx does not mention how children would be raised without a family structure.

- **"There are, besides, eternal truths such as freedom, justice, etc., that are common to all states of society. But Communism abolishes eternal truths, it abolishes all religion, and all morality..."** Sounds like a license to lie, peddle falsehoods and implement censorship.

-Abolish all private property. Marx also predicted that buying and selling would disappear. He also stated that – "labor... [would]... no longer be converted into capital, money, or rent..." Although Marx was less than clear, he seems to suggest that money would no longer be needed. He never explains how people would get compensated for their labor. Furthermore, who would decide how the resources of the world would be utilized? So many economic questions were left unanswered by the political philosopher.

-Marx wanted a "**heavy progressive or graduated income tax.**" At this point, he contradicts himself. I will use his own words against him. How can one pay "**a heavy… income tax…**" if "**labor can no longer be converted into capital, money**…?"

- "**Abolition of all rights of inheritance**." This is self-explanatory.

-Marx called for the "**centralization**" of all banks, transportation, communication, factories, and the "**cultivation of waste land…**" The now-defunct Soviet Union tried this and failed.

- "**Equal obligation of all to work. Establishment of industrial armies, especially for agriculture**." This sounds awful, like slavery.

- "**Combination of agriculture with manufacturing industries; gradual abolition of the distinction between town and country by a more equable distribution of the population over the country**." He never indicates whether this is voluntary or who directs people to give up their property to live in some "**wasteland**." Nor does he indicate if people could freely choose to work in "**industrial**" and "**agricultural armies**." Once again, so many questions left unanswered.

- "**The Communists are further reproached with desiring to abolish countries and nationality**."

At the end of the chapter, Marx seems to conclude that people would readily embrace Communism. "**In place of the old… society… the free development of each is the condition for the free development of all**."

Personal note. I have never read of any such unworkable economic/political system that anyone would freely submit to. All these ultimatums can be found within four pages of the "Manifesto of the Communist Party."

Points of Ponder: Marx, Pavel Morozov, and the destruction of the family.

In the Communist Manifesto, Marx called for the abolition of the family. The philosopher proclaimed that family bonds were "claptrap" (venereal disease) as far as he was concerned. Marx blamed the family for allowing child labor during the Industrial Revolution, which is hogwash.

In George Orwell's novel, *1984*, the central character, Winston Smith, was frightened of children. He worried that he would be denounced by any random child, which would assuredly guarantee his arrest.

The case of Pavel Morozov demonstrated how the Soviets undermined the family structure by indoctrinating children to be suspicious of their parents. Pavel denounced his own father for being a kulak, a supposed rich peasant who was a fictitious state enemy, created by the Bolsheviks. The father was subsequently shot. Pavel was later killed by a mob from his village, which was said to have included family members. Stalin praised the boy in public, but in private, the "Boss" referred to him as "a little swine, for denouncing his own father." Nonetheless, Stalin ordered statues of Pavel, which were made of plaster. The plaster statues were made of wooden frames, many of which were quite flimsy. In a supreme irony, the head sculptor was killed when one of these faulty frames broke and the statue fell on her.

The clash between God and atheistic Marxism.

The Manifesto of Communism calls for the elimination of all "eternal truths… all religion, and all morality…" The Bolsheviks were the first who tried to turn Marxism into a "reality", and as one critic of Communism noted, the USSR was "a state… created… [and]… based explicitly on atheism… [while it] … claimed infallibility." This would make for an inevitable clash with Christianity, which is the "bedrock of Western civilization." The belief in God and the Christian doctrine of original sin, that we are imperfect, put faith in direct conflict with Marxism's notion of infallibility. As Marx wrote in the Manifesto, "communism abolishes internal truths, it abolishes religion, and all morality," which keeps the old political order from crumbling before the communist revolution.

The actions of the crusaders and the Inquisition certainly demonstrate that Christianity has a turbulent past, but these transgressions have been acknowledged. The wicked deeds of the Bolsheviks and other communists are rarely acknowledged by true believers of Marxism. One only needs to visit the CPUSA website to see that fact.

Jean Revel described the diabolical mindset of the early communists. If "evil acts" make the Marxist revolution possible, then evil is a legitimate means for achieving communist victory. "Truth and justice can and must be sacrificed to the necessities of revolutionary combat." This opens the door to fraud on an unprecedented scale, terror, and unspeakable atrocities committed in the name of communist victory.[2]

Communism's death tolls.

Published in 1999, *The Black Book of Communism* estimated that in a little over a century, Communism has caused the death of 100 million people, at a minimum. A majority of those who died perished within the Soviet Union, Mao's China, North Korea, Ethiopia, Afghanistan, and Cambodia after the communist Khmer Rouge took over this Southeast Asian country. Other deaths were connected to the Cold War, a geopolitical struggle between the two superpowers after WWII: the United States and the Soviet Union. The democratic West versus communist countries. It involved low-level conflicts and proxy war conflicts, in which countries or groups were supplied by both groups. The deaths are connected to warfare in Indochina prior to communist victory (Vietnam, Laos, and Cambodia), Africa (Mozambique and Angola), and Latin America.

-Soviet Union: *The Black Book on Communism*, put the death toll at 20 million deaths, a number that has been disputed by historians for being too low. Norman Davies's *Europe* uses R. Medvedev and R. Conquest as sources, and they put the death toll at over 40 million in the former USSR. Death tolls connected to the Forced Agricultural

---

2 Satter, David. "100 Years of Communism- and a 100 Million Dead." Wall Street Journal. 11/7/2017. Pp. # A17. Revel, Jean-Francois. Last Exit to Utopia. Pp. 208-209. Courtois, Stephane, et.al. The Black Book on Communism. p.1-132. Andrew, C, and Mitrokhin, V. The Sword and the Shield; The Mitrokhin Archive and the Secret History of the KGB. P. 39. Acton, Edward. The Present and the Past Russia. Pp. 177, 179. Nelson, Rebecca. The Handy History Answer Book. Pp. 267-268. "Cult of Resentment" Praeger University. Marx, Karl. "Manifesto of the Communist Party". Great Books of the Western World. pp. 426, 427, 428, 429. For Pavel Morozov, see the following. Amis, Martin. Koba the Dread. P. 68, 123-128,138, 208, 193. Radzinsky, Edvard. Stalin. P. 403.

Collectivization, the Ukrainian Terror Famine and the Great Terror are lower in *The Black Book of Communism* than in Norman Davies' *Europe*. There are also categories of mass murder overlooked in the former USSR, which include the mass deportations of minority groups. These deportations consisted of internal exile within the USSR. These forced mass expulsions occurred just before the outbreak of World War II and continued throughout this conflict. Deportations and mass murder also occurred in communist occupied Eastern Europe after the war. The Baltic states also experienced forced relocations when the Soviet Union annexed these countries. An additional 1 million WWII POWs (German, Japanese, Romanian, etc.) should be included within the Soviet death tolls. Davies noted that some of these categories could overlap. Finally, the Russian Civil War was set into motion by the Bolshevik-initiated coup towards the end of 1917. *The Great Big Book of Horrible Things* puts the death toll of the Russian Revolution at 9 million, of which 5 million died from the Bolsheviks' instigated food shortage, which became known as Lenin's Famine. (Please see notes.)

-Communist China: (CCP): *The Black Book of Communism* puts the death toll in communist China at 65 million by the mid-1990s. A recent biography of Mao Zedong suggests that the number of those who perished in the famine caused by the Great Leap Forward could push this death toll higher. Furthermore, the genocide of Tibetans, along with the persecution of the Uighurs and practitioners of Falon Gong, would certainly make this number higher. In 2020, the COVID-19 pandemic, which originated in China, became a global pandemic. The Chinese government's slow response in reporting the outbreak and its lack of transparency about the contagious nature of the virus made the epidemic worse. Now, a growing body of evidence points to a leak at a bioweapon laboratory in Wuhan, China. If these new factors are taken into consideration, the death toll at the hands of the Chinese communists could soar well past 65 million.

- North Korea: In the introduction of *The Black Book of Communism*, Stephane Courtois puts the death toll for North Korea at two million. I believe this number is low. Pierre Rigoulot, who wrote the chapter on North Korea in *The Black Book of Communism*, wrote "100,000 died in party purges...1.5 million deaths in concentration camps...[and]...at least 1.3 million deaths stemming from the...[Korean]... war. The author of *The Great Big Book of Horrible Things* puts the death toll for the Korean War at 3 million. Note, this was a non-provoked war of aggression, backed by Mao and Stalin, and carried out by Kim Il Sung. Separate from the war, the number killed by the regime could have exceeded 3 million. The death toll from the famine in the 1990s does not seem to be included in *The Black Book of Communism*. A quick Google search puts the death toll from starvation between several hundred thousand to a million. *A New York Times* article put the figure at more than two million, while a BBC article indicated that close to 3 million died. The cumulative death toll, including the Korean War and those murdered within North Korea, could be between 4 million to 5 million deaths.

-Cambodia: From 1975 through 1979, the Khmer Rouge killed 1.7 to 2 million people **after the communists toppled the Cambodian government.**

-Eastern Europe: *The Black Book of Communism* puts the death toll at 1 million in Eastern Europe and the Baltic states, which fell under the control of the Soviet Union (USSR) at the end of WWII. Davie's *Europe* lists two categories. "Deportations from eastern Poland... [the]... Baltic States, and Romania, 1939-45... 2 million." Also, "post-war screening of repatriates and inhabitants of ex-occupied territory... 5 to 6 million."

-Afghanistan: The unprovoked Soviet invasion killed 1.5 million Afghans between 1979-1989.

-Indochina, which includes fighting in Vietnam, Laos, and Cambodia. The Vietnamese communist government published a statement, which indicated that 3 million died between 1954-1975. *The Great Book of Horrible Things* puts the number at over 4 million. It should be noted that American involvement did not ramp up until the middle of the 1960s, but communists had been killing in the northern part of Vietnam from the 1940s through the 1950s. It was the communist North Vietnamese who initiated the war in southern Vietnam in 1959 and spread the war into neutral Cambodia and Laos, while supplying the communist rebels in these countries. The Soviet Union and China backed the North Vietnamese. Fighting in Laos from the 1960s to 1973 killed 62,000, while fighting in Cambodia from 1970-1975 claimed 600,000 lives.

-Latin America: The death and destruction in Latin America are connected to the Cold War. *The Black Book of Communism* puts the death toll at 150,000. *The Great Big Book of Horrible Things* puts the total closer to 365,000, which includes the Latin American nations of Guatemala, El Salvador, and Nicaragua.

- Africa: *The Black Book of Communism* puts the death toll in Africa at 1.7 million. This number is probably low. The 1975, communist coup which toppled the Ethiopian government probably led to the death of 2 million people from state-sanctioned murder, a massive famine, and a war against Eritrea. The Ethiopians were supplied with a full array of Soviet weaponry, and were augmented by soldiers and air power from the USSR and Cuba. Death tolls in Mozambique and Angola are a bit murkier. *The Great Big Book of Horrible Things* noted that 800,000 perished in Mozambique and 500,000 or more in Angola. In Mozambique, the fighting between the communist backed government and Western-backed guerrillas, along with a famine, was the chief cause of death. It is worth noting that neither group was committed to the welfare of the Mozambican people. In Angola, the Soviet Union provided direct military aid in the form of weaponry, logistics, and air support. Castro also provided Cuban military support in the form of soldiers, air power, and weaponry. Western aid to the anticommunist forces paled in comparison to communist support. American aid only amounted to several hundred million dollars, while most military support came from South Africa.

-Another 10,000 or so people were probably killed by groups and individuals connected to Communism. This number is probably low. It is believed that the Peruvian terrorist group Sendero de Luminoso could have killed as many as 25,000 people.

So, what is the total number of people killed by Communism? In Matthew White's *The Great Big Book of Horrible Things*, he argues that, without verifiable numbers, larger death tolls should be considered lower. He acknowledges that roughly 67 million died under Communism, which is still an astronomically high number. He further stated that communism states were "unique," so to lump the death tolls together would be too "broad" of a generalization to be considered in totality. He readily conceded that, "if I bundle all communist regimes together... [it would] ... make a new number 1..." killer of human beings.

I disagree that communist states should be viewed separately. Marxism is the North Star that guided these communist states. All communist states should be lumped together. Furthermore, if the death tolls of the Soviet Union, communist China, and other communist regimes have been undercounted, then those who perished could have easily exceeded 100 million victims.

Furthermore, it is the "stock and trade" of Communist totalitarian states to deny how many people were killed under their rule. The Soviets, the Khmer Rouge, the Chinese Communists, and the North Koreans all used mass graves to dispose of victims. Norman Davies provides an example of a secret Soviet mass burial site, located in a forest outside Minsk, Belarus. Authorities have estimated that hundreds of burial pits lie within the forest, and that each mound could contain roughly 3,000 bodies. Soviet authorities never acknowledged the existence of these burial pits. And this is just one area in what was once the vast Soviet Empire.

After the Second World War, the Allies were able to obtain photographs and film footage, which showed Nazi soldiers shooting prisoners. They took pride in their atrocities and photographed their ghastly deeds. The communists rarely allowed photographs to be taken. Visual evidence of Communism's terrible deeds is quite scant, and it is difficult to convey such horror without photographs or videotape. One of the historians of *The Black Book of Communism* wrote that in comparison to the Nazis, "no such parallels existed in the darkness of the Communist world, where terror had been organized in strictest secrecy."

Communism-led death tolls in comparison to other mass killings throughout the ages.

-To put this in comparison, the African slave trade, which consisted of the European Trans-Atlantic slavery, lasted for several centuries, and killed 16 million. The Muslim Slave Trade through the Sahara Desert probably lasted close to eleven centuries and killed 18.5 million.

-The conquest of the Americas lasted close to four centuries and caused the death of 15 million Native Americans. (Most of these deaths fell within the Spanish Empire, with disease being the primary killer.)

- The Christian Crusades in the holy lands lasted almost two centuries and killed maybe 3 million.

-The Second World War killed 66 million people.

-World War I killed 15 million people. [3]

---

3 Courtois, Stephane, et.al. The Black Book of Communism. p. 4, 10, 15, 30-31, 463-465, 495, 498, 542, 562, 563-564. Davies, N. Europe. p.963, 965, 1329. White, Matthew. The Great Big Book of Horrible Things. p. 80-81,98, 161-162, 344, 359, 400, 439-457, 465-473, 474, 475, 486-500, 505. Sedacca, Matthew. North Koreans dying of Starvation following Covid isolation measures. US. News. June17, 2023. http://nypost.com/2023/06/17/north-koreans-are-dying-of-starvation-report/ Natsios, Andrew. "The Politics of Famine in North Korea." United States Institute of Peace. Aug.2, 1999. https://www.usip.org/publications/1999/08/politics-famine-north-korea The BBC article wrote that the North Korean leader "prioritized funding his nuclear weapons program..." (and the funding of the Sung family lavish lifestyle), rather than saving lives. Their priorities are quite clear. Mackenzie, Jean. "North Korea: Residents tell BBC of neighbors starving to death." BBC. June 14, 2023. http://www.bbc.com/news/world-asia-65881803 Crossette Barbara. "Korean Famine Toll: More Than 2 million." New York Times. Aug. 20, 1999. Section A, page 6. Rengifo-Keller, Lucas. "Food Insecurity in North Korea is at its worst since the 1990s Famine." 38 North: informed Analysis of North Korea. Jan. 19, 2023. http://www.38north.org/2023/01/food-insecurity-in-north-korea-is-at-its-worst-since-the-1990s-famine/ Deaths in Communist China. One video from the "China in Focus" video channel. "How communism killed 80 million in China: Chinese Communist Party at 100 years." NTD. I did not include this video, but it certainly cast doubt the official death tolls in communist China. #EpochTV http://ept.ms/3enuN71 For Sendero de Luminoso. Andrew, C. & Mitrokhin, V. The World was Going our Way: The KGB and the Battle for the Third World. pp. 513, footnote 36. Gordon, Michael, Strobel, Warren. "Behind Closed Doors: The Spy-World Scientists Who Argued Covid was a Lab Leak." Wall Street Journal. Dec. 26, 2024. Gallagher, Mike. "Time for Accountability on the Covid Lab-leak Coverup." Wall Street Journal. April 15, 2025. Matthews, Christopher.

Domino Theory.

The Domino Theory was a conceptual understanding applied to the expansion of Communism. As one country falls to Communism, the countries bordering these new totalitarian regimes will fall in their own turn. Critics have derided this notion, but to those opposed to Communism, the theory has valid points. After the Soviet Union was established, the Bolsheviks controlled a vast empire that included most of the old Czarist Russia. During the Russian Civil War, the Soviets attacked the Baltic States and Poland, but were pushed back.

From 1945 to 1975, huge swaths of the globe fell under the yoke of Communism. Eastern Europe was brutally forced into Communism by Stalin after WWII, which included Bulgaria, Romania, Hungary, Czechoslovakia, Poland, and East Germany. Albania and Yugoslavia were communist, but the Soviets did not control these states. The Baltic countries of Lithuania, Latvia, and Estonia, as well as the eastern European country of Moldova, and a slice of Romania, were annexed by the USSR. The Communist "Iron Curtain" was drawn across Eastern Europe; thus, the free became unfree.

The West was able to beat back the communists in Greece and fend them off in Turkey (Stalin demanded control of strategic Turkish territory). Mao Zedong won control over China. Korea was a near miss in 1950, after the unprovoked attack by North Korea on South Korea. Only the actions of the United Nations forces led by the USA were able to stop the communists. By 1949, the Soviets had stolen the secrets of nuclear weaponry and had developed and detonated an atomic bomb. In 1959, Castro's communists took over Cuba, and now the United

---

"Trump Endorses Covid 'Lab Leak' Theory on Government About the Virus." Wall Street Journal. April 19, 2025.

States had a hostile country less than a hundred miles from its coast. In 1963, the Cuban Missile Crisis almost resulted in a nuclear war with the Soviet Union. Things looked grim for the free world, and Communism was on a roll. Roughly two-thirds of Asia and half of Europe were under Marxist control, and by 1959, US authorities knew Southeast Asia could be next. If Vietnam fell, then so could Laos, Cambodia, Thailand, and India. By 1975, Vietnam, Laos, and Cambodia fell under communist control with horrifying results.

Those who have criticized the Domino Theory have had their arguments cut down to size by information that has been made public over the past 30 years. Here are a few critical sources:

- The opening of the Soviet Archives after 1991. Also, the opening of the communist archives of Eastern Europe.
- The US government publication of the Venona Project and the information obtained from Soviet encrypted telegrams.
- A treasure trove of information given to the West by former KGB agent, Vasli Mitrokhin, and many other Soviet defectors.
- Critical research was conducted by historians who wrote *The Black Book on Communism*. Additionally, notable historical research include works by Robert Conquest, Roy Medvedev, and Alexander Solzhenitsyn. The list goes on and on.

Where there is smoke, there is fire: Domino links.

This information sets the Domino Theory on a solid foundation. Historical sources in *The Black Book of Communism* indicate that, as early as 1919, the Bolsheviks aided Bela Kun in Hungary and communist groups in Korea. The Bolsheviks had been working with Chinese communists in the cities until the mid-1920s, when Chang Kia-Shek's Nationalists wiped them out. Undeterred, the Soviets supported communists in the rural areas of China, and Mao emerged victorious in 1949. Mao and Stalin backed Kim Il Sung's war of aggression against South Korea in 1950.

The North Vietnamese received weapons and training from both the Soviets and the communist Chinese. Furthermore, Ho Chi Minh violated the declared neutrality of Cambodia and Laos and **used these Southeast Asian countries as a staging area** to attack South Vietnam. These combined factors were critical in toppling South Vietnam's government in 1975. By the end of 1975, both Cambodia and Laos would be taken over by communist forces, which had been supplied by the Soviets, China, and North Vietnam.[4]

Similarly, Castro's Cuba and the USSR were crucial in the Sandinistas' victory in Nicaragua. Both the Soviets and the Cubans waged a proxy war in this Central American country and turned it into a communist regime. The Mitrokhin Files indicated that the Soviets supplied weapons and money, while the Cubans were crucial for organizing and delivering weapons and supplies to the Sandinistas. It should also be noted that Costa Rica played a role in the communist victory by allowing the establishment of bases for staging raids into

---

4 A Vietnamese leader, Hoang Van Hoan, admitted that in between 1950 to 1954, Communist Chinese advisors had been training soldiers and cadres in North Vietnam. In 1959, the CIA estimated that the Northern Vietnamese had "infiltrated 5,000…southern-born cadres" into South Vietnam. Courtios, Stephane, et, al. The Black Book of Communism. p. 271-275, 280-282, 284-285. 464-465, 565-571. Maclear, Michael. The Ten Thousand Day War. p. 45-56. Spector, Ronald. In the Ruins of Empires. P. 135-137. Morris, Stephen. Why Vietnam Invaded Cambodia. Pp. 90-91. All four of the proceeding sources indicate that North Vietnamese soldiers and South Vietnamese communist insurgents infiltrated and terrorized the countryside executing local elites, terrorizing villagers in the countryside. Greene, Thomas. Comparative Revolutionary Movements. Pp. 108. Kissinger, Henry. Diplomacy. 622-642, 667, 701. LeFeber, Walter. The American Age. Pp. 446

Nicaragua. Nicaragua would eventually be taken over by the communist Sandinistas.

Points to Ponder: Castro wants to set the world on fire with Communism.

Communists were determined to spread Communism across the globe. In 1965, the Cuban communist leader, Fidel Castro, sent his main henchman, CHE Guevara, to Congo to instigate revolution in the African state. Several months after arriving, CHE Guevara's small force was soundly defeated by government-backed military forces. The revolutionary fled, abandoning his forces.

In 1967, CHE Guevara met his end in Bolivia while trying to organize a communist insurgency in this South American country. Guevara believed that Bolivia could become the staging area for a Vietnam-like guerrilla warfare that could be waged in the bordering South American countries. This overly optimistic scenario would supposedly encourage a worldwide communist revolution, and Bolivia would theoretically be the first domino in South America. He expressed no concern if people were killed, and property was destroyed. His plans were pure fantasy.

CHE and his small force entered Bolivia and linked up with local communist rebels. Poor planning, lack of supplies, and clashes with Bolivian forces whittled down his group. Instead of joining CHE's force, frightened Bolivian peasants avoided the group. When supplies ran short, CHE's group took hostages and ransomed villagers for provisions. (Note* the revolutionary kidnapped and robbed the very peasants they were supposed to be liberating. Nice.) The Bolivian military, along with help from the CIA, was able to corner his small band and kill most of the insurgents. On October 7, 1967, CHE Guevara was captured by Bolivian forces and was later executed without trial.[5]

By the mid-1970s, the Soviet Union, Cuba, and Communist China were trying to expand a communist base in Africa. The Soviets and Fidel supplied soldiers, weaponry and supplies to Angola, Mozambique, and Ethiopia from 1975 through 1989. East Germany provided training for establishing secret police organizations. With all this information, "The Domino Theory" looks more like reality. [6]

---

[5] On numerous occasions, Castro, and CHE, made fiery speeches, which made it clear that they were going to bring communist revolution to Latin America. The Cubans sought to spread communism in an overt fashion, unapologetic, and confrontational. Castro dispatched small bands of Cuban revolutionaries to Haiti and the Dominican Republic to foment a communist uprising, but local military forces wiped out both terrorist groups. The Cubans tried to set up bases in Argentina, Peru, Venezuela, Guatemala, and Colombia, but failed. CHE was adamant, "Bolivia must be sacrificed so that revolutions in neighboring countries may begin..." Anderson, Jon Lee. CHE. Pp. p. for general information pp. 422-710; for expanding communism in the Western Hemisphere; p. 365, 375, 376, 377-378, 398, 413-414. For specific pages on CHE's band coercing Bolivian peasants; and Cuban communist backed insurgencies which used terror to coerce villagers to join the communist insurgency. Anderson, Jon Lee. CHE. Pp 684, 691-2 Andrews, C& Mitrokhin, Vasili. The World Was Going Our Way: The KGB And the Battle for the Third World. Pp., 33, 34, 35, 36, 37, 38, 39, 40, 41, 42, 43, 44, 45, 46, 47, 48, 49, 50, 51, 51, 52, 53. Aguila, Juan Del. Cuba: Dilemmas of a Revolution. Pp.117-8, 145; footnote 25. Wright, Thomas. Latin America in the Era of the Cuban Revolution. pp.41, 87-88, 91-94. Clayton, L. & Conniff, M. A History of Modern Latin America. 452. Greene, Thomas. Comparative Revolutionary Movements. pp.110.

[6] In Angola, Cuban officers turned a blind eye to the actions of their soldiers, who raped, murdered, and robbed the populace. The Cuban military smuggled diamonds and ivory out of Africa, and systematic corruption was widespread within their armed forces. Cuban General Rafael Del Pino was so sickened by the corruption, and the military operations in Africa, that he defected to the United States. Pino noted that the Cuban "air force became the favorite instrument of terror... [of the local populace, which] ...were subjected to...criminal and merciless treatment...We...[became]...a mercenary army serving the interests of Soviet imperialism..." The disillusioned general wrote that," Angola ranks as one of the greatest crimes committed by...Castro...against the Angolan people but...[also]...against our own youth, whom he sent to the slaughterhouse..." Hollander, Paul. The End of Commitment. P. 150-155. Pino witnessed ill trained Cuban conscripts; "most of who were black," being sent into combat, and their inexperience got them killed., The Black Book on Communism, estimated, that between 7,000 and 11,000 Cuban soldiers were killed in Africa. Courtois, Stephane, et.al. The Black Book of

Murderous Marxism

Communism. p.663-665. Clayton, L. & Conniff, M. <u>A History of Modern Latin America</u>.
Pp. 454. Revel, Jean. <u>Last Exit to Utopia</u>. Pp. 132. Aguila, Juan Del. <u>Cuba: Dilemmas of a Revolution</u>. Pp.126-128, 141-143, 148, footnote, 68.

Chapter 2
Overview of the Soviet Union 1918-1991.

The history of the Soviet Union can be viewed in several segments. The first segment was the Russian Revolution, which had several phases. In 1917, Russian military setbacks during the First World War facilitated the abdication of the Czar, which heralded the Russian Revolution. Towards the end of 1917, a Bolshevik coup overthrew the Provisional Government, marking the beginning of the Russian Civil War. The Bolsheviks reconquered much of the former Russian Empire. The Civil War also included the Bolsheviks' war of aggression against Poland and the Baltic States, followed by the consolidation of territorial gains. Meanwhile, during the Civil War, the Bolsheviks waged war against the peasantry, which was followed by "Lenin's famine" of the early 1920s.

The second segment entails Joseph Stalin taking over the reins of power after Lenin's death. Stalin (also known as the "Boss") was able to consolidate power and gain complete control over the Soviet Union and held power until he died in 1953. He presided over the monopolization of Russia's agriculture. He orchestrated a system of terror, which entailed mass arrests, mass murder, show-trials, and the incarceration of millions in the massive Gulag concentration camp system. Stalin had old Bolsheviks, his military, peasants, technicians, party members and tens of millions of others murdered or imprisoned.

Murderous Marxism

The third phase is the Second World War. In 1939, the Nazis and Soviets signed the Non-Aggression Pact. Its secret protocols outline how these two totalitarian states would divide up parts of Europe. With the outbreak of the Second World War, both regimes held to the agreement until Nazi Germany attacked the Soviet Union in 1941. The USSR went from being aligned with Nazi Germany to being one of the Western Allies. WWII was destructive and deadly for the Soviet populace, but Stalin would emerge even more powerful, with communist domination of Eastern Europe until the late 1980s.

The Fourth phase. After Stalin, Nikita Khrushchev assumed power of the Soviet Union, from the mid-1950s through the 1960s, and he ended the use of mass terror. Khrushchev criticized the dead dictator in the famous secret speech of 1956. The Cold War between the Soviet Union and the United States began in earnest with the Korean War and intensified under Khrushchev.

The Soviet Union intensified its existing worldwide espionage operations across the globe and supplied communist insurgencies and terrorist organizations. The USSR aided in crushing uprisings against Soviet backed governments in East Germany, Hungary, and Czechoslovakia. The Soviets supplied weaponry and support for communist backed movements in Asia, South America, and Africa, which only led to more destabilization and killing. In 1979, the Soviets invaded and occupied Afghanistan until 1989.

From the 1950s through the late 1980s, the Soviets engaged in" active measures,' which were disinformation operations across the globe. The goal of these secret "active measures or campaigns" was to destabilize governments or sway public opinion against Western democracies, especially the United States.

The Fifth phase. From the late 1960s to the early 1980s, the Soviet Union was marked by inept leadership, a grossly inefficient state bureaucracy and massive corruption that permeated the entire system. These factors were the primary reason for the collapse of the USSR in 1991. While the Soviet Union was no more, the damage from Communism had been done.

Czarist Russia prior to the Russian Civil War.

The Bolsheviks originated in Russia, and they were wild-eyed revolutionaries. They wanted to export the communist revolution to every corner of the world, and Russia was their first step. They used extreme violence and terror to take over Russia. The Bolshevik takeover of the Russian Empire was a matter of timing, good luck, and missteps by others. There were other groups vying for power: socialists, anarchists, traditional Russians, and regional groups struggled for power during the Russian Revolution which started in 1918. Yet the Bolsheviks would prove to be the most ruthless, which contributed to their success in taking control of Russia. (See Lenin's train ride.)

The Russian Empire, prior to the 1917 Revolution, was backwards and rife with corruption. Ruled by the inept Tsar Nicholas II, Russia entered the First World War along with the other European nations. While vast in geographic size, the economy was small and inefficient. It was based primarily on agricultural produce from a huge peasant base, along with other commodities. Infrastructure, such as roads, bridges, and canals, was lacking.

The primitive Russian economy was not able to cope with the strain of supplying its armies during WWI. Due to the military setbacks, Czar Nicholas II took over as the head of the Russian army, but his poor leadership only made the situation worse. As the economy faltered, food shortages and other economic hardships became acute. Different groups sought to challenge the Czar and remove him from the throne.

By the beginning of 1917, a cross-section of Russian society, intellectuals, nobility, and business leaders, forced Czar Nicholas II to abdicate his throne. The Provisional Government was formed but fared little better. The new Russian government chose to continue the war, and the economic situation only worsened. On November 6-7, 1917, the Bolsheviks struck, staging a coup d'état, which took over the government. While they consolidated power after the coup, they had promised land reform for the peasants, the largest class within Russia, and more political latitude for the revolutionary councils, the Soviets. The Bolsheviks allowed the Constitutional Assembly to continue functioning, and when elections were held, they failed to win. It did not matter. Vladimir Lenin, the leader of the Bolsheviks, had no intention of keeping their word. He pulled Russia out of World War I because he was about to make war on the people of the former Russian Empire.

As one historian noted," Lenin and his Bolsheviks were revolutionaries of a most thoroughgoing kind. Once in power, they set about tearing up the old Russia root and branch. Under Lenin... and more under [Joseph] Stalin from 1929 onwards, they reconstructed almost every aspect of Russian life. But they did it by coercion from above..." When the Russian Civil War broke out, the number of people who perished would eclipse the military losses of the First World War. Bloodshed and terror would touch every sector of Russian society.

William Johnson

Points to Ponder: Lenin's train ride.

By the beginning of 1917, World War I had been raging for more than two years, and the German Empire was facing a military stalemate. To the east, the Russian Revolution had forced the Czar to abdicate, but the new Provisional Government of Russia was still in the war. To the West, Great Britain and France were far from being defeated. Furthermore, the German strategy of using unrestricted submarine warfare in the Atlantic Ocean was the primary reason the United States declared war on the German Empire. The Germans understood that once American men and material began arriving at the Western Front, the odds would no longer be in their favor. Desperate to tip the military odds in their favor, the German Empire looked to eliminate one of the Allies.

The Germans knew the Russian Provisional Government was politically weak, so they struck upon a bold plan to knock Russia out of the war by destabilizing the country from within. They arranged for Vladimir Lenin, the firebrand Bolshevik, to be returned to Russia from his exile in Switzerland. The Germans would also hedge their bets by contributing gold to finance Bolshevik revolutionary activity. In April of 1917, a locomotive with a single car left Switzerland and delivered the future leader of the Soviet Union and other Bolshevik revolutionaries to Russia. And the rest, you could say, is history.

Under Lenin's leadership, the Bolsheviks executed a coup in November 1917, eliminating the Provisional Russian Government. The Bolsheviks plunged Russia into a blood-drenched Civil War, which the communists won. Lenin would be the driving force behind establishing the first communist state in the world. Like cancer, Communism metastasized, spreading across the globe, from Russia, then to China, Eastern Europe, North Korea, Indochina, Cuba, Nicaragua, and parts of

Africa. One could effectively argue that **Lenin's train ride could be considered one of the most consequential events connected to the history of the locomotive.**

For Germany, it was a different story; their bet did not pay off. Although Lenin pulled Russia out of the First World War, Germany could not beat the Allies. They signed an armistice with the Allies, ending the First World War, and the provisions of the Treaty of Versailles devastated Germany. Fast forward, over two decades later, the Soviet Union would be critical in the defeat of Nazi Germany. [7]

Terror: the Bolsheviks' most crucial weapon.

By 1918, the Russian Civil War was in full swing, and terror would become the most crucial weapon in the Bolshevik arsenal. The Bolsheviks made their intentions quite clear in official writings and proclamations. Any opposition would be crushed without mercy. The communists would not tolerate different opinions or doubts about the use of brutality. Anything less than full support for the Bolshevik goal of domination was considered an act of civil war against the state. As one Bolshevik leader wrote, **"not only destroy the... enemy, but...**

---

7 Davies, N. Europe. p. 914-917, 919, 920, 921, 962, 988, 1000, 1003, 1010, 1012, 1013, 1027, 1028, 1030, 1036, 1047, 1052, 1058, 1090, 1092, 1106, 1108. Acton, Edward. The Present and Past Russia: Russia. P. 126-187. Merridale, Catherine. Lenin on the Train. Pp.6-7, 15, 140-142, 199-200, 210, 228, 229, 242-244, 247-253, 275. Willmott, H.P. World War I. 226, 227. Keegan, John. The First World War. pp. 332-343. Medvedev, Roy. Let History Judge. P. 340, 358. Kissinger, Henry. Diplomacy. 622-642, 667, 701. LeFeber, Walter. The American Age. Pp. 446. Courtois, Stephane, et. al. The Black Book of Communism. p.18, 22, 23, 24, 25, 39-49, 52. White, Matthew. The Great Big Book of Horrible Things. Pp. 359-361. Andrews, Christopher, Mitrokhin, Vasili. The World was going our Way: The KGB and the Battle for the Third World. Pp. 623: is the index, which has well over 56 pages connected to active measures. Kennedy, Paul. The Rise and Fall of the Great Powers. Pp. 172, 234-5. The backwardness of the Russian Empire's economy prior to the Revolution. Radzinsky, Edvard, Stalin. Pp. 95-98. Lenin's train ride and German gold.

anyone who raises a hand in protest against class war will die..." Lenin fixated on maintaining power when he wrote, **"It is of supreme importance that we encourage and make use of mass terror..."** In another telegram, Lenin wrote that any opposition of the peasantry to mass requisitions of food, **"must be crushed without pity... make an example of these people... (1) Hang (I mean hang publicly, so that people see it), (2) Publish their names. (3) Seize all their grain. (4) Single out hostages..."**

To legitimize terror, the Bolsheviks echoed the Communist Manifesto, when one of their leaders asserted, **"We reject the old systems of moral and 'humanity' invented... to oppress... the 'lower classes'... Blood? Let it flow like water!"** Lenin summed up Bolshevik inhumanity when he wrote this bloodthirsty memo to a communist colleague. **"The basic concept, I hope, is clear... to set forth a statute which is both principled and politically truthful... to supply the motivation for the essence and the justification of terror..." "The courts must not exclude terror. It would be self-deception or deceit to promise this... and to legalize it in a principled way... for applying it broadly in practice."** This is just a smattering of the horrible writings penned by the Bolsheviks. Terror was the central pillar of their goal to attain supremacy.

Note, prior to 1922, Revolutionary Russia was referred to as the Russian Soviet Federative Socialist Republic (RSFSR). After 1922, the first communist state would officially become the United Soviet Socialist Republic (USSR), and the people were referred to as Soviets. The Soviet Union consisted of Russians, Poles, Byelorussians, Ukrainians, and many more different nationalities. For instance, Joseph Stalin was a Georgian.

The purveyors of terror, the Soviet secret police. Before the Nazis, there were the Bolsheviks.

Well over a decade before the Nazis, the Soviets created institutions dedicated to terror. By 1918, the Soviets had built what would become the first modern-day version of the secret police, along with a massive prison and concentration camp system. Nazi institutions of repression were dwarfed by the Soviet versions. Furthermore, the Soviets pioneered using trains to transport millions of victims throughout their vast system of concentration camps. During the Russian Civil War, the Bolsheviks periodically used poisonous gas to break peasant resistance to the confiscation of their crops. They also developed large crematoriums to make the bodies of their victims disappear. One could say that the Nazis copied the Soviet model of terror.

The Soviet secret police made other secret police look like amateurs.

To understand the murderous efficiency of the Bolsheviks during the Russian Civil War, one must understand the development of their secret police. Arguably, the Soviet secret police were more vicious than the Nazi's Gestapo. Established in 1918, they spearheaded the most terrifying aspects of Soviet history. The Soviet security apparatus (secret police) was quite large and was known by a variety of different (acronyms) names: Cheka, OGPU, NKVD, GPU, MGB, MVD, KGB, to name a few. The Soviet secret police had a variety of departments with different functions. Throughout the history of the KGB, it underwent reorganization, mergers, separations, and occasionally overlapped with the military intelligence services. They were always deadly effective. Whatever acronym you chose, the Soviet secret police struck fear into the hearts of the USSR's populace. For this reference book, I will refer to the Soviet secret police by their final name, the KGB.

The ranks of the KGB grew dramatically during the Russian Revolution. By June 1918, the Bolsheviks had 12,000 agents, and by the end of the year, the number had grown to 40,000. By the beginning of 1921, their ranks had swelled to over 280,000, a sevenfold increase in just over two years. In contrast, the US Federal Bureau of Investigation currently has 35,000 employees, of whom a little over 10,000 are special agents. By 1939, the Soviet secret police had 366,000 members, which included the staff of the Soviet Gulag system. In contrast, the Nazis' Gestapo had 7,500! The KGB was one of the largest employers in Europe at the time.

The Black Book of Communism noted that the Soviet secret police were not only brutal but also debauched and rife with corruption. Extortion and bribery were rampant. Alexander Solzhenitsyn, the author of *GULAG Archipelago* and survivor of the Soviet concentration camps system, railed against the corruption of the secret police. Besides mass murder, torture, Soviet records indicated that the KGB routinely robbed, looted, and sexually assaulted women on a massive scale within their concentration camp system. The scale of sexual violence was beyond description. Drunkenness was widespread, and cocaine use was not uncommon.

Goodfellas, don't leave any witnesses.

In the Mafia-related movie, "*Goodfellas,*" a group of gangsters robbed a cargo area at JFK airport, making off with millions in cash and jewelry. When the police got a lead on the robbers, the ringleaders of the gang started killing off their accomplices so they could not "rat them out" to the authorities. In short, leave no one to talk. Such was the revolving door of Soviet secret police leaders in the USSR, from 1918 to 1954. The Soviet Union had nine different leaders of their security apparatus (secret police) during this time span. Feliks Dzerzhinsky, the first head of the KGB, was born into a Polish aristocratic family and died of cancer in 1926. One of the few secret police heads to die of natural causes. V. Menzhinsky headed up the KGB from 1926 to 1934, and he supposedly died from a heart condition. Gregory Yagoda (1934-1936), one of Stalin's most brutal secret police chiefs, carried out mass killings until he was arrested, tortured, and shot. Before being killed, Yagoda claimed to have poisoned his predecessor, Menzhinsky. Yagoda's successor, Nikola Yezhov (1936-1938), was no slouch either. He carried out mass killings until he was arrested and shot. (It was rare that such Soviet higher-ups would have been killed without the approval of Stalin.) Yezhov's successor, Lavrenti Beria, was the head of the Soviet secret police four different times between 1938-1953. After the death of Stalin, he was shot in 1953. Of the next four KGB leaders, two were shot, one died of natural causes, and the successor of Beria, Sergei Kruglov, survived his chairmanship. Still, historians cannot agree if he died from a heart condition, poisoning, or was run over by a train.

Beria, mass murder, serial rapist and serial killer all wrapped up in one.

Lavrenti Beria was a complete sadist; he had absolutely no qualms about killing. Literally, his rise to power was built on a mountain of bodies. In one instance, he invited a group of KGB officers to a "lavish banquet," and during the festivities, he had them arrested and shot dead in the basement. Beria was so paranoid that he even bugged Stalin's apartment. The secret police chief had a prisoner, physicist Lev Theremin, make the eavesdropping device, which was placed in the

Soviet leader's residence. Besides being a mass murderer and the periodic head of the Soviet secret police, Beria was a serial rapist and murderer. The number of his victims could easily number in the hundreds or more, and the KGB compiled 47 volumes of evidence of his grisly killings. Since he was an efficient mass murderer and slavishly devoted to Stalin, he was able to operate freely. Case in point, there is a photograph of Beria, with Stalin's daughter sitting in his lap. Stalin can be seen in the background looking over paperwork, seemingly unconcerned that his daughter sat in the lap of a serial killer. After the fall of the USSR, a building once occupied by Beria was renovated, and workers discovered bones of murder victims buried on the property.

Points to Ponder: Yagoda's ghoulish hobby.

Yagoda had a fascination for morbid memorabilia, specifically bullets that were used to kill early Bolshevik revolutionaries. Yagoda held onto the bullets dug out of the corpses. Supposedly, he named the bullets after the person who was executed. Ironically, when Yagoda was shot, his successor, Yezhov, had the bullet removed from him, and he kept the projectile as a souvenir. When Yezhov was shot, the bullet that killed him was supposedly retrieved.

Points to Ponder: Hitler's only secret police leader.

Historical comparison. In contrast, Heinrich Himmler was appointed by Adolph Hitler to head his personal bodyguard, the Schutzstaffel, or SS. What started as a group of several hundred men that safeguarded the Führer in the 1920s grew to over 200,000 men by 1939. By the beginning of the Second World War, Himmler headed a security apparatus, which not only encompassed Hitler's elite guard, but also the military wing, the Waffen SS and the dreaded Nazi secret police, the Gestapo. During WWII, the Gestapo would strike fear into

Murderous Marxism

the hearts of the people and countries the Nazis conquered. Until the final days of the Second World War, Heinrich Himmler would be the only leader of this Nazi security apparatus.

Before Himmler became the leader of the SS, he raised chickens, was a fertilizer salesman, and was fascinated by the occult. After Germany attacked their former Non-Aggression Pact ally, the USSR, the Soviets joined the Allies' fight against the Third Reich. During the war, the three main allies: Great Britain, the United States of America and the USSR held several conferences, one of which was held at the Soviet city of Yalta in 1945. The United States' President, Franklin Delano Roosevelt, was in attendance when he observed a man amongst the attendees whom he did not recognize. He asked Stalin through an interpreter who the man was, and the "Boss" quipped, "That's Beria... He's our Himmler." [8]

---

8 Solzhenitsyn, Alexander. The GULAG Archipelago, 1918-1956. Pp. 151, 153, 154, 155, 156, 157, 158-9, 161, 314-317, 352, 353, 435, 436. Radzinsky, Edvard. Stalin. p. 345. Courtois, Stephane, et. al. The Black Book of Communism, p. xvi, 52, 57-58, 64, 69, 72, 74, 75, 78, 79, 82, 83, 84, 85,102 103-104, 139, 140-142. Davies, N. No Simple Victory. P. 191. Blauvelt, Timothy. Patronage and betrayal in the post-Stalin succession: The case of Kruglov, and Serov. Communist and Post-Communist Studies, Volume 41, Issue 1, March 2008, p105-120. Quote from p.117; "He died in obscurity, falling under a train in 1977." Vronskaya, Jeanne, and Chuguev, Viktor. (Editors). A Biographical Dictionary of the Soviet Union,1917-1988. pg. 210, 375. "Files shown on Stalin henchman," The Associated Press: Reprinted in: The News & Observer. Jan. 18, 2003, p. 16A. When William Shire first met Himmler, he thought the future head of the German secret police was a school teacher. Shire, William. The Rise and Fall of the Third Reich.172,176, 204, 299-300, 373-374, 428, 864. PBS: The American Experience. The Man behind Hitler: Heinrich Himmler 1900-1945. Article. Simon Whistler. "Lavrentiy Beria: Stalin's Architect of Terror." Biographics. Video: You Tube. This source outlines the history and organizational history of the Soviet secret police. Andrew, C., Mitrokhin, V. The World Was Going Our Way. The KGB And the battle for The Third World. P.495-501. Davies, N. Europe. p.929, 931, 932. Montefiore, Simon. Stalin. pp.198, 483. Katamidze, Slava. Loyal Comrades, Ruthless Killers: The Secret Services of the USSR 1917-1991. Pp.10,11,12. The web site for the Federal Bureau of Investigation. White, Matthew. The Great Big Book of Horrible Things. Pp. 368-369, 454, 529. Good Fellas:

The Russian Civil War.

In early November 6-7, 1917, the Bolsheviks executed a coup, seizing control of the Russian government. Vladimir Lenin allowed the Provisional Government to function, but none of the legislation passed by the Duma (Russian Parliament) would be implemented. By March of 1918, Lenin had pulled Russia out of WWI. Some historians have asserted that the Bolsheviks wanted to focus on building the first communist state. That seems a stretch. Not everyone was on board with the Bolsheviks' unilateral power grab.

Furthermore, the Bolsheviks were not interested in power sharing; they wanted sole control of Russia, despite a sizeable part of the population that was reluctant to cede power to them. Lenin no doubt realized that the Bolshevik coup would provoke an armed response. He probably pulled Russia out of WWI because he would need the manpower to take over and control Russia.

The Russian Civil War was more than a battle between the Bolsheviks (Reds) and the Whites (the Czarist forces); it involved several different groups that sought to overthrow the Bolsheviks.

The Russian Civil War also included the Bolsheviks reconquering former territories that had declared independence after the collapse of the Russian Empire. The Bolshevik forces also attacked Poland and the Baltic states but were unsuccessful. Not every facet of the Civil War will be covered.

1990, Warner Brothers. Glinsky, Albert. Theremin: Ether Music and Espionage. Pp. 256, 257, 258, 259, 262.

The Bolsheviks go back on their word and lie straight through their teeth.

Karl Marx's writings promised a workers' paradise, and the Bolsheviks were supposedly going to deliver it. The reality was quite different. By the beginning of 1918, the Bolsheviks had begun imposing heavy taxes, regulating, confiscating property, and plundering the former Russian Empire. Communist centralized planning of the economy failed miserably. Economic indexes and production fell, in some cases, dramatically.

Protests and labor strikes erupted across Russia because the Bolsheviks had broken their promises to the industrial workers. *The Black Book on Communism* noted that by force of arms, the communists monopolized all food distribution. They threatened to withhold food ration cards from workers if they did not obey their ultimatums. During the revolution, food rations were also cut, so workers had to search for food to survive. The Bolsheviks added insult to injury by declaring that missing work was to be considered a crime. Workers received meager wages and food ration cards that barely met subsistence needs. The communists made food distribution a weapon, in which they could apply murderous leverage over the populace. Workers' paradise sounds more like a living nightmare.

In the rural areas, the confiscation of peasants' agricultural produce and high taxes sparked thousands of revolts. Food confiscation, on this scale, could mean life or death for impoverished peasants. Any protests were considered counter revolutionary. Even passive dissent was brutally suppressed. In both rural and urban areas, the Bolsheviks responded with savagery, mass arrests, and imprisonment. Many thousands were summarily executed, many without trial.

In 1921, Bolshevik brutality was the primary factor behind a mutiny at the Kronstadt Naval Base, which soon encompassed the entire city. Striking workers and regular citizens also joined the mutineers. They demanded a say in government, free elections, an increase in food rations, free speech, and the release of political prisoners. The Bolsheviks violently crushed the mutiny, and the city was retaken. Those who rebelled were shot or imprisoned.

Points to Ponder: The Communist Party of the United States of America (CPUSA).

Yet when one reads the CPUSA website, they will see article after article, in which writers screech how they want to defend workers' rights. The hypocrisy of the CPUSA knows no bounds. They refuse to acknowledge that the early Bolsheviks treated workers terribly. While workers in the USSR toiled away, they received meager wages and had to stand in line for hours for food and other staples. Hunger was a constant companion. There were shortages of housing, and at times, two families might be crammed into a small dwelling.

Furthermore, the opportunity to advance oneself was nonexistent. Complaining could cost you your life. In contrast, communist elites in the USSR were well paid, had spacious apartments and received fantastic benefits. You would never know this by reading the CPUSA website.

The Czar and his family are murdered, and Disney makes a movie.

In the spring of 1917, Czar Nicholas II, his family, and the royal entourage were taken hostage by the Bolsheviks and moved to the city of Ekaterinburg. In the summer of 1918, the Bolshevik leadership

Murderous Marxism

ordered the murder of the Romanov family. Nicholas II, his family, their servants, which included their doctor, and the family dog were secretly killed. There was no trial for the royal family or the others. If you Google the death of Nicholas II, many times you will often read that the Russian royal family was executed. Execution indicates that there was a fair trial, and guilt was proven. None of that occurred. In the book, *The Last Tsar,* Russian historian Edvard Radzinsky wrote about the final days of the royal family. Scouring archives and numerous other sources, the historian pieced together what he believed to be the final days of the Romanovs.

The royal family was taken to the basement of the house where they were being held, and murdered. Some of the killers had been drinking, and their shooting was less than accurate. According to Radzinsky, the Czar, his wife, and the servants probably died immediately, while some of the children supposedly survived the initial barrage of bullets. Radzinsky believed that some of the children were shot multiple times, bludgeoned, and bayoneted. The Bolsheviks then robbed the corpses of all valuables, which included the royal jewels. The bodies were loaded into trucks and driven into a forest, stripped of clothing, doused with acid and gasoline, then set ablaze. The remains were buried in two hastily dug pits. No body, no problem! Their brutality resembled the actions of gangsters, not the heroic revolutionaries they later claimed to be.

Later rumors would arise about a woman claiming to be one of the Romanov daughters, Anastasia. She claimed to have escaped and wandered about Europe for years with amnesia. As this urban myth grew, some people started to believe this woman's tall tale. DNA testing ended the charade and proved the woman claiming to be Anastasia was an imposter. Several movies were made about the Romanov daughter, who supposedly escaped the Bolsheviks. The most popular and profitable movie about the lost Romanov princess was Walt Disney's animated version: *Anastasia*. The Disney version was highly sanitized, and the historical accuracy was turned on its head, with little or no mention of communist complicity in the murders of the Romanovs.

It begs the question: what crime was the royal family guilty of? The royal women could not inherit the throne, so why were they killed? Why were innocent servants murdered? Some have pathetically theorized that the inept Nicholas II might have somehow rallied forces against the Bolsheviks, which was an unlikely scenario. The reasoning was probably quite simple. Like out of a Mafia movie, the Romanovs had to be killed because their mere existence could potentially become an obstacle to the Bolsheviks' takeover of Russia. The servants were murdered so they would never talk.

In 1924, the Bolsheviks renamed the city of Ekaterinburg to Sverdlov. Yakov Sverdlov was one of the ring leaders tasked by Lenin to murder the Romanov family, but he never lived to see the dedication of the city named after him. According to "official" sources, "Yakov Sverdlov died after a sudden illness..." in 1919. Robert Massie, a British historian who specialized in Russian history, wrote that "persistent rumors" indicated that Sverdlov died after being physically assaulted. In 1987, a documentary on Soviet TV supposedly had film footage of his funeral, which distinctly showed "his head... in the open coffin... bandaged." If the video recording is accurate, it begs the question: Were the Bolsheviks killing off accomplices to "tie up loose ends," or was it a coincidence that Sverdlov just died suddenly?

Points to Ponder: The killings of Western kings.

During modern times, other Western monarchs have been killed, or should we say executed. The King of England, Charles I, was beheaded after his semi-tyrannical rule ran afoul of Parliament, which sparked the English Civil War. He was defeated, captured, put on trial, and convicted. Only then did he lose his head. Louis XVI of France had the misfortune of being incompetent and not sufficiently ruthless when the French Revolution broke out. He tried to flee the country, but was captured, put on trial, convicted, and lost his head when he was guillotined. The Romanovs were never given any judicial due process; just murdered.

Points to Ponder: Women trying to assassinate the bloody revolutionaries!!

The murderous rule of revolutionaries can sometimes inspire people to assassinate them. Lenin's rule was no different. In 1918, a young woman named Fanny Kaplan shot the Bolshevik leader but only succeeded in wounding him. Kaplan was arrested and readily admitted that she had acted alone and was subsequently shot. Lenin was badly wounded, and some have opined that his injuries might have contributed to the stroke that killed him six years later.

Women assassinating tyrants has some precedent. Over a hundred years earlier, during the early blood-soaked days of the French Revolution, Charlotte Corday stabbed to death the firebrand revolutionary pamphleteer, Jean-Paul Marat. She was arrested and freely confessed to killing Marat. Charlotte was later condemned to death and was guillotined. Both women acted alone, with the hope that their actions would alter history and bring tyranny to heel. Neither of the attempts achieved its goal.

The Red Terror.

When the Russian people resisted the Bolshevik takeover, the communists enacted what became known as the Red Terror, which entailed the use of savage brutality to win the Russian Civil War. The Bolsheviks claimed that the Red Terror was more of a spur-of-the-moment reaction to break the resistance of the masses. One of the contributing writers to *The Black Book of Communism*, Nicolas Werth, wrote that the Bolshevik excuse was a concocted falsehood. Werth wrote that "the truth was that the Red Terror was the natural outlet for the almost abstract hatred that most of the Bolshevik leaders felt toward their 'oppressors' who they wished to… [kill off] … not on an individual basis, but as a class." Dzerzhinsky, the first head of the Soviet secret police, the KGB, said that victory hinged on "forcing certain classes into submission, or by exterminating them altogether." This passage seems to lay bare the Bolsheviks' true intentions. Very little seems to separate these early communists from the future Nazis.

Within a few months after the outbreak of hostilities in 1918, the Bolsheviks murdered, without trial, between 10,000 and 15,000 people. Striking workers and peasants rebelling against the wholesale confiscation of their agricultural produce were shot down. In contrast, over ninety years (between 1825 and 1917), Tsarist Russia executed 6,321 prisoners. *The Black Book on Communism* noted that the Bolsheviks' secret police murdered in "the space of a few weeks" two to three times that amount. As a Soviet dissident and writer, Alexander Solzhenitsyn noted in his book, *GULAG Archipelago*, the Bolsheviks used distorted language to mask their murderous acts. **As people were** murdered without trial, the Soviets referred to it as "extrajudicial killings." [9]

Bolshevik atrocities mount, especially in Ukraine.

Ukraine's location on the northern coastline of the Black Sea has made it a strategic region between Asia and Europe. An abundance of fertile land that produced bumper crops of grain and ports that allowed ships to travel from the Black Sea to the Mediterranean Sea made this a coveted region. Different groups battled to control Ukraine for well over a thousand years. In the eighteenth century, the Russian Empire took Ukraine by force of arms. With the collapse of the Russian Empire after WWI, Ukraine gained its freedom, only to see this newfound independence threatened by the Bolsheviks. In 1919, during the height of the Russian Civil War, a White General Anton Denikin attempted to

---

9 Supposedly some of the Tsar's daughters were on their hands and knees screaming as they were shot and bayoneted. Initially the bodies were thrown into a small, abandoned gold mine, but were later retrieved. The Bolsheviks took steps to obscure the identity of the corpses so if discovered, the royal family could not be identified. The bodies were stripped of clothing then doused with acid and burned. What was left of the corpses were buried in two pits. The basement, in which the murders took place was photographed. Radzinsky's book contains a tremendous amount of detail about the murders; all quite sad. Later the bodies of the Czars family were discovered, and DNA testing verified that the remains were that of the Czar and at least part of his family. Not all the bodies were discovered. Radzinsky, Edvard. The Last Tsar: The Life and Death of the Nicholas II. Sverdlov, pp. 134, killing of the Romanovs. Pp. 339-340, 360-375, 398-424, 435-438. Amis, Martin, Koba the Dread. p. 53,54,55. Colley, Rupert. "Fanny Kaplan- the woman who tried to kill Lenin" Feb. 10th, 2015. http: //rupertcolley.com. White, Matthew. The Great Big Book of Horrible Things. Pp. 359-368. Davies, N. Europe. Pp. 549, 550, 551-553, 677, 699, 710-711, 928-929, 931. Solzhenitsyn, Alexander. The GULAG Archipelago, 1918-1956. Pp. 625. Courtois, Stephane, et. al. The Black Book of Communism, p. xviii, 39-70, 71, 73, 74, 75, 78-85. Anastasia. Walt Disney; Movie. 1997. Medvedev, Roy. Let History Judge. 247-254. Good Fellas: Movie. 1990. Katz, Brigit. "DNA Analysis confirms authenticity of Romanov's Remains," Smithsonian Magazine: Online. July 17, 2018. Information about Fanny Kaplan. Vronskaya, Jeanne & Chuguev, Vladmir. A Biographical Dictionary of the Soviet Union 1917-1988. Pp. 164., Sverdlov pp.429.

record Bolshevik atrocities in the Don, Kuban regions of Ukraine over a period of several months. He recorded:

-White officers were thrown into a blast furnace.

-Others were bound and drowned in the Black Sea.

The Communists targeted non-combatants as well as soldiers with a single-minded ferocity. Denikin described the grisly death of unarmed peasants:

"Corpses with the hands cut off, broken bones, heads ripped off, broken jaws, and genitals removed."

-Photographs show stone-faced peasants standing next to decapitated heads and mutilated bodies.

A former KGB agent, Vasili Mitrokhin, defected to Great Britain after the fall of the Soviet Union. He had been the agent assigned to the Soviet Archives, and he spent years secretly copying files. His voluminous notes chronicled the gruesome details about Bolshevik atrocities, which "sickened" the former agent. Mitrokhin noted that the early KGB committed these savage acts in Ukraine.

-Made "gloves out of human skin."

-Some were stripped of clothing, "placed in barrels, with nails hammered towards the inside", and the containers were rolled down hills.

-Others were impaled.

-Some prisoners were placed in "cages of rats… [that]… were fixed to prisoners' bodies and heated until the rats gnawed their way into the victims' intestines."

Murderous Marxism

The Black Book of Communism estimated that between 1919 and 1920, the Bolsheviks deported, imprisoned, or killed between 300,000 and more people in Ukraine and surrounding areas. It was out of a population of three million. When prisons were filled, they resorted to using firing squads and mass drownings. Prisoners were loaded onto barges and thrown into "the Volga River, with stones around their necks." At one point, when the Bolsheviks were retreating from Ukraine, they spared few. "They burned villages by the hundreds and carried out mass shootings." (*The Black Book of Communism* contains photographs of rotting corpses, which were the handiwork of the Bolsheviks.)

By 1920, most groups that opposed the new communist regime had been crushed, and the Bolsheviks "intensified" their war against the large peasant groups that resisted the confiscation of their crops. Russia is vast and has a tremendous amount of territory that refused to submit to the Bolsheviks' draconian mandates and taxation. The communists used every means of terror to achieve their goal of subjugating the peasantry, "including large-scale executions of hostages and... bombing... villages with poisonous gas..."

Points to Ponder: Mass murder and atrocities. What is Old is New. The Bolsheviks used French Revolutionary terror tactics.

Communists have admired the blood-drenched actions of the radicals of the French Revolution. They drew inspiration from these revolutionaries who overthrew the old regime of the French monarchy. From 1789 through the mid-1790s, these radicals engaged in a period of blood-letting that shocked their European contemporaries. The historical parallels are striking. Just like the Bolsheviks, the revolutionaries went to great lengths to kill off real or imagined opponents. The French revolutionaries shot people in "large batches," but that became expensive, so they developed an economical way of mass killing. They devised barges that could be sunk and later refloated. As one historian noted, these reusable death chambers became known as the "terrible Noyades." Thousands died horrific deaths in these drowning machines. Fast forward a century and a half, and the Bolsheviks also used barges to drown their victims. They also gassed and used mass shootings to kill off prisoners.

Points to ponder: The Nazis used the guillotine and gas.

The Nazis also drew inspiration from the French Revolutionaries. The French radicals used the guillotine to execute victims, and it was a perfect terror weapon and a macabre form of entertainment. Mobs howled with excitement as victims were taken to a raised platform that held the guillotine. The victim was strapped down, and a blade would plunge down a vertical track, slicing off the doomed person's head. The Nazis also used the guillotine to execute prisoners, but it was not used as a public spectacle as it had been during the French Revolution.

During the nineteenth and twentieth centuries, German corporations had been leaders in both the chemical and pharmaceutical industries. Unfortunately, it would be this expertise that the Nazis used to develop methods for committing mass murder. The Germans had used mass shootings during the Second World War, but this was expensive and laborious to carry out. The Nazis struck upon the idea of gassing victims, which turned out to be an efficient, cold-blooded method for mass killings.

The history behind the primary gas used to kill Jews and others during the Holocaust is bizarre. Master chemist Fritz Haber was the "father" of the German Army's gas warfare program during the First World War. Haber's involvement was not without controversy. His wife became so upset at his participation in Germany's gas warfare program that she committed suicide. After the end of the war, the Allies considered declaring him a war criminal, but in a strange twist of fate, Fritz Haber won a Nobel Peace Prize for chemistry in 1918. However, he did not receive the award until the next year. During the interwar years, Haber would take part in the development of a pesticide for killing rodents, which became known as Zyklon B. When the Nazi's came to power in the early 1930s, Fritz Haber fled Germany because he was Jewish. He later died in 1934.

During World War II, the Germans struck upon the idea of using Zyklon B to gas victims. To keep victims from fighting back, the gas chambers were disguised to look like showers in the concentration camps. Jewish people and other victims would be ordered to disrobe, then crowded into the fake showers, then gassed with Zyklon B. Their bodies, in most cases, were incinerated in industrial-sized crematoriums.

The Slaughter of Tambov.

To totally subjugate the peasantry in the Tambov region of western Russia, Bolshevik General Mikhail Tukhachevsky signed "Order No. 121" on June 11, 1921. It was brutality; incarnate. Tukhachevsky ordered:

-People were to be shot on sight if they did not give their names.

-Villagers were forced to inform anyone that they thought might possess weapons; if no one was forthcoming, hostages would be shot.

-If a weapon was found or a resistance member was discovered, the eldest son would be shot.

-People who resisted and fled had all their possessions confiscated.

The Bolsheviks used 100,000 soldiers to crush resistance in the Tambov region. Bolshevik commanders were ordered to set up and operate "**death camps where prisoners were gassed**." To clinch victory, Tukhachevsky ordered, "**The forests…are to be cleared by the use of poisonous gas. This must be carefully calculated so that the layer of gas penetrates the forests and kills everyone hiding there. The artillery inspector is to provide the necessary amounts of gas immediately…to carry out this sort of operation.**"

The Reconquering of the old Czarist Empire: 1918-1922.

The historian Norman Davies noted that some historians were blindly sympathetic to the Soviets and accepted that the Bolsheviks could, with impunity, conquer areas that had declared their independence, such as Ukraine, the Donbas region, Siberia, and other territories. In the end, the Bolsheviks, by force of arms and mind-numbing brutality, won the day and snatched back most of the former Russian Empire of the czars.

After the Bolshevik coup, the British, French, Americans (and later the Japanese) were suspicious of Soviet intentions. They had the right to fear the Bolsheviks. The Bolsheviks reoccupied Siberia, a vast region with tremendous natural resources, which would serve as a strategic link for them to the Pacific Ocean.

WWI was coming to an end, and the German, Austrian and Russian empires were in the process of falling apart. The geopolitical order was shifting dramatically. From these disintegrating empires, new nations emerged in Eastern Europe, and their respective economies were weak.

Poland saves Europe from the Soviets, and few take notice.

During the Russian Revolution, the Bolsheviks took the opportunity to attack Poland in 1919. With the end of WWI, Poland had become an independent country after being ruled for over a century by the empires of Germany, Austria, and Russia. It was at this point; the Soviets saw an opportunity to reconquer Poland and take their revolution into the heart of Europe.

In the summer of 1920, the Bolsheviks launched a military offensive into Poland. The commanding Soviet General, Tukhachevsky—the butcher of Tambov—supposedly said, "To the West! Over the corpse of White Poland lies the road to world-wide conflagration." His optimism was short-lived. The Poles defeated the Soviets in the Battle for Warsaw. A British diplomat who witnessed the battle noted that if the Poles had lost, "not only would Christianity ... experienced a dangerous reverse, but the very existence of western civilization would have been imperiled." The Polish victory quite possibly saved parts of Europe from communist domination. History seems to have overlooked this fact. More history down a memory black hole?

During this war, Soviet brutality is summed up in a photograph in *The Black Book of Communism*. The photograph shows a lone captured Polish officer. He had been stripped, suspended from a tree by his left leg, and a sharpened stake, several feet long, had been rammed into his rectum. Soviet soldiers could be seen milling about, admiring their handiwork. This example of savagery was unlikely to be the only atrocity committed by the Bolsheviks; just one of the few captured on a phonograph.

American intervention in Siberia.

In the summer of 1918, US President Woodrow Wilson dispatched an American expeditionary, of close to 10,000 men into Siberia. Their mission was supposedly to support the withdrawal of the Czechoslovakian forces that were in the region. Wilson's excuse seems implausible, given the complexities of events unfolding during this period. The American Expeditionary Force turned out to be a useless gesture.

The emergence of a new communist terror state spurred Wilson to half-hearted action to check the Bolshevik drive to resurrect the Russian Empire under a communist regime. The pathetically small American expeditionary force had little chance of altering the trajectory of the Bolsheviks' re-conquest of the former Czarist Empire. It also gave the Bolsheviks the plausible excuse to use brutality, while claiming that external forces were conspiring to snuff out the fledgling communist state. The West and democracies were cast as villains, and Wilson's only achievement was to give the Bolsheviks a fig leaf of legitimacy. By 1920, American forces had withdrawn from Siberia.

"Lenin's Famine"

The Soviets intensified their seizure of foodstuffs from the peasantry. The communist attacks were so destructive, they thoroughly disrupted agricultural production on an unprecedented scale. Between the summer of 1921 through 1922, some 30 million people were starving throughout the former Russian Empire. Photographs show children...dead from starvation. The images were haunting, with their skeletal remains, taut skin, half-open mouths, and their lifeless eyes...open...staring into oblivion. Other photographs show starving children sitting on a bench or crouching. They were gaunt, unwashed, clothed in rags, and many had vacant stares; their facial features resembled those of "small birds" rather than children.

Lenin was unfazed. His diabolical mind deduced that "Famine... [could be used to destroy] ... the outdated peasant economy... [and]... usher in socialism... [and]... destroy faith not only in the Tsar, but in God too." The Bolsheviks wanted religion abolished because you cannot worship God and serve Marxism.

Points to Ponder: The Americans and outside relief agencies provide aid for the starving people.

The starvation became so dire that the Bolsheviks allowed foreign relief to be delivered. If not, they would have destroyed the very population they sought to control. The "Red Cross, the Quakers, and the American Relief Association (ARA)... [managed]... by Herbert Hoover," a future President of the United States, provided the much-needed foodstuffs. The Soviets tried their own relief, but they were barely able to feed 3 million people a day. In contrast, the Red Cross, the Quakers, and the ARA were able to supply 11 million people per day. By the end of 1922, at least 5 million Russians had died of starvation. Yet mass starvation and death on this scale were just the beginning of the nightmare for the populace of the newly created USSR. Ironically, it was the Americans and other relief groups that relieved a great deal of suffering instigated by the communists. Note, Herbert Hoover received a card from an area near Pinsk, thanking him for saving their lives.

The Bolsheviks win.

By the end of 1922, the Bolsheviks were in control of most of the former Russian Empire. In summary, it was the Bolsheviks who instigated the Russian Civil War with their coup in November 1917. The

Provisional Government of Russia was less than perfect, but it was trying to create a representative government. It was the Bolsheviks who set into motion the fighting. Although all sides engaged in violence, documentation clearly indicated that the Bolsheviks engaged in the systematic and organized application of terror during this conflict. Once in control, groups that had supported the Bolsheviks, the peasants, urban workers, and other revolutionaries were betrayed by the communists. When these groups objected to the subjugation, the Bolsheviks prevailed with the application of terror or what they called "war communism." Subsequentially, the Bolsheviks tried to export communism to almost every corner of the world. Some historians seem to find any plausible reason to excuse this blatant power grab, along with the barbaric tactics used by these communists to maintain power. Liberal and other supporters of the Soviet Union sang their praises. With the death of Lenin, Joseph Stalin took over the Soviet Union, and terror would take on a whole new dimension.

1922: Post Russian Civil War: Lenin wants to destroy all religion.

Lenin despised religion, and he worked tirelessly to stamp out systems of faith. A survivor of the Soviet concentration camp system wrote that the communists equated Christianity with "noxious fumes… poisoning the revolutionary will." Lenin wrote that the massive famine that stemmed from the Russian Revolution could possibly facilitate the outbreak of cannibalism. He theorized that the horrified masses would lose their faith in God, the czar, and their peasant lifestyle. By Lenin's reckoning, only by reducing people to depraved animals could they become proper revolutionaries. The Bolshevik leader wrote that church property must be taken with "ferocious and merciless energy" and brutal force must be used "in suppressing all resistance…", "the greater number of... clergy that we manage to execute... the better." The clergy were put on trial for worshipping God. Thousands were killed in rigged court proceedings. In 1922 alone, church records indicate that almost 8000 priests, nuns and monks were murdered, while thousands were sent to concentration camps. Places of worship were turned into arsenals, warehouses, while many were destroyed. Stones from demolished churches were used for building material, as were headstones from graveyards. An official 1936 census estimated that 15,835 churches remained out of an original number that exceeded 58,000 religious buildings; Jewish and Muslim faiths suffered losses similar in proportion.

Soviet authorities pumped out a great deal of propaganda, condemning faith. A quick Google search of early Bolshevik anti-religious propaganda shows numerous posters that disparaged the worship of God. The communists held parades that mocked Christianity and Judaism. Authorities wore "blasphemous" outfits, some of which were "semi-pornographic" with special emphasis on degrading "priests, nuns and rabbis." Instead of embracing these parades, many citizens stared in horror; too afraid to speak up. They just walked away, allowing the atheistic spectacle to carry on with only a few people watching.

Point to Ponder: Another Bolshevik milestone: crematoriums to dispose of murder victims.

It is generally believed that the Nazis were the forerunners in developing massive furnaces to cover up their ghastly crimes against humanity. In reality, the Soviets pioneered the use of large-scale crematoriums to dispose of bodies. Soviet crematoriums never approached the industrialized furnaces used by the Nazis. Nevertheless, the Soviets were still the first to use this method to eliminate the corpses of their numerous victims. In Moscow, the crematoriums were on call, well into the early morning hours, because that is when the Soviet secret police did most of their killings.

In some cases, bodies arrived with official paperwork stipulating that the victims' corpses were to be incinerated immediately. One worker at the Moscow crematorium noted that, "some of the bodies were still warm. Some of them were not even dead when we put them into the furnace."

No body, no faith?

The Soviet crematoriums were supposed to serve another insidious function: destroy the Russian people's faith in religion. Marx considered religion the "opiate of the masses." The Communist Manifesto did call for the abolition of all faith, along with philosophy and internal truths. If people have faith, they would be reluctant to worship the new atheistic Marxist state. In Russia, faith in God was (and still is) all-important, and the Orthodox Church was a critical social pillar of this country.

Furthermore, the Orthodox Church considered cremation taboo, so the Bolsheviks' calculus was quite simple. The atheistic Bolsheviks theorized that by incinerating the body, there would be no need for graveyards or headstones. With no remembrances, faith would wither and fade. In the end, the Soviets' plan failed to take root. [10]

Communist comparisons: Eastern Europe and the destruction of faith after WWII (1945-1948).

In the waning days of WWII, the Soviets captured Eastern Europe, and they set about breaking these nations. The Soviets carried out mass arrests of clergy and other laymen. Many were either executed or given lengthy prison sentences. Quite a few died from torture or hard labor in concentration camps. In one case, a Muslim lawyer was killed for coming to the defense of a Christian clergyman. All religions were targeted: Judaism, Islam, but the main scapegoat was Christianity because it was the dominant faith in Eastern Europe. Show trials of the clergy were used to showcase the power of the communist state over faith.

Another communist tactic was to degrade and humiliate the clergy publicly. Priests and other seminarians had their heads forced into

---

10 White, Matthew. The Great Big Book of Horrible Things. Pp. 359-367. Davies, Norman. Europe. 706-707, 914-917, 919-921, 929, 932, 934-935, 937. Courtois, Stephane, et. al. The Black Book of Communism, p. 70, 72, 73,74, 86-129. Andrew, C, and Mitrokhin, V. The Sword and the Shield; The Mitrokhin Archive and the Secret History of the KGB. P. 29, 30, 31. Solzhenitsyn, Alexander. The GULAG Archipelago: 1918-1956. Pp. 33, 300, 301, 302, 305, 306, 307, 308, 309, 342-352, 435, 436. Katamidze, Slava. Loyal Comrades, Ruthless Killers: The Secret Services of the USSR 1917-1991. Pp. 9,10. Moore, Jonathan. Hung, Drawn and Quartered. Pp. 144-166. Greene, Thomas. Comparative Revolutionary Movements. Pp. 106-7. Everts, Sarah. "A Brief History of Chemical War." Science History Institute Museum & Library. Haber had converted to Christianity, but he still feared for his life when the Nazis came to power. Bowlby, Chris. "Fritz Haber: Jewish chemist whose work led to Zyklon B" BBC Online. April 12, 2011. Davies, N. No Simple Victory. Pp. 327-8, 360-363. Amis, Martin, Koba the Dread. p.29,30,185, Merridale, Catherine. Night of Stone. p. 115, 116, 117, 130-139, 141, 162, 201. LaFeber, Walter. The American Age. 289-294. Radzinsky, Edvard. Stalin. Pp.172.

buckets of human waste, which they were forced to eat. If they vomited, the appalling process was repeated. Torturers would scream, that "the Virgin Mary was... the Great Whore," and... "Jesus was the c_ _t that... died on the cross." In other instances, clergymen were made to parade in public, wearing garments smeared in feces. Other displays of public humiliation consisted of young seminarians being forced to kiss a fake male organ strung around their neck of an older clergyman. The humiliated priests would then be forced to utter the phrase, "He has risen." The communist reasoning was simple and crude. Killing, imprisoning, and degrading the clergy and making religion look weak, and the communist state was made to seem all-powerful. Communist thugs surmised that people would readily join the Marxist fold. These blasphemous displays only served to horrify people, and they certainly did not achieve their desired goal.

Points to Ponder: Dancing with a Corpse; the Spanish Civil War (1936-1939).

Communism's obsession with degrading religion seems to have no bounds. Prior to the outbreak of the Spanish Civil War, social tensions were running high in Spain. In the 1920s, and later in the 1930s, groups influenced by communists and other radicals killed clergy, desecrated churches, smashed open crypts, and removed the semi-mummified remains of nuns and other clergy. One historian noted a "famous incident of a worker dancing with a disinterred... [corpse of a] ... nun." Catholicism was (and still is) a central pillar of the Spanish identity, and the populace was shocked at the violation of their faith. This sacrilegious behavior, which was inspired by Marxist atheistic fervor, only inspired the fascist Nationalist forces of Francisco Franco to engage in a no-holds-barred strategy to destroy the communist backed Republican forces of Spain. At this point, communist history was repeating itself. The Bolsheviks murdered clergy and desecrated churches and made every effort to stamp out religion.[11]

Communist Comparison: Communist post-WWI bloodshed: Germany, Hungary, and Bulgaria.

At the end of the First World War, communists sought to capitalize on the chaos caused by the global conflict. The Bolsheviks attacked Poland and Estonia but were defeated. Lenin gave direction and support to communist leaders in Hungary, but to no avail. Germany was a different story. Rosa Luxemburg led an independent communist revolt, which was easily put down. Bulgaria experienced acts of terrorism committed by communists.

Germany after the First World War.

At the end of the First World War, the Empire of Germany found itself on the losing side of this great conflict. (From 1918 through 1933, Germany would be known as the Weimar Republic, but I will refer to it as Germany.) Although the war ended with an armistice, a formal cessation of hostilities, the victorious Allies forced Germany to accept and sign the terms of the Treaty of Versailles, which officially ended the First World War. The treaty had a primary guilt clause, which labeled Germany as the primary aggressor for the outbreak of the war. Germany lost all colonies, was limited to a small army with limited weaponry, but the major blow came in the form of massive war

---

11 Beevor, Anthony, The Battle for Spain. p. 17, 46-47, 154. Davies, N. Europe. p. 985. White, A. The Great Big Book of Horrible Things. Pp. 397-399. Courtois, Stephane, et. al. The Black Book of Communism, p. The Soviets in Spain, 333-352, attacks on religion by the Soviets and the communists in eastern Europe. 382, 409-413, 421-422.

reparations owed to the Allies. The war reparations devastated Germany's economy and fueled social discontent.

Post-war Germany's political instability was linked to its economic problems from the First World War. The Treaty of Versailles mandates entailed: the loss of German industrialized regions, massive war reparations, which fanned hyperinflation of their currency. As unemployment soared, Germany was more susceptible to radicals who sought to overthrow the government. The region of Saxony was in a state of turmoil (it was known as Red Saxony), with communists and anti-communists "fighting in the streets." In 1919, Rosa Luxemburg and her followers launched the "Spartacus Revolt," which turned out to be an ill-fated communist coup in Germany. Authorities crushed the small revolt, and the plotters were arrested. Shortly after their arrest, Rosa and several of her conspirators were seized and brutally murdered.

In 1920, Germany would experience a violent communist workers' uprising in the Ruhr Valley and a right-wing coup known as the Kapp Putsch. While the communist uprising was violently suppressed, the Kapp Putsch "fizzled out" after a week, and the ringleaders fled the country.

Adolf Hitler was an Austrian who served in the German army during WWI. He rose to the rank of corporal when the war ended. Hitler, like many in Germany, felt that the government had stabbed them in the back by agreeing to the provisions in the Treaty of Versailles. The future leader of the Third Reich would be inspired by Italian fascism. In 1922, Benito Mussolini successfully marched on Rome and muscled his way into power in Italy. Motivated by Mussolini's successful, Adolf Hitler led what became known as the Beer Hall Putsch in 1923. The coup failed. After exchanging gunfire with the police, the conspirators fled. Hitler was arrested and sentenced to prison in 1924 but was later released in the same year. Hitler learned from his failure, so he sought the road to political power through democratic means. By 1930, the Great Depression had rocked the world economy. That same year, the German government asked Adolf Hitler to join the government, which was his road to ultimate power.

Hungary: Post WWI.

Hungary had been part of the Austrian Empire, and it gained its independence after the war. The new nation was beset with tremendous economic problems and general unrest from being on the losing side of WWI. Hungary lacked strong leadership and an unreliable justice system, which gave communists and radical groups the opportunity to instigate revolution. The communists attempted twice to seize power in the fledgling nation. On the second attempt, Bolshevik-backed communist leader, Bela Kun, was able to get a tentative grip on power. He and other Hungarian communists were in direct contact with the Soviets. In a message to Kun, Lenin wrote, "The **_Dictatorship_** of the... [workers]... requires the use of swift violence to crush the resistance of exploiters, capitalists." Another publication from the communists demanded that, "only workers... [should be] ... allowed to live." The communists did away with the police and the army, and terror was the byword of the day. They created an organization, known as the "Terror Group of the Revolutionary Council of the Government... [which]... became known a 'Lenin's Boys'." This group unleashed a wave of terror, murdering hundreds of people.

Bela Kun's Bolshevik Hungary was short-lived; it lasted from the spring of 1919 until the summer. Anti-communist Hungarian forces under the command of Miklos Horthy and units from the Romanian Army drove the communists out of Hungary. Bela Kun would flee to the

Soviet Union and would later be murdered during "the Great Terror" that was unleashed by Joseph Stalin. Talk about irony.

Post-WWI Bulgaria.

In the early 1920s, communists attempted to instigate violence in Bulgaria, but the authorities crushed them. Communists resorted to terrorist attacks and assassinations. In 1924, communists planted a bomb in a cathedral in the capital of Sophia. It exploded during a funeral, toppling the steeple, killing 140 and wounding many more. The government either hunted down or drove the communists underground. Bulgaria became a right-wing Eastern European country with a monarch.

What lessons did Europe learn from Hungary after WWI?

The Soviets made worldwide communist revolution a top priority, especially in Europe. It gave credence to fascist accusations of Bolshevik plots and conspiracies. By the end of 1918, the Soviets had already created the Comintern, an international organization that was openly dedicated to global communist domination of the world. Lenin also intended this organization to be a tool of subversion. When possible, the Bolsheviks would use the Red Army, as they did in Estonia towards the end of WWI. The Bolsheviks proclaimed that the Comintern was dedicated to "insurrection and proletarian dictatorship."

Furthermore, the proclamation laid down "twenty-one conditions" that would be used to foment "class struggle," which the communists hoped would lead to "civil war… in almost all the countries in Europe and America…" When the moment was right, the communists would throw out the rule of law, which they considered to be a "bourgeois" or middle-class tool to repress the emerging dictatorship of the working class. Underground communist organizations would take their orders from the Bolshevik-controlled Comintern and instigate revolution when the time was right.

To be clear, a larger historical picture was taking shape in Europe in the years following the First World War. The small, fledgling European countries that emerged from the crumbled empires of Austria, Germany and Russia learned a savage lesson about communist activities in Hungary. The Soviet Union would not wait for revolution but would try to instigate it in Europe and around the globe. Eastern Europe would have to use brutality to keep communists at bay; unfortunately, repressive control would be their weapon of choice.

Lenin dies, and the torch is passed, and the "Boss" takes over.

With the death of Lenin in 1924, Joseph Stalin, the son of a "drunken" Georgian cobbler, was able to gain control of the USSR. Stalin started his revolutionary career as a bank robber, but he consolidated political power by using the "organs" of the state, the bureaucracy, and the secret police. The future leader of the USSR had many names. Stalin's real name was Iosif Vissarionovich Dzhugashvili. His childhood name had been Sosa, while his communist party nickname was Koba. Stalin's last name was an alias, which in Russian means steel. His brutality made Lenin seem tame; eventually, he became known as the "Boss." [12]

---

12 Courtois, Stephane, et. al. The Black Book of Communism, pp. 74, 272-276, 278, 279-280. In Radzinsky referred to Stalin in his biography of the Soviet leader. Radzinsky, Edvard. Stalin. p. 150-151, 190-191. Davies, N. Europe. p. 677, 915, 932, 934, 941-943, 949, 959, 966-7, 969-976. Solzhenitsyn, Alexander. The GULAG Archipelago: 1918-1956. p.625. Shire, William. The Rise and Fall of the Third Reich. Pp. 18, 57-58, 71, 83, 86-88, 91, 93, 94, 97, 98, 99, 100-119, 162, 167,168, 192, 194, 214, 217. Information on

Points to Ponder: Worship the embalmed corpse of the revolutionary leader!

In early Christianity, people collected "holy relics," articles that were supposedly connected to Jesus and other Christian saints or events. Some holy relics are still venerated. In that vein, communist regimes were fixated on preserving their revolutionary leaders, even after death. They took a novel path, embalming their revolutionary leaders, and in the process, turning them into their own version of holy relics. The early Bolsheviks considered Lenin a pseudo-religious figure, a communist "messiah..." An early Bolshevik referred to him as a "political Jesuit." A mere statue would not do for the communists; Lenin would be immortalized as an "imperishable god." After his death, he was embalmed and put on display in a mausoleum in Moscow, with honor guards that marched around the building. When Stalin died, his body was embalmed and placed next to Lenin's body, but given his blood-drenched history, he was disinterred and reburied in the Kremlin wall. Besides Lenin, Mao Zedong and Ho Chi Minh were also preserved and put on display. In one sense, this gruesome display of Lenin's cadaver seems to be a form of state-sponsored worship: a communist holy relic. Today, the honor guards are gone, but it is still opened to the public. Ironically, Lenin's embalmed corpse has lasted for a century, which was much longer than the murderous Marxist regime that he helped to establish. [13]

Bela Kun. Vronskaya, Jeanne & Chuguev, Vladmir. <u>A Biographical Dictionary of the Soviet Union</u> 1917-1988. Pp. 215-6, 416-417.

13 Radzinsky, Edvard. <u>Stalin.</u> Pp. 212-215, 239. Davies, N. <u>Europe</u>. p.274-275, 612. Maclear, Michael. <u>The Ten Thousand Day War.</u> p. 250. Pantsov, Alexander & Levine, Steven. <u>Mao: The Real Story</u>. p.574. Amis, Martin. <u>Koba the Dread.</u> pp. 58.

Stalin's grand scheme, rob the peasants and use the cash from crop exports to industrialize the USSR.

The Russian historian, Edvard Radzinsky, surmised that Joseph Stalin had a grand scheme in mind after the death of Lenin. After the Bolsheviks' bloody victory during the Russian Civil War and Lenin's catastrophic war on the peasantry, the communists created the New Economic Program (NEP). It was a shallow gesture by the Bolsheviks to allow the peasants to engage in small-scale market transactions while being strictly regulated. They had no intention of allowing the NEP to be permanent, but they needed time to fatten up for hog before it was slaughtered.

Radzinsky theorized that during the 1920s, Stalin used his time to consolidate power and develop his new grand scheme for the Soviet Union. The "Boss" would rob the peasants of their land and equipment. They would then be forced to work on their stolen land, virtually unpaid, and hand over their crops to the state. If a famine ensued and people starved, that was acceptable to the "Boss." The Soviets would then sell the agricultural produce to other countries for hard currency, which would underwrite a crash Soviet industrialization program. If it had to be done on the bones of millions of dead peasants, so be it. Stalin would use their deaths to develop the Soviet steel industry, which would be used to build trucks, tractors, and trains. No price was too high to pay for the greater good of communism.

Joseph Stalin ordered the full-scale collectivization of Soviet agriculture, which also included the Ukrainian Terror Famine. Collectivization entailed the communist Soviet government seizing all the agricultural land and equipment. It started at the end of 1929 and went into full operation in 1930. The communists used brute force to monopolize all agricultural production. Collectivization and the Ukrainian Terror Famine unleashed an apocalyptic famine, which gripped the Soviet Union. Peasants who had bought their land at great cost, lost everything, and were forced back into serfdom (mostly unpaid work) "at the point of a gun." The confiscation of the peasants' land probably constitutes one of the most blatant instances of state-sponsored robbery in history.

To justify this theft to the public at large, Soviet propaganda invented a new class enemy, "kulaks," or rich peasants, which is a contradiction of terms. Peasants who worked diligently were vilified, and poorer (or lazy) peasants were encouraged to hate and denounce their neighbors. These supposed "kulaks" were arrested by authorities and sent to concentration camps. To be clear, the communist plan was to gain support for the state by scapegoating a part of the peasantry. Another goal was to so thoroughly frighten the peasants that they would never contemplate disobeying an order. The final indignity was that the Soviet government denied that the famine took place. The denials went in for years, but no one can keep such a terrible truth under wraps forever.

To this very day, the CPUSA routinely fabricates fictitious enemies on its website. They demonize Republicans, and the 47th US president, Donald Trump, as "fascists", "racist, sexist and homophobic…" Anyway, to gin up support for communism. Such is the mindset of the CPUSA; honorable opponents do not exist.

Communist comparison: harnessing hated.

Points to Ponder: George Orwell and the "Two-minute Hate."

Historical comparison. George Orwell's novel,"1984," was spot on with its description of the brutality and inhumanity of modern totalitarian dictatorships. Published in 1949, Orwell probably used the communist Soviet Union as his example of a totalitarian regime for his novel, and it was quite a fitting comparison. The Soviet Union fixated on creating fictitious enemies of the state, like kulaks. Fictitious enemies helped the communists divert attention away from failed authoritative policies and state incompetence. Mao and his communists followed the same playbook. They held "bitterness meetings," and attendance was mandatory; people had to participate. These "bitterness meetings" literally leaped from the pages of *1984*. Orwell wrote that the "Two Minute Hate" sessions were "impossible to avoid... [it created] ... a desire to kill, to torture, to smash faces... [hatred]... seemed to flow through the whole group... like an electric current, turning one... into a... screaming lunatic. And yet the rage that one felt... could be switched from one object to another. Mao's goal of using hatred to gain control worked by manipulating the peasants. The communists gained an iron grip on the countryside, as did the Soviets in the USSR in the 1930s.

Points to ponder: Hatred and the Nobel Peace recipient.

In 1973, the Nobel Peace Prize was jointly awarded to the US Secretary of State, Henry Kissinger and the North Vietnamese Communist leader, Le Duc Tho. The recipients were bestowed the Nobel Peace Prize for concluding the Paris Accords, a peace plan, between North Vietnam, South Vietnam, and the United States. It was during these negotiations that Le Duc Tho, in a moment of candor, admitted to Kissinger that the key to communist victory was creating hatred between social groups. "If one wishes to convince the peasants to take up arms, first of all, you have to fill them with hatred for the enemy." And this was straight from the mouth of a Nobel Peace Prize recipient. A Vietnamese communist magazine in the 1950s was more to the point: "the landowning classes will never be quiet until they have been eliminated." As one historian noted, the Vietnamese communist thinking was akin to the Communist Chinese sayings about "supposed" class enemies. "Better ten innocent deaths than one enemy survivor." Once again, creating hatred was a critical factor in the communist victory.

Points to Ponder: CHE Guevara and hatred.

CHE Guevara, the revolutionary, who was critical in Castro's victory in Cuba, made it clear that he understood the brutal effectiveness of terror and harnessing the bitter resentment of one's opponents to advance communism. Guevara wrote that it was "extremely useful that hatred turns men into effective, violent, merciless, and cold killing machines..." Once again, history repeats itself. For communism to succeed and become the law of the land, hatred is a prerequisite. We saw the same type of activity with Mao in China and Ho Chi Minh in Vietnam.[14]

---

14 Radzinsky, Edvard. Stalin. Pp. 216-219, 238, 239, 240, 244, 245, 246. Solzhenitsyn, Alexander. The GULAG Archipelago: 1918-1956. p.24-26, 55, 56. Medvedev, Roy. Let History Judge. Pp. Kulaks, 149,150, 289. Vronskaya, Jeanne & Chuguev, Vladimir. A Biographical Dictionary of the Soviet Union 1917-1988. Stalin, pp. 417. Courtois, Stephane, et. al. The Black Book on Communism. Kulaks pp. 9, 10, 16, 46, 51, 60, 72; Mao; hatred and bitterness meetings, pp. 477-480, Vietnam hatred pitting one part of rural villagers against others. Pp. 569, CHE Guevara hatred, pp. 652. Orwell, George. 1984. P. p.11. Davies, N. Europe. Pp. 960, 961, 962, 964. Merridale, Catherine. Night of Stone. Pp. 165-167. CHE Guevara hatred; Aguila, Juan Del. Cuba: Dilemmas of

The Soviets' forced collectivization of agricultural: one of the greatest robberies in world history.

When authorities went into the countryside to seize the peasants' crops, they were met with resistance. While there were rebellions, the peasants never had any chance of prevailing against the Red Army and the KGB. Soviet authorities sent troops into the countryside to terrorize the people and confiscate food. All resistance was brutally crushed. There is one photograph of these "shock troops" smiling as they are digging up the farmland, looking for a few scraps of food that peasants tried to hide away. This massive confiscation of agricultural produce led to mass starvation. The new fictitious enemy of the state, the kulaks, were arrested and executed or received lengthy sentences in the GULAG concentration camps. In many cases, being sent to the GULAG was a death sentence. The following are examples of Soviet brutality.

-Peasants could be arrested for holding back a half a dozen ears of corn, or a couple of slimy heads of cabbage.

-One photograph in *The Black Book of Communism* shows a forest fire, intentionally set by the Soviet authorities to flush out villagers who were hiding. Many died from fire and smoke. Those who emerged from the inferno were either shot, imprisoned, or forced to work the land.

-In one instance, several peasants were sentenced to death and shot for cutting grass from a gulley to feed their livestock.

-A woman widowed by the famine was given ten years in the GULAG for taking a few potatoes so she would not starve.

---

a Revolution. Pp. 118. Soloman, Alex. "YCL in 2024: Fighting Fascism at Home and Abroad." Communist Party: USA, ONLINE. Dec. 3, 2024.

- "Horse manure was eaten, partly because it often contained whole grains of wheat."

-Cannibalism, which appeared during *"Lenin's Famine"* during the early 1920s, reappeared again with a vengeance. The corpses of people who died of starvation had their livers removed. "Parents in desperation, killed their children, de-fleshed the bodies, salted the flesh, to preserve this terrible meal." Cannibalism became so rampant that the Communist government printed posters that said: "Eating your children is an act of Barbarism." (Irony; barbarians calling desperate, starving people barbarians.) In the Baltic slave camps, some 325 cannibals from Ukraine were still serving lengthy sentences in the late 1930s. The list of horrific events during forced collectivization could fill volumes of books.

A "Tidal Wave" of peasants to the GULAG.

Solzhenitsyn wrote that a "multimillion wave of dispossessed kulaks" was sent straight into the GULAG system. Two million were deported, and tens of thousands died in transit. Whole families were swept up in this wave. Men, women, and young children were sent to the vast Soviet concentration camps. Many would never survive their sentence. (More on this later.)

The Ukrainian Terror Famine.

The Holodomor, or the Ukrainian Terror Famine, was worse because the deaths struck a single region in the early 1930s. Starvation and disease cut through the population like a scythe. Although numbers vary, *The Black Book on Communism* asserted that four million perished, while other sources put the death toll at 6 to 7 million people. Half of these were children. A rare photograph from 1933 shows victims in the city of Kharkiv. In the photo, several people clad in rags are sprawled out on a sidewalk. Clearly, they are dying, and people are just walking by them, seemly indifferent to their plight. Note, if you tried to help any of these starving people, you could be arrested and maybe lose your life. A Ukrainian official spoke with a high-ranking Soviet official about mitigating the suffering, but the official was unmoved. He was indifferent to trainloads of dead prisoners that showed up in railway depots or peasants, who lay dying of starvation in their villages. Many know that six million Jews died in the Holocaust, many of whom were transported to their deaths on trains. The same thing happened to the Ukrainians, yet few have ever heard of the Holodomor. More history down the black hole?

Exported Grain and Famine Underwrote Soviet Industrialization.

Communists rail against industrialization, yet they are silent on the Soviets stealing produce from the peasants to underwrite industrialization in the USSR. The grain taken from the peasants was sold to Western Europe, and the proceeds were used to subsidize Soviet industrial development and mechanization. In 1931, the Soviets sold 864,000 tons of grain to Western Europe, and in 1932, the total was well over 900,000 tons. In 1933, a couple of hundred thousand tons were sold—and that was the worst year of the famine. It can safely be said that Soviet industrialization was built on the bodies of many millions of innocent victims from Stalin's forced collectivization of agriculture. Yet in the end, collectivization failed, and Soviet grain production would never achieve its full potential because of Stalin's draconian mandate. It did not matter to Stalin because he was about to unleash the Great Terror, and any potential critics of his failed agricultural experiment did not have long to live.

Points to ponder: Marxist snake oil salesman heads up science in the Soviet Union.

In the Soviet Union, the state had the last word when it came to science. After forced collectivization destroyed Soviet crop production, Stalin enlisted the aid of a fraudster, Trofim Lysenko, to "remedy" the agricultural base decimated by the "Boss." Lysenko was a conman who masqueraded as a scientist, and he assured the Soviet leader that his scientific methods would rescue Soviet agriculture. Lysenko advocated a host of loony schemes, from subjecting seeds to frigid temperatures to grafting incompatible plants; the list went on and on. All his scientific evidence was falsified, and when farmers tried to implement his methods, the crop failures only worsened, and more people starved to death. Instead of shooting the impostor posing as a scientist, Stalin had the farmers executed or imprisoned. The insanity did not stop there.

Lysenko declared that genetics (which encompasses DNA) was a Western capitalistic plot. Soviet geneticists and scientists who did not "renounce the chromosomal theories" of heredity were brutally persecuted or shot. Years later, Lysenko was interviewed by a Western scientist and was asked to explain how genetic traits could skip a generation. Lysenko replied that "Fertilization is a process of mutual devouring... [and when] ... digestion is not complete... we belch... unassimilated hereditary material is belched out..." Lysenko would go on to have a dazzling career, winning numerous scientific awards, but as one historian noted, "Soviet science was blighted for years."

Scientific insanity was not confined to the USSR. Presently, "woke' policies have spread in the West, especially in Great Britain and the United States. Woke government authorities, educators, and some supposed researchers claim that there is no biological difference between women and men. For instance, they claim that biological men can become pregnant and have children. If a man thinks he is a woman, then he is a woman, and vice versa. Political commentator Matt Walsh's video, *"What is a Woman?"* points out the craziness of transgender movement. Clearly, scientific insanity is not confined to totalitarian states but can manifest itself in democracies that allow government agencies to run wild and influence the scientific community.

Death Tolls from the Great Famine and Forced Collectivization.

Mere words cannot readily convey the human suffering and massive death tolls of Forced Collectivization, especially in countries that have never experienced famines. The death toll for Stalin's famine varies. *The Black Book* on Communism puts a minimum death toll at six million or more. During the Second World War, while Stalin was meeting with British Prime Minister Winston Churchill, the "Boss" supposedly admitted that 10 million had perished during Forced Collectivization. The historian Norman Davies noted the research of R. Medvedev and Robert Conquest, which estimated that Collectivization and dekulakization could have killed 10 million to 14 million victims. At the same time, the Ukrainian Terror Famine could have caused an additional 6 to 7 million deaths.

Robert Conquest's *The Harvest of Sorrow: Soviet Collectivization and the Terror Famine* tried to give the reader a sense of how many people died by noting that for every letter in his book (411 pages), twenty lives were lost. That type of math seems a bit abstract. A better example would be the ancient Roman Colosseum, which could hold 50,000 people. Ten million Soviet victims would be the equivalent of 200 Roman Colosseums; 14 million people would be 280 Colosseums full of spectators. Think about that the next time you are watching an NFL football game, and you scan all the spectators in the stadium. [15]

Points to Ponder: Special shops and communist elite privileges.

As the peasants starved, Stalin and the rest of the communist elites had whatever they wanted. Marxists screech that capitalist society is fundamentally unequal. No one ever claimed that it was perfect, but within a capitalist society, one had the potential to improve one's life. There are many rags-to-riches examples in the United States. On the other side of the coin, communist countries were (and still are) notoriously discriminatory when it comes to wealth redistribution. Income inequality was endemic. The communist elites lived quite well, while rank-and-file citizens had to stand in line for the necessities. As officials rose through the ranks of the state bureaucracy, they received more special perks. Luxuries also included "superior healthcare facilities, beautiful homes that included pools," and the opportunity to vacation at beautiful resorts reserved for the privileged. Stalin and Mao, along with other communist leaders, had numerous houses and apartments at their disposal. Workers saw none of these benefits.

Specialty shops symbolized inequality in communist regimes, and the Soviet Union was the first to create these stores for the privileged elites. Leaders and bureaucrats could obtain consumer goods, such as

---

15 Courtois, Stephane, et. al. The Black Book of Communism. P 146-168. Amis, Martin. Koba the Dread. p., 3,4,5, 63-64, 121-127,129, 130. Radzinsky, Edvard. Stalin. P. 257-260. Solzhenitsyn, Alexander. The GULAG Archipelago: 1918-1956. p.24-34, 54,55, 437. Davies, Norman. Europe. Lysenko, Pp.830. This historian gets his figures for the death tolls for collectivization and the Ukrainian terror Famine, from R. Medvedev, and R. Conquest, p.965, 1,329. Jones, Steve. In The Blood. pp. 20-24. Montefiore, Simon Sebag. Stalin. p.84. Medvedev, Roy. Let History Judge. Pp. 230-240. Medvedev, Roy & Zhores. The Unknown Stalin. Pp.190-207. Matt Walsh's video, What is a Woman?

citrus fruits, delicatessen meats, luxury pastries, expensive cuts of meat, and expensive liquors. The general population never had the opportunity to obtain any of these delicacies.

In North Korea, three generations of the Kim family have ruled with an iron fist since the late 1940s. Since this pseudo-communist monarchy seized power, they have amassed a fortune, which fuels its lavish lifestyle. Presently, the third ruler of North Korea, Kim Jong Un, has a net worth that "has been estimated at more than $5 billion since 2013," and *Forbes* ranked him "<u>as the world's 36th most powerful person</u>." The actions of the Kim family have completely eclipsed the worst actions of any capitalists, yet few self-proclaimed Marxists point this contradiction out.

Juan Reinaldo Sánchez was a firm believer in communism and the personal bodyguard for Fidel Castro. He personally witnessed Castro amass a fortune, and he would later co-author a book, *The Double Life of Fidel Castro: My 17 Years as Personal Bodyguard to El Líder Máximo*. Sanchez reported that Castro feigned poverty, but had twenty luxury houses, a yacht, fishing boats, secret bank accounts, and much more. He rejected the hypocrisy and eventually got out of communist Cuba.

Corrupt, hypocritical Marxists are not confined to communist regimes. As mentioned before, Black Lives Matter (BLM) roared onto the American political scene after the death of George Floyd and the subsequent rioting that occurred in 2020. Social upheaval and the potential use of boycotts enabled BLM to use its newfound political clout to pressure American corporations into donating tens of millions of dollars to the civil rights organization. There was little accountability for how these funds were spent. When confronted about outrageous spending, one BLM co-founder admitted that she spent several million dollars to purchase luxury homes in Los Angeles and other locations.

Another BLM executive was accused of swindling approximately 10 million dollars in funds from the organization.

Furthermore, the group admitted to doling out millions of dollars in questionable contracts to friends and family. By the end of 2020, BLM admitted to raking in $80 to $90 million, and several years later, that sum has dwindled to $29 million. (Please see the notes below for more details.) [16]

Communist Comparisons: Communists made famines.

A Soviet propaganda poster shows an old man with a young boy riding on a train. They had a panoramic view of the countryside, which looked quite impressive. Ships, trains, manufacturing facilities, and

---

[16] Davies, N. Europe. Pp. 1,122. Hollander had many more examples of the specialty shops in his book. Hollander, Paul. The End of Commitment. Pp. 64, 67, 68, 95, 96, 97, 98, 137. Radzinsky, Edvard. Stalin. Pp. 300-301. These pages outline how the Soviet elites were highly paid, and the workers received very little. Income inequality was rife in the defunct USSR. Engerman, David. Know Your Enemy: The Rise and Fall of America's Soviet Experts. Pp. 103. The second ruler of North Korea, Kim Jong Il had some 20,000 DVD movies. In contrast, any commoner could receive prison time or the death penalty. (Just this past year, seven people were executed for watching illegal DVDs a decade earlier.) Kim Jong Il consumed $700,000 worth of Hennessy Paradis Cognac in a year. Besides movies, Kim Jong Il and his son enjoyed riding Harley Davidson motorcycles (at $13,000 to $17,000 a piece, not counting luxury models). They have 20 Jet Skis ($5,000 to $12,000 apiece), and nine Orlov Trotter horses ($5,000-$13,000 apiece). French, Paul. "The House of Kim". History of Communism. 3rd ED. P.86-93. Villasanta, Arthur. "Kim Jong Un Net Worth: How Is North Korea's Leader Spending His Billions?" International Business Times, World. May 23, 2019. Sang-Hun, Choe. "North Korea Executes People for Watching K-Pop, Rights Group Says…" The New York Times. Dec. 15, 2021. "Sanchez, Juan. The Double Life of Fidel Castro. P. 7-11, 15, 16, 17, 18, 57-61. Corruption of Cuban communists. Aguila, Juan Del. Cuba: Dilemmas of a Revolution. Pp.190. Pantsov, Alexander & Levine, Steven. Mao: The Real Story. Pp. 363, 365, 366. Campbell, Sean. "Black Lives Matter Secretly Bought a $6 Million House." New York Magazine: Money, Intelligencer. April 4th, 2022. Gaskins, Kayla. "BLM finances under fire: Only 33% of donations given to charities as execs paid millions" The National Desk. May 31, 2023. Watson, Michelle. "Black Lives Matter executive accused of 'syphoning' $10M from BLM donors, suit says" CNN. Sept. 5th, 2022. Kokal, Mitch. BLM Dealing With Founder's Financial Fallout." John Locke Foundations. June 11, 2024.

waves of grain could be seen against a beautiful landscape. The old man exclaims in the caption, "The dreams of the people have come true..." Other such Soviet propaganda posters show happy peasant farmers harvesting bumper crops of grain. This was pure fiction.

Communist-made famines have killed millions and devastated countries. The Bolshevik (sometimes known as Lenin's) famine of the Russian Civil War killed 5 million. Stalin's forced Collectivization (10-14 million dead), the Ukrainian Terror Famine (6 to 7 million dead), Mao's Great Leap Forward famine (30 to 45 million dead), and subsequent famines in Cambodia (close to a million dead) and North Korea (1.5 to 2 million dead). In communist Ethiopia, from hundreds of thousands to over a million died. Most sources indicated that at least a million perished in Ethiopia. Death tolls for communist famines could easily reach 50 to 60 million plus victims.

The Great Leap Forward: the greatest communist famine of all time.

The Great Leap Forward ranks as one of the world's greatest catastrophes orchestrated in the name of communism. Mao Zedong had no specific plan in mind when he called for the reorganization of steel manufacturing and agriculture in China. He surmised (wrongly) that Marxist revolutionary fervor would inspire the Chinese to expand grain and steel production rapidly. From 1958 through 1962, Mao engaged in a crash program of agricultural expansion. What they got was an apocalyptic man-made famine that killed tens of millions of people. The Chinese communists readily conceded that at least 20 million perished in the Great Leap Forward (GLF). A leading Mao biographer, Alexander Pantsov, felt that this number was unrealistic, and that probably 30 million was a more accurate number, maybe as high as 40 million died.

A Chinese journalist re-examining scholastic material on the GLF believes that 36 million died. Whereas some Western scholars, plumbing the resources of Chinese archives on the GLF, set the butcher bill at 45 million. Hair-brain central planning, unrealistic quotas, and backbreaking work while starving added to the misery.

When the GLF famine became apocalyptic, people ate anything they could get their hands on to stay alive, which included bark, grass, frogs, lizards, and so on. Many small villages ceased to exist. Pantsov wrote that people became so desperate that they took extreme measures to save their loved ones. As people fled, some distraught parents dug deep pits on the side of roads and put their bewildered children into the holes, so they could not follow them. The hope was that someone would take in the abandoned children and feed them. So many children were abandoned, the communists banned people from taking in children who had been deserted.[17]

---

[17] Smith, Gayle. "Ethiopia and the Politics of Famine Relief," Middle East Report 145 (March/April 1987). In Ethiopia, while under communist control, a famine, which started from drought, became a murderous tragedy that the regime tried to conceal from the world. When the world began to realize the depth of this calamity, celebrities raised money for Ethiopia. Michael Jackson and a host singers and stars were hoodwinked into making a popular video, "We are the World." The video was a success, but famine relief was not. Courtois, Stephane, et. al. The Black Book of Communism. p. The GLF: 487-498, Cambodia pp. 583-586, Ethiopia, 693-695. See death tolls in this book for starvation in North Korea. Li, Dun. The Ageless Chinese; A History. pp. 524, 532-534. Mao also tried to reorganize steel making, by creating small backyard furnaces. The Chinese leader had the officials confiscate peoples metal tools and cutlery. They produced small quantities of inferior metal, and the experiment failed miserably. During the GLF, the communist tried to eliminate filth, which included killing sparrows. That ended in failure because the insect population increased dramatically destroying crops. The sparrows were not there to eat the bugs. Pantsov, Alexander, with Levine, Steven. Mao: The Real Story. P447-448, 450-464, 470-82 (page 472 for the children in the holes. Pages 470-476 are especially heartbreaking. White, Matthew. The Great Big Book of Horrible Things. pp.488-489. Orwell, George. *1984*. Pp. 25-26.

GULAG: the Soviet Concentration camp system, established well before the Nazis.

Over a dozen years before the Nazis built their first concentration camp, the Soviet Union had established a vast slave labor system across the USSR. The Soviet system had hundreds of camps and was known by the acronym *GULAG*. The famous dissident and prisoner of this Soviet system, Alexander Solzhenitsyn, described this slave labor system in the title of his bestselling book, *GULAG Archipelago*. He referred to the GULAG as the *"Sewage Disposal System,"* which was used for the mass incarceration of prisoners, known as *"zeks."* The Sewage Disposal System worked. Millions of innocent victims were flushed into the GULAG system. The system also served a double duty. In addition to imprisonment, it also served as a slave labor camp system, which became an integral part of the Soviet Union's attempt to industrialize. Furthermore, the potential threat of imprisonment in the GULAG struck fear into the populace.

By September of 1918, the Soviet Union had established its first batch of concentration camps, which was almost fifteen years prior to the Nazis building their first camp in 1933. *The Black Book on Communism* noted a Nazi memorandum on the organization of concentration camps, which was based on the Soviet system. The memorandum stated that the "Reich Security Head Office... [should issue to all] ... commandants a full collection of reports concerning the Russian concentration camps." The Germans compiled reports that went into "great detail" about information they gleaned from former zeks, who had escaped from the Soviet system. The information was considered crucial to laying the foundation for creating the Nazi concentration camp system. The report noted that the Soviets used slave labor to the advantage of the dictatorship, and in the process, "destroyed whole people." Sounds like a plan for a systematic mass murder started with the Soviet Union.

The Soviet Union's GULAG was just as brutal as the Nazis camps. Both totalitarian regimes had a variety of different camps: prisons, forced labor, prisoner of war, transit camps, camps for women, and camps for skilled labor. This is far from a complete list. The Nazis concentration camps also included extermination camps, which had a timetable for murdering the victims. The Soviets' concentration and forces labor camps had no timetable for death, but authorities did use a crude arithmetic to estimate the life span of zeks. A strong prisoner could last two years, but historian Roy Medvedev insisted that some of the more brutal camps were designed to break a zek within several months. Many zeks died shortly after arrival.

Other factors shortened the life span of zeks. Many prisoners received small food rations, forced to work long hours under physically taxing conditions. Camps located in Siberia and the Arctic regions added another level of misery to the GULAG system.

Prisoners were frequently murdered in the Soviet camps. Guards shot prisoners who fell behind while being marched from one location to another. It was routine for the guard to shoot batches of prisoners on orders from Moscow. In other instances, when an epidemic was imminent, guards shot prisoners to keep the contagion from spreading.

Auschwitz was probably one of the most infamous Nazi concentration camps. It had an extermination camp, a concentration camp, and a forced labor system. As prisoners entered Auschwitz, they would see a large sign, *"Arbeit macht frei,"* work will set you free. In contrast, few have heard of Kolyma, a Soviet concentration camp system that was just as deadly as Auschwitz. When zeks entered one of

Murderous Marxism

the Kolyma system's many camps, they also saw a sign with the inscription. "Labor is a matter of honor, valor, and heroism." Located in Northern Siberia, it consisted of several dozen slave labor camps, which primary focus was mining gold and logging. (Note* The Bolsheviks never tried to reconcile how a Marxist totalitarian state dedicated to the destruction of capitalism, but still mined gold that was sold on the international market.) It is a sobering thought that the death ratio of people in Kolyma was equal or greater than the death ratio in Auschwitz. Auschwitz has been preserved as a historical site to remind the world of the genocidal legacy of the Nazis, while camps like Kolyma have been either bulldozed or overrun by vegetation.

Points to Ponder: Anne Frank and Avraham Shifrin.

While many people have heard of Anne Frank, few have heard of Avraham Shifrin. Anne wrote, *The Diary of a Young Girl*, which became a world bestseller book that has been published in many languages. Commonly known as "Anne Frank's diary," it chronicles the hopes and aspirations of a young Jewish girl trying to stay alive while hiding in a concealed apartment during the Nazi occupation of Holland. The ending was tragic. Someone denounced Anne and the others, and the Nazis arrested them. She was sent to a concentration camp, and she died in the Holocaust. Her father, who survived the war, returned to the hideout, and discovered his daughter's diary and had it published.

In contrast, very few have heard of Avraham Shifrin, who was also Jewish, but in contrast, he was a survivor of the Soviet GULAG system. He emerged from the murderous Soviet camps and wrote about his experiences. Avraham wrote the *First Guidebook to the Prisons and Concentration Camps of the Soviet Union*. His accounts are filled with heart-wrenching sorrow and death. Yet this observation begs the question: Why have so many heard of the Nazi death camp of

Auschwitz, yet few know of the brutal Soviet camps of Kolyma and Vorkuta? These Soviet camps have probably claimed just as many victims as the Nazi camps but have slipped into historical obscurity. Like Anne Frank, Avraham Shifrin's name should be known, but many historians seem to have little appetite for exposing the horrors of the Soviet Union's GULAG system. More history down the black hole of memory?

The Atomic GULAG.

By 1945, Soviet spies and collaborators were able to steal the secrets of atomic weaponry from the United States. (See the Venona Project). The Soviet leader immediately ordered the development of a nuclear weapons program, which entailed yet another massive slave labor complex, which became known as the Atomic GULAG. The program was massive, and prisoners numbered in the hundreds of thousands. They mined uranium, built nuclear reactors, built the camps, and processed radioactive material. The work was extremely hazardous, and safety protocols and protective equipment were almost nonexistent. Avraham Shifrin was a prisoner of the GULAG system and a writer who compiled data on almost all the Soviet camps and prisons. He considered the atomic camps to be extermination camps because of the lethal conditions for prisoners. Tens of thousands were either killed by accidents, toxic gases associated with processing uranium, or direct exposure to nuclear materials. Those with protracted radiation poisoning died slow, agonizing deaths. Since the Soviet nuclear program was top secret, prison sentences became a lifetime confinement for zeks. Their sentences were only moderated by the death of Stalin. Besides being living nightmares, the Atomic GULAGS also devastated the surrounding environment, which transformed regions into apocalyptic wastelands.

Soviet Slave labor.

Who filled the GULAGS? Mostly political prisoners, known under the Soviet penal code system as "58s." Other prisoners included soldiers, party members, technicians wrongly accused of damaging equipment, kulaks, intellectuals, and the list goes on and on. Not having the proper identification papers, making a joke, looking suspicious, being related to someone who was imprisoned, or just being caught in a Soviet secret police sweep could land you in the GULAG. One man was sentenced to ten years in the GULAG because he was the first to stop clapping after one of Stalin's speeches. Slave labor became the fate of many of these prisoners. Solzhenitsyn wrote that zeks were "Unpaid laborers... [for]... the lowest possible cost... endless chains of people were turned into convicts... a ready supply of "20th century slaves" for communist state industries. How many were sent to the Gulags? "Solzhenitsyn gives a figure ('a modest estimate') of 40-50 million who were given long sentences in the gulag from 1918-1953," and as many as 17 million could have died in the camps.

By the early 1930s, many Europeans were aware of the GULAG system. A 1931, a British poster showed an emaciated Soviet prisoner dying while cutting lumber. Starvation, accidents, disease, and simply being worked to death claimed millions of lives. Prisoners died mining copper, gold, coal, along other commodities. Prisoners were also used for massive construction projects, such as the "White Sea – Baltic and Moscow-Volga Canals projects. Much of their labor and lives were squandered on projects that never produced any tangible results. The White Sea-Baltic Canal failed because it was too shallow to move large cargo vessels, and it was frozen for months on end in the brutal Arctic climate. Hundreds of thousands of zeks died building these infrastructure projects.

A few of the examples of Soviet brutality.

-One sadistic camp commandant of Kolyma would march between rows of prisoners and would arbitrarily shoot one after another zeks. "Guards followed with a change of pistols... [the bodies of the dead were] ... stacked by the camp gates." Prisoners were assured they would suffer the same fate "if they tried slacking."

-In one camp, Solzhenitsyn explained how the zeks would conceal the bodies of prisoners who died so that they could collect their food rations. They only turned the bodies over to the guards when the stench of the corpse became unbearable.

-In prison camps for women, Soviet authorities raped many thousands of female prisoners. In many instances, women traded sex for food.

- "Garbage eaters" or "goners" were prisoners who had gone insane due to the conditions in the camps. They would readily eat rotting garbage, no matter the condition. There were instances in which these "goners" consumed "scraps thrown into a latrine." Beating and threats seemed to have little effect on them, so the guards let them eat the fetid garbage.

-Prisoners tried to encourage infections on limbs, so they could go to the camp hospital, which could potentially be a death sentence. One man chopped off half of his foot to get out of work.

-Cramming multiple zeks into cells meant for only a few prisoners. Although the communists were not the only ones to fill prison cells beyond capacity, the Soviets took it to unheard levels. A cell meant to hold 28 men could have well over a hundred zeks jammed into a cell. A solitary confinement cell meant for one or two prisoners would have over a dozen men jammed into a tiny confinement space. (I lost count of the instances recounted in historical texts on communism, in which cells were crammed to overcapacity.)

- Although the Soviets denied having prisons for children, they had dozens. Avraham Shifrin's guidebook on the GULAG prison system identified 119 prisons and camps for women and children. The rape of girls and boys was rampant.

-In 1975, one man, a "58," was sentenced to five years in prison for believing in God.

-There were dozens of psychiatric prisons used to detain "58s." These prisons added a new dimension of psychological torture for prisoners.

- One isolation cell prison was roughly the size of a phone booth and resembled a safe. When closed, the prisoner could see no light nor hear sound.

-Urkas were common criminals sentenced to the GULAGS, and they added an extra level of misery to the lives of the zeks. They included murderers, rapists, and other violent criminals: the worst of the worse. The guards treated them better than the 58s (political prisoners). The urkas were made trustees and were used to police the zeks. They could rape, murder, assault and steal from the zeks with impunity.

**I cannot possibly relate every act of barbarism in the Soviet camps. Acts of horror committed in the Gulags would fill thousands of pages.

Soviet trains transported their victims years before the Nazis.

"Slave Caravans" is the phrase used by Solzhenitsyn to describe the Soviet transportation system for prisoners. Years before the Nazis used trains to move their doomed victims, the Soviets had transported millions of zeks to the GULAG. As the zeks were loaded onto the trains, the guards took valuables such as money and cigarettes. The authorities also added an extra level of misery by transporting the political prisoners with convicted felons (Urkas). The criminals beat up the prisoners and robbed them of what was left of their meager belongings. As with the Nazis' trains, prisoners were crammed in so tight that sitting or lying down was impossible. It was not uncommon for a zek to die standing up, while bunched up against other prisoners. They were given very little food or water, and latrines were nonexistent. Prisoners froze in the winter and were subjected to brutal heat in unventilated cars in the summer.

Hell ships.

During the Second World War, the Japanese transported captured Americans and other Allied POWs on what became known as "hell-ships." The conditions were horrific, and many POWs died. Although unknown at the time, the Soviets pioneered the maritime delivery of zeks to their far-flung concentration camps. Given the vastness of the USSR and the lack of roads, the Soviets also used ships to transport zeks on riverboats, especially to the interior part of Siberia. Ocean-going vessels were also used to deliver prisoners to different destinations on the eastern coast of the USSR.

Solzhenitsyn described the terrible conditions on these vessels. Zeks were crammed into filthy holds; disease was rampant, while food and water were almost non-existent. When food was supplied, it was taken from filthy communal buckets. Solzhenitsyn described how zeks lay "there in piles or crawled around like crabs in a basket." On some ships, latrines were open barrels that overflowed; on other vessels, toilets were nonexistent. In some cases, prisoners were crammed together on the ships, just like on the freight trains. To relieve themselves, prisoners "urinated in [to] glass jars which were passed hand to hand and emptied through the portholes... anything more substantial went right into their pants."

On one occasion, an ocean-going Soviet prison ship caught fire. A Japanese vessel spotting the smoke rushed to the aid of the distressed ship, but the Soviet captain refused help. To conceal the seriousness of the ship fire, the hatches were deliberately locked down, trapping the prisoners below decks. If the guards had opened the hatches to save the zeks, it would have been revealed that the ship was a prison transport. By the time the crew got the blaze under control, many prisoners had died, and the bodies were simply thrown overboard. [18]

Points to Ponder: Lev Theremin's eerie music and his deal with the devil.

---

18 The spelling for the acronym for GULAG is "G(lavnoe) u(pravlenie ispravitel'no-trudovykh) lag(erei), Chief Administration of Corrective Labor Camps." Courtois, Stephane, "et.al. The Black Book of Communism. Pp. 15, 26, 27, 73, 80, 104, 118, 136, 138, 186, 190,191, 203-207, 209, 222, 226, 227, 234, 238-241, 251-252, 257. Davies, Norman. Europe. This historian gets his figures from R. Medvedev, and R. Conquest, p. 963, 1016, 1018, 1023, 1026-7, 1201, 1329, 1330. Solzhenitsyn, Alexander. The GULAG Archipelago: 1918-1956. p.24-25, 54, 445, 489-532, 536, 562. Radzinsky, Edvard Stalin. p. 353-355, 413-414. Robert Amis's book has numerous examples of the mind-numbing brutality in the Soviet camps. Amis, Robert. Koba the Dread. p.66,67,70,71, 80,81, 82, 83, this page gives examples of cramming prisoners into cells, well beyond the rated capacity. Pp. 235. This book details the Atomic GULAGS. Medvedev, Roy & Zhores. The Unknown Stalin: His Life, Death, and Legacy. Pp.121-141, 160-180. Medvedev, Roy. Let History Judge. Pp. 243, 500-516, 659-660. Shifrin, Avraham. The First Guidebook to Prisons and Concentration Camps of the Soviet Union. pp. 15-65. Davies, N. No Simple Victory. Pp. 327-8. Glinsky, Albert. Theremin: Ether Music and Espionage. Pp. 220-222, 223, 224, 225, 227, 228.

The "theremin" is a unique musical instrument with a bizarre history. This electrical instrument is operated without human contact. It has been made famous for providing the eerie soundtrack music for popular movies like *Ghostbusters*, *The Day the Earth Stood Still*, and Alfred Hitchcock's *Spellbound*. Originally, it was designed as a potential surveillance device, a proximity sensor used to detect movement. It was invented in 1920 and patented eight years later by Russian physicist, Leon Theremin (Lev Sergeyevich Termen), in the Soviet Union. From its inception, the USSR was obsessed with stifling popular dissent, and the Soviets used every tactic to control their population, which included the new field of electronics. The theremin never proved to be a practical monitoring device that could replace guards.

Subsequently, this quirky gizmo was developed into a musical instrument. When a performer passes their hand close to the device, it emits an otherworldly noise, which has been described as "ether music." Besides being used for concerts, the theremin has been primarily used in various movies to provide suspenseful background music. With the permission of the Soviet authorities, Lev Theremin toured the United States, giving concerts, and in the process, he became moderately successful. Lev lived in the US for over a decade, and with the help of friends, started a company that manufactured several different types of the theremin. During the 1930s, the Great Depression had hobbled the American economy. Theremin's business had fallen on hard times when he mysteriously disappeared in 1938. His wife, friends and business partners had no idea that Lev had agreed to leave the US and return to the USSR. After returning to the Soviet Union, the inventor was arrested and sent to probably the most brutal concentration camp system in the Soviet Union, Kolyma. At this point, Lev had a stroke of fortune. After several months at Kolyma, he was transferred to a *sharashka*, a Soviet prison for scientists and engineers.

Murderous Marxism

The *sharashka* was the brainchild of Stalin's most deadly secret police chief, Lavrenti Beria. Theremin would go on to invent other devices, one of which was a remote listening system, known by the code name "Snowstorm." The actual eavesdropping device was placed in a wooden facsimile of the US seal. In the summer of 1945, the "bugged" wooden seal was presented by Soviet school children to the American ambassador in Moscow. Nicknamed the "thing," the listening device eavesdropped on American diplomatic conversations until accidentally discovered in 1953.

Lev Theremin would outlive the Soviet Union. He had been a loyal communist but was still arrested and imprisoned. Prior to the collapse of the USSR in 1991, he was able to travel outside the Soviet Union, basking in his reputation for inventing a musical instrument which bears his name. Russian historian Edvard Radzinsky interviewed the over 90-year-old scientist, and during their conversation, Lev made a bizarre statement about his longevity. He declared that he would live to be 100.

Furthermore, the physicist told Edvard, "I am young. Dr. Faustus is simple: old age hides when you are working." Dr. Faustus was a fictional medieval scholar who traded his soul to the devil for magical powers and longevity. Ironically, Bulat Galeyev, a Russian biographer of Theremin, titled his book about Lev, *The Soviet Faust*. Galeyev asserted that, "in order to pursue... [his]... abiding passion for scientific creation, he was essentially forced to sell his soul to the devil, meaning the KGB..."

Final footnote: In 1993, after returning from a trip, the scientist discovered that his laboratory in his apartment had been completely ransacked, his equipment destroyed, and his personal papers had been stolen. Edvard Radzinsky noted that, "someone was evidently very interested in the ideas of this strange twentieth-century Dr. Faustus." One might wonder whether the break was a random act or something else. The police were never able to catch the culprits. Theremin died soon after the burglary. He never made it to 100. [19]

Communist Comparisons: Concentration camps in China, Cambodia, and North Korea.

Laogai: the hidden Chinese prisons and centers for profit.

In the DuPont Circle area in Washington, DC, there is a small brick mansion, which barely stands out against the grand buildings of the United States capital. The Laogai Museum is located several miles from Georgetown University and the Capitol Building. The museum is dedicated to reminding the world of the existence of a vast network of Chinese Communist concentration camps. As with the Soviet Union, the Chinese communists built an immense prison camp system known as the Laogai, which has been referred to as "The Hidden Gulag." Modeled after the Soviet GULAG system, the Laogai system was created in 1950, and it became a symbol of communist power over the populace. *The Black Book of Communism* puts the death toll of the Chinese Gulag at 20 million. It is estimated that 99% of those imprisoned were charged with "endangering the state." Few books have been written about the Chinese concentration camps, and the word laogai was not added to the Oxford English Dictionary until 2003.

---

19 Radzinsky, Edvard. Stalin. Pp.407-409. Bridgwater, William. ED. et. al. The Columbia Encyclopedia. pp.701. Glinsky, Albert. Theremin: Ether Music and Espionage. Pp. 2, 27-39, 73-91, 149-154, 162-163, 168-173, 177-179, 186-194, 200, 211-227, 253-254, 256-263, 271-273, 336-337. Tiedemann, Garrett. "A History of the Theremin in Movie Music." Your Classical Radio. July 15, 2016.

The System.

The Laogai system contains close to "a thousand large camps" and probably just as many "detention centers." It has been estimated that "50 million people" have been incarcerated in the Laogai between 1950 through the mid-1980s. The camps vary, with some being slave labor camps that could potentially be "larger than some American cities." There are also various forms of detention camps, prisons, reeducation camps, and black jails. Black jails are informal detention centers, in which communist authorities will snatch people off the streets and hold people for a short period of time.

The Laogai system makes communist China competitive in the world market.

As China opened its economy in the 1980s, the communists used the prisoners of the Laogai to aid, in part, the economic development of its burgeoning industrial base. The communists exploited slave labor to make profits, which came through corruption of the entire communist economic system. A *1988 Criminal Reform Handbook*, issued by the Ministry of Justice, states that the Laogai "organizes criminals in labor and production, creating wealth for society..." Since the 1980s, the financial growth and wealth creation have catapulted communist China into a world economic juggernaut.

Japanese, South Korean, and Western corporations eager to gain access to the massive Chinese consumer market looked the other way when it came to slave labor in China. Karl Marx's *Communist Manifesto* railed against the excesses of capitalism and the exploitation of labor. Yet, it is the very aspect that a supposed communist detests, capitalism, that underpins Communist China's economic success. It is also done in cooperation with Western corporations, such as Nike, Coca-Cola, and

Apple, which have profited handsomely from the large Chinese market. Chinese firms enjoy cost-saving labor and access to massive markets for their products and services. This newfound wealth that has enriched the Chinese Communists rests in part on the slave labor system of the Laogai. Karl Marx is probably doing back flips in his grave.

Chinese Communist Party Organ Harvesting.

The Office of the Commissioner of the United Nations Human Rights Commission has disclosed that it has gathered credible evidence indicating that the Laogai camps have added a new scope to human exploitation. Besides forced sterilizations and medical experimentation, organ harvesting has added a new dimension of horror to these camps. It has also become a new growth industry that probably rivals the historical legacy of Josef Mengele. There are numerous UN reports of CCP oppression and their Nazi-like contempt for human life. Victims include Uighurs of western China and believers of Falun Gong. If you Google "organ harvesting" in communist China, you will get numerous hits. Yet, few in the West know of this barbaric medical growth industry, which probably generates enormous profits that could easily surpass several hundred million dollars a year. Since donating organs is culturally taboo in China, it gives credence to the involuntary harvesting of human organs. The Chinese communists assert that the organs are from criminals, but these claims are difficult to believe. While volumes of reports have been published on this gruesome industry, it probably still operates unabated.

Pol Pot and the "killing fields" of Cambodia.

Pol Pot and his Khmer Rouge thugs turned Cambodia into vast killing fields, full of mass graves. No other communist regime surpasses them for the sheer percentage of people murdered in comparison to the population. **Cities and other urban areas were emptied of people, and the country was turned into a vast gulag/prison system, and most of the population was de facto prisoners.** Between April 1975 through the beginning of 1979, roughly forty-five months, approximately 1.5 to 2 million Cambodians were brutally killed. Pol Pot (his real name was Saloth Sar) sought to transform this agrarian country into a state of pure communism. His only achievement was in killing almost 1 in 4 Cambodians, which was close to a quarter of the population. By the time the Khmer Rouge was swept from power, the small country was set back decades.

North Korean Prison Camps, and Concentration Camps; Pure Hell on Earth.

Prisons in North Korea have become diabolical laboratories, in which methods of torture, physical abuse, humiliation and murder were honed to fiendish perfection. Some of these prisons are comparable to the Soviet Gulags or German concentration camps. Victims were quietly arrested, then imprisoned, many times without trial. Prisons vary. "Help posts" were for minor political crimes, such as not showing enthusiasm for the supreme leader, or anti-social behavior, the ineffective (whatever that means), liars or those who were considered lazy. Hard labor camps were for common criminals. Some prisons near border areas were created to imprison individuals who were deemed unreliable and might try to flee the totalitarian hellhole. The "special dictatorship zones" were the worst concentration camps. Whole families could be arrested and imprisoned for years. One individual, who was able to escape to South Korea, had been imprisoned because his grandfather made positive remarks about living in a capitalist country. He had been nine years old when he and other family members were thrown in prison. The communist regime in North Korea also banishes invalids, dwarfs, and mentally disabled persons to remote areas within the country.

Life in the camps of the *special dictatorship zones* is a nightmare. *The Black Book of Communism* had numerous examples of prisoners being subjected to every form of cruel torture and death. They suffered horrific beatings, starvation, electrical shocks, and at times, were forced to fight each other for the amusement of the guards. Executions were frequent. Guards could be promoted if they could shoot a prisoner who was trying to escape. In some instances, guards desiring advancement forced prisoners to climb the perimeter fence so they could shoot them. Camp 13 was a particularly harsh detention center, with sadistic guards and vicious guard dogs. On at least two separate occasions, guard dogs mauled prisoners to death. Prisoners were also used for live target practice. The doomed were forced to run, and the guards shot them down. At the same camp, personnel reported the possibility of bodies being incinerated, and one guard spoke of seeing small bits of hair and flesh in one tunnel, but was afraid to say anything, because he could "get a black bean (a bullet) in the head."

Analysis: When a communist regime is so fixated on keeping its populace imprisoned within its country, it becomes a de facto prison, and the people are slaves. The prison and concentration camps could be considered a living hell.

Sendero de Luminoso slave labor camps.

Sendero de Luminoso is a radical communist group that is engaged in a campaign of terror across a remote area in Peru. Starting in the 1980s, their attacks have killed tens of thousands, and they have destroyed numerous government facilities and infrastructure. They fund themselves, in part, by engaging in drug trafficking. Sendero has also created its own small, forced labor camps (GULAGS). Given the remoteness of the Shining Path's area of operation, they were able to establish these quasi-prison camps without the government's knowledge. Villagers were abducted and forced to tend Sendero's agricultural fields, while subjecting them to Marxist indoctrination. The Peruvian government only became aware of these camps when some prisoners escaped and alerted the authorities. In 2015, the Peruvian military was able to carry out several rescue operations, freeing over fifty villagers from two different camps. Most of the abductees were Ashaninka Native Americans, and some had been held captives for years. Besides enslavement, the captors raped women. The children who were born from these sexual assaults were also forced to do manual labor or become rebel fighters.

Marxists claim that their ideology strives to free the lower classes from the shackles of the industrialized world and capitalism. So why is the Shining Path enslaving the very people they are supposed to be helping? [20]

---

[20] Kempton, Nicole, Richardson, Nan, Andrew, Nathan, Wu, Henry. Laogai, The Machinery of Repression in China. P.1-152. Courtois, Stephane, et.al. The Black Book of Communism p. 497-513, North Korea, 553-560. Ochab, Dr. Ewelina "U.N. Concerned about Organ Harvesting in China." Forbes. Dec. 18, 2022. Smith, Saphora. "China forcefully harvests organs from detainees, tribunal concludes." NBC, World. June 18th, 2019. United Nations Human Rights: Office of The High Commissioner; Media Center. China: "UN human rights experts alarmed by 'organ harvesting' allegations." June 14th, 2021. United Nations. John King Fairbanks, the famous Sino-historian, unbelievably, never mentions the Laogai. He spoke briefly about brainwashing, which he called "thought reform." Fairbank, J. Great Chinese Revolution;1800-1985. P.255-256. Courtois, Stephane, "et.al. The Black Book on Communism. Pp. 328, 675-681. "Peru rescues 39 'slaves-workers' from Shining Path farm" BBC News. July 28th, 2015. Post, Colin. "15 more rescued from second Shining Path 'production camp'" Peru Reports. August 2, 2015. Laffin, Andrew, C. & Mitrokhin, V. The World was Going our Way: The KGB and the Battle for the Third World. pp. 59, footnote 36, p. 513.

Stalin and the Great Terror.

From its beginning, the Soviet Union used terror to frighten the populace into subservience. In the late 1930s, Stalin would take terror to its pinnacle. The Great Terror was "the largest-scale peacetime... bloodletting in European history..." Why did the "Boss" ramp up terror? Given the destructiveness of Stalin's program of forced agricultural collectivization, doubts about his governing were quietly voiced. Concerns circulated among party members, although there was never any overt confrontation with the "Boss". They had a reason to be concerned. Stalin was paranoid, vindictive, and utterly without conscious. He nursed grudges and had a totally overblown conspiratorial mindset. In Stalin's mind, enemies were around every corner. If Stalin felt that his subordinates were not sufficiently diabolical and conspiratorial in their mindset, he would berate them, calling them "blind kittens."

When the USSR collapsed and the secret Soviet archives were opened to the public, historians combed through documents hidden away for decades. Before the fall of the USSR, historians sympathetic to the Soviet Union made the excuse that Stalin was unaware of the mass killings done in his name. Documentation clearly indicated that Stalin took a direct role in the Great Terror, personally signing death warrants for thousands of victims. In *The Black Book of Communism*, there is a photograph of a document signed by Stalin, in which he demands that 5,000 more victims needed to be added to the list.

The process of destruction.

Stalin created sheer unending terror by manipulating the "organs" of the government, specifically the secret police. The KGB compiled information on everyone, especially party leaders who were not blindly devoted to the "Boss." Stalin would fixate on a potential rival, isolate them politically, and, through the state-controlled media, vilify the individual or group. He would then strike. The KGB arrested the doomed person[s], brutally tortured them, and forced them to sign a bogus confession. Some of the prisoners had to rehearse their confessions so they sounded sincere when confessing to their supposed crimes against the state. Sometimes they were executed immediately or would be used as witnesses in other show trials. Based on their false confessions, more people would be arrested, tortured, shot, or imprisoned. Many of the Bolshevik bigwigs were shot, a few got lengthy prison sentences, and they conveniently died while imprisoned. Some survived. This process of eliminating real or imagined rivals would be repeated, again and again.

The "Boss" escalated the terror to unprecedented levels. He purposely undermined trust between people, especially the older Party leaders. As one historian noted, "Stalin... [instituted a] ...system of elimination: each victim killed his predecessor and was killed by his successor. Thousands of senior Party officials were... involved... in the work of destruction." Everyone feared the "midnight knock" at the door. Arrests and torture were routine. Summary death sentences were carried out daily. Doomed prisoners, trying to save themselves, denounced others, hoping they would only get lengthy prison sentences. No one could be completely trusted; no one was safe. It should be noted that under "the Communist Party... denunciation... [was]... an obligation, whereas the Nazi Party did not..." Sympathetic historians used terms like purge and liquidate to downplay the Great Terror, but this communist bloodbath ended with the murder of roughly 700,000 to over a million victims.

Probably one of the most frightening aspects of the Great Terror was the disappearance of individuals, whole families, or groups of people. In the totalitarian novel, *1984*, George Orwell used the euphemism, vaporized to describe the disappearance and the probable murder of individual[s]. It was an accurate description. One day, they were there; the next day, they were gone. If you tried to inquire about someone's disappearance, that could trigger your own arrest. In one instance, a family was moved into an apartment on short notice. Since there was a lack of housing in the USSR, they probably felt fortunate to get the apartment, but happiness soon turned to horror. They discovered a teakettle, still warm, from the prior inhabitants who had probably been arrested just a few hours earlier.

The first targets: the old Bolsheviks.

In early 1934, after the Seventeenth Soviet Party Congress was convened. Stalin's paranoid nature caused him to see enemies around every corner, so he plotted to eliminate any potential rivals, real or imagined. Party members were elected to the Central Committee by secret ballot. Stalin got the most votes, but some of the party members opposed him, and the "Boss" would never allow such a slight. Out of the "1,996 delegates, 1,108 would… [be killed by the end of] … the Terror," The congress had 139 senior Party members in attendance, of whom 108 would be executed, and this was just the beginning. One of the surviving senior Party members claimed that most of the individuals who counted the voting ballots were shot.

Murderous Marxism

Stalin most definitely orchestrated the murder of a close Party leader named Kirov, who was supposedly his friend, a man he called "brother." On this pretext, the "Boss" claimed a vast conspiracy against the state existed. Many of the old Bolsheviks were arrested, pressured into implicating others, who in turn were arrested, tortured, and eventually shot. Solzhenitsyn wrote that Stalin "would rather that 999 innocent men should rot than miss one genuine spy."

Dictatorships crave enemies of the state. What better way to divert the people's attention away from the murderous failings of totalitarian dictatorships? When "actual enemies" were in short supply, fictitious enemies were created to focus the people's attention in another direction. The communists were no different and were probably the worst at creating fake enemies. Soviet authorities blamed kulaks (rich peasants) for wrecking Soviet agriculture, technicians for supposedly destroying equipment, and spies were everywhere. Family members of those arrested could also be arrested for being socially dangerous or "harmful elements." Alexander Solzhenitsyn outlined almost a dozen different social categories that the Soviets considered dangerous to the USSR. By vilifying a group or person, the "Boss" was able to galvanize public support; mind-numbing terror also helped. To this end, Stalin found his perfect boogeyman, Leon Trotsky.

Trotsky

Leon Trotsky was one of the original Bolshevik leaders during the Russian Revolution. He was a fervent Marxist leader who had no qualms about utilizing terror tactics and ordering killings. Initially, he was considered a hero of the Russian Revolution. With the death of Lenin, Stalin was able to consolidate power and isolate Trotsky politically. He directed the state-controlled media to vilify Trotsky, and he went from hero to villain. Trotsky was not the only individual vilified by Stalin, but probably the most famous example. He was expelled from the Soviet Union and bounced around the globe until he finally found asylum in Mexico. Stalin had agents follow him, looking for the opportunity to kill him. In 1940, after an initial assassination attempt, a Soviet sponsored hit man was able to talk his way into Trotsky's presence and smash him in the head with a cut-down ice ax, killing the old Bolshevik. Trotsky's assassin, Ramon Mercader, served twenty years in a Mexican prison, and after his release, he lived for a time in Communist Cuba. In the Soviet Union, he was "decorated with the Order of Lenin for his murder of Trotsky and... [later, after Mercader died, he] ... was buried quietly in Moscow." Stalin did not stop his witch-hunt after Trotsky was killed. Many of Trotsky's family members were arrested and killed. Trotsky's name would be invoked in many thousands of rigged trials, in which the victim was accused of conspiring with the former Russian revolutionary to try to overthrow the state or plotting to kill Stalin. Trotsky had called Stalin "the gravedigger" of the party; little did he know that it would come to encompass the entire Soviet Union, and later Eastern Europe.

Terror strikes everyone.

The atrocities committed during the Soviet Great Terror are too numerous to tell, but here are a few examples. Some examples of Soviet atrocities fell outside the period of 1937-1938.

-One political commissar was arrested and shot for refusing to torture.

-Another commissar was shot for not killing enough.

-A twelve-year-old boy who complained about being raped by his interrogator was shot immediately.

-In Georgia, a region from which Stalin was from, 425 party officials were shot or imprisoned out of 644 between 1936-1938.

-One Georgian authority had his eyes gouged out and eye drums punctured in front of his wife.

-Another Georgian official, who had been poisoned, was exhumed from his grave, and his wife was tortured to death in front of her son. The son was then imprisoned and later shot.

-One KGB killer casually described his role in committing mass murder. In Siberia, doomed prisoners were held in a jail, and then they were transported to a waiting pit. "They'd climb out, huddled... [and]... we shot them, and if anyone was moving, we finished them off... It was hard work; you earned the vodka that they gave you later... '*I slept well*,'"

The "Boss" goes after family members of acquaintances.

Stalin took a perverse pleasure in inflicting pain on those who were most loyal to him. Not all brutality was connected to the Great Terror. It could happen at any time. It cannot be repeated enough: no one was safe.

- Stalin's first wife, Ekaterine Svanidze, was the mother of his first son, Yakov. She died in 1907 from tuberculosis when she was 22 years old. Once Stalin was in power, he had his brother-in-law, who was supposedly his friend, shot as a spy. His brother-in-law's wife was imprisoned and later died in a camp. The sister of Stalin's wife was also given a lengthy sentence, and she died while imprisoned.

-Stalin's second wife, Nadezhda Alliluyeva, committed suicide under mysterious circumstances in 1932. She supposedly shot herself in the heart, but state media claimed that she had died of a medical condition. Sources indicated that Stalin treated his wife terribly, and that is what probably drove her to commit suicide. She was thirty years old. The sister of his second wife was imprisoned and later released. She was lucky; her husband was also imprisoned, then later shot.

-Stalin orchestrated the arrests of the wives of his Foreign Secretary V. Molotov and Mikhail Kalinin; both men were part of his inner circle. To placate Stalin, Molotov denounced his wife after her arrest. Both wives were lucky; after torture and imprisonment, they were released.

-Nikita Khrushchev, who would later lead the Soviet Union after the death of Stalin, had his daughter-in-law imprisoned, but later she was released.

-Then there was the sad case of Stalin's chief secretary, Alexander Poskrebyshev. His wife, Dr. Bronislava "Bronka" Poskrebysheva, a medical doctor, was arrested after pleading for the release of her brother, who was imprisoned. Since Poskrebyshev had worked with Stalin for years, he begged for the release of his wife, but the "Boss" was unmoved. He supposedly replied, "Don't worry, we'll find you a new wife…" Bronka was later shot, as was her brother, and her body was buried in a mass burial pit. Poskrebyshev's daughter had been told that her mother died of natural causes. Later, a classmate, who knew of Bronka's fate, told the daughter that her mother had been murdered. At times, Stalin could not restrain himself from psychologically torturing the chief secretary. This diabolical psychopath would needle Poskrebyshev by asking how his daughter was faring. Even after the murder of his wife, Poskrebyshev unfailingly served Stalin. He would later remarry but remained devoted to Bronka. Supposedly, when the chief secretary looked upon a photo of his murdered wife, or heard her name, he would "burst into tears." No one was safe.

Stalin wipes out the Comintern and the Soviet military.

During the Great Terror, members of the International Communist Organization, the Comintern, became Stalin's next victims. A majority of the members were not citizens of the USSR, but lived in Moscow, or they travelled to the Soviet Union for conferences. Thousands were killed on the orders of the Boss. The secret police raced around quietly, arresting Comintern members and killing them in the middle of the night.

Several years before the slaughter of the Comintern, the KGB and other foreign communist agents carried out assassinations and kidnappings outside of the USSR; most of these murderous crimes took place in Europe.

In 1930, Bolshevik operatives, along with local agents, kidnapped a former Czarist general, Alexander Kutepov, on the streets of Paris. The intent was to smuggle him out of France and put him on trial, which would have probably ended with his execution. The general never made it; he died while being transported back to the USSR. Given his advanced age, the rough handling by the agents probably caused the old man's heart to give out. In 1937, another Russian émigré and associate of Kutepov, Y. K. Miller, was kidnapped in the middle of the day in Paris. Two stories emerged about his fate. The first being that he was shot, and his corpse was buried. The Mitrokhin Files indicated that agents were able to smuggle Miller back to the USSR, put him on trial, and he was executed.

During the 1930s, Soviet agents and diplomats understood that if they were summoned back to Moscow, it would probably be a certain death sentence, so many refused to return. The KGB went to great lengths to pursue these individuals. In the late 1930s, Ignace Reiss was a Soviet agent who defected and penned an open letter accusing Stalin of numerous crimes. He was lured into a meeting and murdered by Soviet agents in Switzerland. Ironically, the Soviet intelligence supervisor who arranged Reiss's assassination was later arrested and shot.

Walter Krivitsky was a "resident" agent in the Netherlands who defected after being recalled to the USSR. The KGB tracked him down and murdered him in the United States. Another Soviet intelligence officer who quit his post in Turkey in 1929 was tracked down and killed in Belgium in 1938."

In 1974, John Barron, a journalist for *Reader's Digest*, published *KGB: The Secret Work of Soviet Secret Agents*. His book lays bare the dastardly acts of the KGB during its 73-year existence. In chapter 13, *The Dark Core*, on one page alone, Barron relates the murder and disappearance of almost two dozen individuals outside the Soviet Union. The killings were the handiwork of the KGB. Most of these victims were either former intelligence officers, defectors, or individuals who displeased Soviet leadership. What they have in common is that the Soviet leadership considered them turncoats, which warranted them being permanently silenced.

The Mitrokhin Files indicated that John Barron's work so unnerved the KGB leadership, they ordered a full-scale investigation, which generated several hundred reports on the journalist and his sources. Barron's details on the fiendish activities of the KGB prompted the leadership of the secret security agency to ramp up at least two different disinformation campaigns about the writer. Known by the Soviet euphemism "active measures," the disinformation campaigns were used to discredit Barron. Their actions were ineffective. Unfortunately, the most effective method of silencing Barron entailed left-of-center historians ignoring his journalist work. More information was figuratively tossed into a historical black hole.

There are numerous other examples of Soviet agents kidnapping and assassinating individuals outside the borders of the Soviet Union. Still, probably the most notorious was the murder of the former revolutionary Bolshevik leader, Leon Trotsky, in Mexico City in 1940.

From 1937-1938, Stalin purged the Soviet military; tens of thousands were arrested, and the number executed is not the exact number, but probably numbered in the hundreds. The upper echelons of the military were wiped out. The true extent of the damage from Stalin's purging of the Soviet military would not be felt until their other Nonaggression Pact signatory, Nazi Germany, attacked the USSR in the summer of 1941.

Quasi-communist comparisons: What is old is new. Putin critics have a nasty habit of being murdered.

Even with the fall of the Soviet Union, a spate of assassinations and poisonings has been linked to a former KGB leader, who is currently the president of Russia, Vladimir Putin. The Russian journalist, Anna Politkovskaya, a critic of Putin, was believed to have been poisoned, but recovered. She was later shot to death in her Moscow apartment. In 2015, another Putin political opponent, Boris Nemtsov, was gunned down on a bridge in Moscow. Several other Putin critics were poisoned or fell ill under mysterious circumstances. Vladimir Kara-Murza, a journalist, was believed to have been poisoned twice: once in 2015 and another time in 2017. In 2018, a former Russian spy, Sergei Skripal, who defected to Great Britain, was poisoned with a nerve agent, along with his daughter; both barely survived. Yet another Putin critic, Alexei Navalny, fell ill, and it was believed that he had been poisoned. Later, he would be arrested on trumped-up charges, convicted, and sent to a remote penal base in Siberia. Although the details are murky, Navalny was found dead under mysterious circumstances in his cell. Most world leaders decried the death of the Putin critic as murder.

Probably the most infamous of Putin's critics to be poisoned to death was Alexander Litvinenko, a former Soviet KGB agent. With the fall of the USSR and he began working for the Federal Security Service of the Russian Federation, or FSB, which is a reconstituted version of the KGB. It is believed that Litvinenko feared for his life after he had a falling out with authorities linked to Putin. He fled to England in 2000. In 2006, Litvinenko fell ill after meeting with a former Russian associate. It was discovered that he consumed tea, laced with a highly rare and extremely lethal radioactive substance, polonium-210. Litvinenko lost all his hair and died a slow, agonizing death. Before Litvinenko died, he accused Putin of having him killed.

More points to Ponder: Putin attacks Ukraine, and many more Russians connected to the government die.

Since Vladimir Putin launched an attack on Ukraine in February 2022, quite a few Russian oligarchs, who were critical of the invasion, have been killed. Furthermore, Russian government officials who have supposedly displeased the Russian president have also mysteriously died. As this was being written, Yevgeny Prigozhin, the chief of the Wagner Group, a Russian mercenary outfit, died in an inexplicable aircraft accident. Prigozhin had initially supported Putin's invasion of Ukraine. After his mercenaries suffered heavy casualties during a poorly planned military operation, Prigozhin went from a supporter to a critic of the war in Ukraine. Prigozhin gave several interviews, in which he rebuked Putin's handling of the war.

Although events are unclear, the mercenary leader allegedly staged a short-term mutiny against the Russian president. Supposedly, Prigozhin and Putin had patched up their differences. That was until a plane, in which the mercenary chief was travelling, plunged into the earth killing all on board. Witnesses said they heard an explosion, and video footage showed the doomed aircraft with one wing ablaze, spiraling into the ground. An article in the Wall Street Journal (WSJ) explored the rash of deaths of people associated with the former KGB chief. The (WSJ) article noted that these deaths have attracted a morbid internet following, so much so, that Wikipedia has a content article with a list of all those who have died. Maybe all these accidents and unexplained deaths were just coincidental, or maybe old habits die hard.

Death tolls of the Great Terror and beyond.

Historian Robert Conquest, a critic of the Soviet Union, argued that during the Great Terror, six million people were arrested, 3 million executed, and 2 million perished in the GULAG. *The Black Book on Communism* noted that a million and a half were arrested, and almost 700,000 were executed. *The Great Big Book of Horrible Things* stated that 7 million were arrested, a million were executed, and two million died in the GULAG between 1937-1938. Even the lower numbers represent enormous death tolls.

Can we trust the numbers? Case in point. In 1937, Stalin had a census taken of the USSR. He expected to see a population of 170 million, and the census recorded a population of 163 million. Supposedly, the heads of the census were arrested and shot. Two years later, another census was taken, and the population magically grew to 167 million; supposedly, Stalin bumped the number up to 170 million.

The low census figure could feasibly reflect those killed during Collectivization, the Ukrainian Terror Famine, and the Great Terror.

Why such a wide variance? In George Orwell's *1984*, the state constantly falsified information, and the USSR was no different. Given the secretive nature of the USSR and the obvious blatant manipulation of vital statistics, there is a good reason to doubt the supposed official death toll of 20 million that died in the Soviet Union. Mass graves are a good indication of communist intentions to cover up their murderous deeds. After the fall of the USSR, these gruesome discoveries came to light.

-200,000 were found in a mass grave near Kyiv.

-30,000 bodies were discovered in a mass grave near Saint Petersburg.

-25,000 bodies were discovered buried near Levashevo, just northeast of Saint Petersburg.

-25,000 bodies were discovered in a mass grave in a town near Moscow.

- Bones have been discovered at the Moscow Zoo.

- In a forest in Belarus, authorities discovered pits containing the bones of 3000 victims... **_each_**, and "they could see scores, if not hundreds" more pits in the forest. Authorities gave up and erected a cross for the unknown number of murder victims.

- In a pit in the Ural Mountains, another 80,000 remains have been discovered: almost all with a bullet hole in the back of the head. A local noted that people were taken, "and shot with their children at this place." It is doubtful the children were spared. The list goes on and on, and this does not take into consideration yet undiscovered mass graves. Remember, the Soviets rarely left any witnesses.

Stalin's killer: 2010 Guinness Book of World Records "Most Prolific Executioner."

Vasily Blokhin was a true instrument of death, a state-sanctioned killer; totally without conscious. A photograph of Blokhin shows him in uniform with a chest full of medals, but these commendations were not for gallantry on the field of battle. Blokhin was Stalin's most favored executioner, specializing in what the "Boss" called "black work." He headed a special KGB detachment that killed 100,000s of thousands of prisoners on Stalin's orders. It is estimated that Blokhin was personally responsible for killing tens of thousands of people, which included some of the top Bolsheviks. Records indicated that of the over 20,000 Polish prisoners who were murdered in the Katryn Forest, Blokhin personally shot close to 7,000 of these prisoners in roughly twenty-eight days. In comparison, in 1943, "some 6,821 US Marines and sailors" were killed on the Pacific Island of Iwo Jima, in almost five weeks of horrific fighting. The 2010 *Guinness Book of World Records* dubbed Blokhin as the "Most Prolific Executioner."

Murdering in the dead of night.

Killings were usually carried out in the middle of the night, in soundproof rooms. In some killing rooms, the antechambers were painted red to conceal bloodstains. Many of the actual execution chambers had wood on the walls to keep bullets from ricocheting after the projectile passed through the victim's skull. The floor was slanted to provide drainage, and a hose was available to wash away blood.

While carrying out executions, Vasily was clad like a character from a horror movie, with a leather apron, gloves, boots, and a cap to keep him from being drenched in blood. By the end of a hard night of killing, he had to have been covered with gore. He, along with his attendants, drank a great deal of vodka, which helped them carry out their "black works." Vasily preferred to use German pistols because they were of superior quality, rarely failed, and if the bodies were ever discovered, they provided plausibility deniability of Soviet culpability. The KGB thought of everything.

The executioner dodges the bullet but loses his job.

After the execution of KGB Chief Nikolai Yezhov, his replacement, Lavrenti Beria, drew up a new list of people to be killed. Blokhin's name was on the list, but Stalin spared him. It was unusual. The "Boss" was always keen about liquidating anyone who knew too much. The Soviet leader was not sentimental, but he recognized Blokhin's murderous talent, and he was probably reluctant to lose one of his most efficient cutthroats. On Stalin's orders, Vasily was "secretly" awarded, the Order of the Red Banner, which came with a raise in his "pay." There would probably be many more people to purge, but Vasily's career was cut short when the "Boss" died in 1953. Given his grisly job, the Soviet leadership was eager to distance itself from Stalin's executioner. Blokhin was demoted, and he later turned into an alcoholic. Although the historical record is not clear, it is believed that Vasily went insane, and supposedly, he committed suicide in 1955. Alcoholism, insanity, and suicide. One could speculate that vodka could not blot out the faces and voices of the approximately 20,000 people he murdered.

Blokhin's tombstone.

Vasily Blokhin's grave has a fancy tombstone with his image etched upon the monument. There are several ironies about his final resting place. The Manifesto of Communism called for the abolition of religion, and the Soviet Union was an atheist country. The Bolsheviks wanted to ban headstones and cremate victims, to undermine people's faith. Ironically, Stalin's chief executioner not only had a headstone, but it was engraved with an Orthodox Christian cross. Ironically, most of Blokhin's victims never got a grave, tombstone, or any type of remembrance. They were murdered in secret and their bodies were buried in secret mass graves, or they were incinerated, and the ashes dumped in mass burial pits. [21]

---

21 Solzhenitsyn, Alexander. The GULAG Archipelago, 1918-1956. p. 247, 284, 285, 286, 407, 440-1, 442, 443, 444. Amis, Robert. Koba the Dread. p. 97, 101, 112, 134,135,144-145, 147-149, 153, 166-174, 175, 178, 179,180. Merridale, Catherine. Night of Stone. p. 199, 200. Montefiore, Simon. Stalin, The Court of the Red Tsar. P.316-320. Inscription under a photograph, in between page 290-291. Vronskaya, Jeanne, and Chuguev, Viktor. (Editors). A Biographical Dictionary of the Soviet Union,1917-1988. Pp. Stalin's first wife, pp. 416, Stalin second wife pp. 11. Reiss, pp. 349. Courtois, Stephane, et, al. The Black Book of Communism. p. xvi, 184-202, 306-309, 754. Radzinsky, Edvard. Stalin. p.307-308, 392-394, 409-411, 419, 436-438. White, M. The Great Big Book of Horrible Things. p. 385-387 Davies, N. Europe. 960, 963. Andrew, C, and Mitrokhin, V. The Sword and the Shield; The Mitrokhin Archive and the Secret History of the KGB. pp. 19, 41, 42, 68, 69, 72, 75. "Blokhin executed Mikhail Tukhachevsky, and Gregory Yagoda. Cahill, Paul. "Interesting Histories: Vasily Blokhin-A True Monster." April 18, 2017. Online. Vasily Blokhin, history's most prolific executioner. Rare Historical photos. Nov. 23, 2021.Online. Dunn, Morgan. "How Josef Stalin's Favorite Executioner Personally Killed 7,000 Poles During the Katyn Massacre." All That's Interesting. ATI-ATI. Dec. 14, 2020. https://allthatsinteresting.com/vasily-blokhin . Young, Peter. ED. The Atlas of the Second World War. pp. 164. Katamidze, Slava. Loyal Comrades, Ruthless Killer's: The Secret Services of the USSR 1917-1991. Pp. 79-84. Roy Medvedev chapter, "Stalin's Usurpation of Power, and the Great Terror" has conservatively hundreds of examples of sinister killings during this period of the 1930s. Medvedev, Roy. Let History Judge. Pp. 327-512. Specifically pages 427-430. Hinshaw, Drew, et. al. "Russians Keep Turning Up Dead All Over the World." Wall Street Journal. March 3, 2024. Online. Gardener, Frank, et. al. "Wagner chief Yevgeny Prigozhin presumed dead after Russia plane crash." BBC News. Aug. 23, 2023. Sept. 15, 2023. He

William Johnson

Communist Comparisons: Mass Terror.

Communist countries utilized terror, especially when they were trying to gain control of a nation or to maintain power. Not every communist regime utilized terror like Stalin. After the Second World War, the Soviets used terror to assert control in Eastern Europe. After Stalin died in 1953, the use of terror ebbed, and the fear of the communist state supplanted it. In Afghanistan, the Soviets utilized terror in the form of military-inflicted atrocities. (See communist attacks Muslims.) In China, Mao used terror at times, and the Cultural Revolution terrorized many, but never rose to the level of killings during Stalin's Great Terror. In Vietnam, Ho Chi Minh used terror in the countryside, but French and American involvement alienated parts of the populace during this period in Indochina. A hopelessly corrupt South Vietnamese government that governed ineptly only contributed to the communist victory by the North Vietnamese. Communist victory did spawn panic, and two million fled South Vietnam after the fall of Saigon. Castro's communists in Cuba and the Sandinistas used fear and brutality, but not the constant mind-numbing terror used by Stalin. The Marxist regimes, which seized control of the African nations of Angola and Mozambique, used terror. Still, they were disorganized in the application of violence, while their anti-communist opponents were no better in their actions. North Korea, Cambodia, and Ethiopia was a different story. Varying degrees of sheer terror were used for years to decades within these regimes.

---

died at the Wolf Polar prison in Northern Russia. Norman, Greg. "Putin critic Alexei Navalny dead at 47, Russian officials say" Fox News." Feb. 16, 2024. Roth, Andrew. "The Mysterious, violent and unsolved deaths of Putin's foes and critics." The Guardian. Feb. 16, 2024. Hinshaw, Drew & Parkinson, Joe. "Could the US Have saved Navalny" Wall Street Journal. August, 7, 2025. Barron, John. KGB: The Secret Work of Soviet Secret Agents. Pp. 306-331.

The Cultural Revolution, Ripping the fabric of Chinese society.

The Cultural Revolution, like the Great Leap Forward, was the brainchild of Mao. Since the GFL had not transformed China into a communist utopia, the Great Helmsman decided to steer the country in another direction. Mao was convinced that for communism to triumph in China, the old ways, ideas, culture, and customs would need to be destroyed. Only internal cultural turmoil, pitting one segment of the population against another, could uproot the old ways. Mao failed to understand (probably did not care) that China is a traditional culture, with one foot planted in the past, the other in the future. The Cultural Revolution almost ripped the fabric of Chinese society, traumatizing a generation.

He blatantly manipulated the young people of China, who were the most malleable, the ones who would embrace revolutionary fervor and do anything for the Great Helmsman. He had no definitive plan, just an idea to change China. As one historian noted, he "plunged... [China]... into chaos; and... the Great Helmsman was... unconcerned." All Chinese institutions and beliefs were to be attacked: authority, culture, and history; all were to be forcefully transformed. It must be noted; parents, the elderly, teachers, education, and people of authority are venerated in Asian culture, and China was no different. To assail these institutions and these deeply held values is to attack the essence of Chinese society.

By the summer of 1966, "a wave of violence swept the country." Mao's followers, the Red Guard, acted on his every word. The elderly, artists, writers, professors, those who represented the old order, were targeted because they supposedly stood in the way of Mao's vision of the future. Juveniles attacked people on the streets, and hundreds of thousands of people were brutally beaten and killed. Tens of thousands of people committed suicide. People were publicly disgraced, which is culturally taboo in China. They had been forced to wear dunce caps while being paraded through public streets. Teachers were especially singled out for humiliation when they were detained in de facto jails on school property. Once again, victims were beaten, and many died. The Red Guard took over universities, schools, factories, libraries, museums, and any place in which they could force their will upon a group. They destroyed ancient artifacts, paintings, monuments, and anything that represented the past. These wild revolutionaries desecrated graves and even defiled the grave of a Confucius scholar, digging up the body and burning the remains. Chinese history was under assault.

Enough is enough, the end of the Cultural Revolution.

Eventually, the chaos caused by the Red Guard hit a tipping point. The social trauma and the disruption of everyday life became so great that Mao began to regret the forces he unleashed. The loss in productivity for the economy was staggering; whole industries were crippled. The Red Guard had paralyzed large swathes of the country, and the population wanted the anarchy to stop.

By 1968, Mao realized that the Cultural Revolution was out of control, and the People's Liberation Army (PLA) crushed the Red Guard and the other splinter groups that had joined in on the chaos. The Cultural Revolution (as with the Great Leap Forward) failed miserably, and the only legacy was sheer unmitigated misery. Between one and two million died, with most of the casualties being the Red Guard and members of other splinter groups.

Points to Ponder: American Cultural Revolution?

In 2023, a Colorado teacher, and self-proclaimed communist, called for a "forceful Cultural Revolution" on social media. He wanted like-minded individuals to attack whiteness in the United States. This brazen communist had almost got his wish three years earlier when the George Floyd riots broke out in 2020. After the death of George Floyd at the hands of law enforcement, dozens of American cities across the country experienced a wave of violence. Journalist Andy Ngo covered the violence in *Unmasked: Inside ANTIFA's Radical Plan to Destroy Democracy*, and he details how this group, along with BLM and other anarchists, tried to instigate general insurrection across the USA. Arson and looting were widespread, especially in the US cities of Portland and Seattle. Video footage shows rioters attacking police for days on end, destroying property and setting blazes. In Minneapolis, rioters burned down a police station. In many instances, law enforcement stood by because authorities caved to the political pressure asserted by Black Lives Matter and other liberal supporters. The legacy media was also complicit, especially when they kept referring to rioters as protesters. In one Orwellian moment, a CNN reporter, standing in front of an inferno, proclaimed that the rioting was "mostly peaceful protests."

The anarchy of the George Floyd riots, and Mao's Cultural Revolution have striking similarities. Both had been politically motivated, and the ensuing havoc was a means to an end. Mao used the chaos of the "Cultural Revolution" to attain a pure state of communism. Some historians have opined that the Chairman probably wanted to maintain his grip on power by politically isolating potential rivals who questioned his catastrophic decision to unleash the Great Leap Forward. In the United States, liberal politicians probably wanted to harness the social upheaval of the George Floyd riots, so they could ram through DEI and CRT programs, while getting no political pushback from opponents. Different political systems, but the same devious tactics. [22]

North Korea: Soul sucking Hell.

The Black Book on Communism described the damage inflicted by the decades of brutality of the regime.

"How can one calculate the soul-destroying effects of constant, mindless propaganda? How can one put a figure on the absence of freedom of expression, freedom of association, and freedom of movement...a child's life destroyed simply because his grandfather received... [an unjustified] ... prison sentence... a woman... forced to have an abortion in atrocious conditions... people... obsessed by the

---

[22] The Red Guard thugs also targeted private homes, stealing everything they could lay their hands on. By the end of 1966, well over 120,000 homes were forcibly entered and robbed. The amount of loot stolen was staggering; 65 tons of gold, which in 1966 would have been valued close to $55 million. In 2021 this number would be well over $2.65 billion. The thugs also plundered close to 20 tons of silver, over a half million precious stones, 50 million Yuan (China's currency), and millions more in foreign currency, which was handed over to the communist government. Estimates on the amount of plunder stolen are thought to be conservative, because it is doubtful that the Red Guard turned over everything they had stolen. It could be argued that the plundering by these communist inspired thieves constitutes one of the largest strong-armed robberies in history. Pantsov, Alexander, with Levine, Steven. Mao: The Real Story. P. 508-536. Li, Dun. The Ageless Chinese; A History. P. 525,534,535. Fairbanks, John King. The Great Chinese Revolution. Pp. 316-320, 323-324, 328-329, 331-333. De Witte, Melissa. "China's Cultural Revolution was a power grab from within the government, not from without, Stanford sociologist finds," Stanford Report. Oct. 29th, 2019. Online https://news.stanford.edu/stories/2019/10/violence-unfolded-chinas-cultural-revolution . Grossman, Hannah. "Colorado teacher calls for 'FORCEFUL cultural revolution' targeted at 'whiteness': 'This is sacred'" Fox News. May 18, 2023.". The Major Cities Chiefs (MCCA) is a 40-page comprehensive report on the violence and destruction of George Floyd riots. MCCA Report on the 2020 Protest and Civil Unrest. 2021. PDF. Kingson, Jennifer. "Exclusive: $1 billion-plus riot damage is most expensive in insurance history." AXIOS. Sept 16, 2020. Ngo, Andy. Unmasked: Inside Antifa's Radical Plan to Destroy Democracy. Pp. 51-55, 58-65, 67-72, 75-76, 95, 120, 138-139, 203-205.

possibility of starvation... lack of heating... acute shortages and privations."

Any trivial miss-step, an ill-chosen word, the wrong facial expression, watching a Western video, or not showing enthusiasm for the supreme leader could end with a person's execution. For well over seven decades, purges, prison camps, famine, and governmental neglect have dominated the everyday life of North Koreans. See the section on North Korean prisons.

In comparison, South Korea has prospered since the war. Their economy is considered a miracle. South Korea is a small country, but it is an international leader in the manufacture of electronics, consumer goods, cars, steel manufacturing, and heavy equipment. Which country would you rather live in? [23]

Cambodia: terror, mass murder and the Khmer Rouge.

The communist takeover of Cambodia ushered in an apocalyptic nightmare for the small Southeast Asian country. This reign of terror lasted from 1975 through 1979. With breakneck speed, the Khmer Rouge utilized terror, rigid social control, and the destruction of civil society to achieve pure communism. They closed all schools, banks, prisons, and private businesses, and outlawed money in roughly two weeks. All religion was abolished, as Marx insisted upon in the Communist Manifesto. Vast swaths of Cambodian society were subjected to involuntary servitude by the communists. Urban areas were emptied, and people were marched, at gunpoint, into the countryside and were forced to do manual labor. They became slave

---

23 Courtois, Stephane, et al. The Black Book of Communism. p. 551, 552-553. White, Matthew. The Great Big Book of Horrible Things. p. 447.

laborers who toiled away in agricultural fields and construction projects. Cambodia, in essence, became a giant prison camp for much of the population. There was no freedom of movement. If someone tried to escape and was captured, punishment was usually a summary death sentence. The tremendous Cambodian jungle expanse became a de facto wall of this country-wide prison. Only Pol Pot and his army of thugs had anything resembling freedom.

Humanity is banned.

The Khmer used Mao Zedong's Communist China as a template for the new communist utopia. They incorporated parts of Mao's Great Leap Forward, and the Cultural Revolution and the consequences were catastrophic.

Pol Pot literally incorporated parts of the Communist Manifesto, such as banning individuality and the family. Anything that could distract from communist solidarity was forbidden. People who spoke correct grammar, had an urban accent, wore glasses, had advanced education, or technical skills could be executed. Almost all human activities, such as eating meals, growing crops, family relations and other social interactions were eliminated or subjected to state-run dictates. The communists tried to undermine social cohesion by deliberately attacking the family structure. Wives were separated from husbands, and children from parents. For survival purposes, spouses shunned each other, and parents had to push away children. Smiling, singing, public shows of affection, complaining, or talking back were forbidden. An act of love or compassion could end in a summary death sentence. As one Cambodian prisoner noted, "people's hearts turned to stone." What was left of human activity was not much. Terror and death were constant companions.

Murderous Marxism

So many ways to be murdered.

Terror underpinned the power of this new Marxist regime. The Khmer Rouge used savage methods to snuff out the lives of their fellow countrymen. Victims were shot, hung, throats slashed, others were smothered with plastic bags, or their brains were dashed out. An especially brutal method of execution was saved for communist cadres. They were buried up to their chest, and firewood was heaped about them. The prisoner was then drenched with a couple of gallons of gasoline and set ablaze; a horrifying way to die. Many times, the families of the doomed cadres were also killed. The Khmer soldiers routinely wiped-out whole villages. The *Black Book on Communism* noted that some sadistic guards even killed defenseless orphans by either smashing their skulls in or drowning them. Sadism was an asset, never in short supply.

The Khmer Rouge bloodbath: the Americans made them do it.

Some sympathetic historians have tried to assert that the Khmer Rouge committed mass murder because of the American bombing campaigns in Cambodia during the Vietnam War. In short, it was the United States' fault for the Cambodian genocide. I reject this notion. During the Second World War, massive bombing raids were an everyday occurrence that happened across the globe. If bombing drove the Khmer Rouge into a genocidal frenzy, then hordes of British, French, Italians, Germans, and a host of other people should have been running around killing people. The island of Malta was one of the most bombed places during WWII, yet we have no documentation of Maltese killers roaming this isle butchering people. Laos was bombed worse than Cambodia, but the communist Pathet Lao never committed anything close to the apocalyptic killings carried out by the Khmer Rouge. In contrast, Stalin unleashed the Great Terror, which entailed mass murder during peacetime; no bombs were ever dropped on the USSR.

In the Mitrokhin Files, Soviet KGB officials adamantly blamed Mao's actions in China for planting the seed of mass murder in the minds of the Khmer Rouge. The Great Leap Forward and the Cultural Revolution inspired Pol Pot. Trying to blame the US for the killings in Cambodia is just another example of a falsehood dreamed up by the charter members of the "I hate America club," to deflect from the dastardly actions carried out in the name of Marxist-communism.

Points to Ponder: ***The Killing Fields*, an Academy Award, and the murder of Dr. Ngor.**

On February 25, 1996, Dr. Haing S. Ngor was murdered during a robbery at his home in Los Angeles, California. He was best known for winning an Academy Award, for Best Supporting Actor, in the 1984 movie, *The Killing Fields,* a film about the Khmer Rouge genocide in Cambodia. Ngor was a native-born Cambodian who survived the communist reign of terror. Trained as a medical doctor, he was imprisoned in 1975 and had to conceal the fact that he was a physician (and wore glasses) because he could have been killed. Tragically, he had to watch helplessly as his wife and newborn child both died during childbirth. Had he tried to intervene and use his medical knowledge, all three would have probably died. To survive, he ate bugs and other small creatures, and he also endured torture.

Ngor was able to escape from Cambodia, and he later immigrated to the United States. He landed a supporting role in the movie *The Killing Fields,* portraying Dith Pran, a Cambodian journalist imprisoned by the communists. He, in essence, was playing himself in the movie. He never remarried, nor practiced medicine again. The gang members, who gunned down Ngor, were arrested, tried, and convicted on April 16, 1998; "the same day Pol Pot's death was confirmed in Cambodia." Had the Khmer Rouge not taken over Cambodia, Ngor probably could have had a regular life with his family. Sometimes life is quite sad, and Ngor witnessed mind-numbing horror, gained fame from his suffering, only to be murdered by street thugs. Sounds like a Greek tragedy.[24]

Ethiopia, the Red Terror.

The Marxist takeover of Ethiopia constituted one of the most appalling examples of communist brutality in Africa. The "Ethiopian Red Terror" lasted from 1974 through 1990. On December 21, 1974, Ethiopian officers staged a coup, overthrowing the aged Emperor Haile Selassie. One of the ringleaders, Mengistu Haile Mariam, supposedly strangled the eighty-year-old emperor and had his body buried under a latrine. Mengistu, a Marxist, was able to consolidate power through murder and intimidation. By 1975, he had aligned Ethiopia with the Soviet Union. The Soviet, Cuban and East Germans all sent advisers to

---

[24] Courtois, Stephane, et al. The Black Book on Communism. p. 577-635. Andrews, C. Mitrokhin, V. The World was Going our way: The KGB and the Battle for the Third World. p. 264. White, Andrew. The Great Big Book of Terrible Things. Pp. 492-495. Liefer, Richard. (April 27, 1996). 3 Teens Are Charged with Murder of "Killing Fields' Actor Haing Ngor" Chicago Tribune. Retrieved Sept 15,2016. Ngor, Haing S. Encyclopedia Britannica from the original 2012-07-20, Noble, Kenneth, B. (27 February 1996). Cambodian Physician Who Won an Oscar for Killing Fields' is Slain. The New York Times., Ebert, Rodger (March 24, 1985). The Day Haing S. Ngor won the Oscar." RogerEbert.com., Yi, Daniel, Krikorian, Greg. "Three Men Convicted of Killing Ngor", Los Angeles Times. April 17, 1998. Donahue, Deidre. "Cambodian Doctor Haing Ngor Turns Actor in the Killing Fields' and Relives His Grisly Past" People.com. Archived from Original. On 2016-03-03. Morris, Stephen. Why Vietnam Invaded Cambodia. Pp. 69-74.

instruct the Ethiopians on methods of surveillance, interrogation, intelligence gathering and large-scale intimidation of the population.

Mengistu was able to manipulate student youth groups in Ethiopia to do his dirty work. The regime murdered indiscriminately, claiming that the victims were threats to the revolution. *The Black Book of Communism* noted that many thousands were killed, and their bodies were dumped in mass graves, "on a Stalin-like scale." To add insult to injury, officials demanded that families pay for the bullet that ended their loved one's life. One of their favored methods of killing was the garrote, a cord used to strangle the victim, known as "Mengistu bowtie."

Sometimes the terror was overt, such as leaving corpses in open urban areas. In the spring of 1977, Amnesty International reported in the article, *Human Rights Violations in Ethiopia*, [25]

"'1,000 children have been killed, and their bodies are left in the streets and are being eaten by wild hyenas...You can see the heaped-up bodies of the murdered children, most of them age... [from the] ... eleven to thirteen, lying in the gutter, as you drive out of... [of the capital]... Addis Ababa.'"[26]

In 1984, an Ethiopian political officer, Asrat Destu, visited the USSR, and the Soviet leadership pressed him to explain why Mengistu was still slaughtering people when he was obviously in control of

---

25 Courtois, Stephane, et al. The Black Book of Communism. Pp. 687-690. Andrew, Christopher, & Mitrokhin, Vasili. The World Was Going Our Way, The KGB and the Battle for The Third World. Pp. 456- 459.

26 Courtois, Stephane, et al." The Black Book of Communism. 691. Amnesty International reported in the article, Human Rights Violations in Ethiopia, pp.9-11, 14-15. Andrew, Christopher, & Mitrokhin, Vasili. The World Was Going Our Way, The KGB and the Battle for The Third World. P.456-457.

Ethiopia. He replied, "We are doing what Lenin did. You cannot build socialism without red terror..." Shortly after returning to Ethiopia, Asrat was murdered during a "meeting..." As with Stalin in the Soviet Union, no one was safe in Mengistu's Ethiopia either. It was estimated that 500,000 Ethiopians were killed between 1977-1978. The real killer would be a famine, made worse by the diabolical attempt to control the Ethiopian population and battle an Eritrean insurgency against the regime. [27]

Communist atrocities in Eritrea.

In 1952, the United Nations brokered a deal that incorporated Eritrea into Ethiopia. This UN mandate alienated the Eritrean people, who took up arms against Ethiopia. By 1964, fighting had intensified, and by 1977, the Eritrean fighters were able to make substantial gains against the Ethiopians. In 1978, Mengistu accepted Soviet military aid in a bid to crush the Eritreans.

Soviet and Cubans military firepower tipped the war in favor of the Ethiopians. The combined military might drove the rebels from the towns and cities. The Eritreans suffered numerous atrocities, which rarely grabbed the attention of the international community. In the Northern Province of Tigre (also known as Tigray), massive aerial bombing raids were carried out as reprisals for resistance. In one instance, 2,500 people were killed in a single bombing raid.

---

27 Andrew, Christopher, & Mitrokhin, Vasili. The World Was Going Our Way, The KGB and the Battle For The Third World. P.456-459 P.467-468. Courtois, Stephane, et al. The Black Book of Communism. Pp. 691-694. White, Matthew. The Great Big Book of Horrible Things. pp.488-489. African Union. AUHRM Project Focus Area: Ethiopian Red Terror. 2024. PDF.

Rape, murder, terror, and pillaging by Ethiopians forces were endemic. At times, villagers were rounded up and crammed into churches or barns, which were burned to the ground. Few heard the screams of those being scorched to death, and newspaper articles rarely reported these massacres, let alone conveyed the horror. Atrocities were numerous. Fields were mined and forests were destroyed. The forced relocation of people (See Deportations) intensified the famine, deepening the misery and starvation.[28]

Stalin was on top of the world by 1939.

By the end of the 1930s, Stalin was on top of the world; he was master of the USSR, and the Soviet peoples were obedient slaves. Through mind-numbing terror, he had collectivized agricultural and killed off any potential rival, real or imagined. He slaughtered members of the Comintern, decimated the armed forces, and created such an atmosphere of fear that people denounced friends and relatives. One woman supposedly denounced close to 8000 persons.

As he consolidated power within the USSR, geopolitical events beyond the Soviet Union would present Stalin with an opportunity to expand Soviet influence beyond the USSR's borders. The Second World War and the subsequent annexation of Eastern Europe would expand Soviet influence to the edge of Western Europe.

---

28 Courtois, Stephane, et al. The Black Book of Communism. Pp. 691-695. Laffin, John. Brassey's Dictionary of Battles. Pp. 160-161. Evil Days. 30 Years of War and Famine in Ethiopia. "An Africa Watch Report". Sept. 1991. Pp. 110-128. (This publication has page after page of Ethiopian atrocities in Eritrea.)

Stalin sees a storm brewing, another major conflict just over the horizon.

A Russian historian, Edvard Radzinsky, wrote that Stalin might have been planning to instigate a "Great War" sometime in the early 1930s. In the Soviet archives, the historian found notes that suggested "traces" of a plan for a great worldwide conflict. Although these sources were less than specific about Soviet intentions, they potentially give a glimpse into Stalin's mindset. Instead of working for noble causes, such as international peace, the Boss wanted to facilitate a major war. Warfare always seems to have presented opportunities for the communists. (See, The Domino Theory, pg.13-15 and Lenin's Train Ride, pg.18)

He was not the only one who saw trouble brewing in the form of another potential outbreak of hostilities. During the 1930s, Europeans were concerned about another war, but could seemingly do nothing to head off the outbreak of an armed conflict. Since the end of the First World War, Europe had been wracked by unrest from communist and fascist groups battling each other, especially in Germany. Furthermore, a flawed Treaty of Versailles shackled it to Germany, and the "Great Economic Depression" further undermined stability in Europe during the 1930s. In the early 1920s, Benito Mussolini had taken over Italy, and the Nazis rose to power in the early 1930s. The brutal Spanish Civil War, between the communists and socialists, seemed to indicate a looming crisis just over the horizon. The Nazi annexation of Austria and Czechoslovakia seems to indicate that a terrible conflict was unavoidable.

Points to Ponder: European Dictatorships.

NOTE: In between 1919 and 1939, Europe experienced the formation of 17 dictatorships, the first being the former Russian Empire, which became the first communist state, the Soviet Union. During this period, Spain had two different dictatorships, which brought the total number of dictatorships to eighteen. Sixteen of these dictatorships were anti-communist. Not all dictatorships were as brutal as the Nazis or the Soviets, but usually repressive.

Hitler and Stalin: let the dance begin.

Arguably, two of the most diabolical dictators of the twentieth century hatched a deal to split up parts of Europe. It was at this point that these two dictators, Joseph Stalin, and Adolf Hitler, teamed up and began plotting. On August 23, 1939, Nazi Germany and the Soviet Union inked the Non-Aggression Pact. On the surface of the document, the two countries agreed not to attack each other or ally with other nations to gang up on the other. What the world did not know was that the German-Soviet Non-Aggression Pact contained secret protocols, which made this marriage of "mutual territorial ambitions so dangerous." The pact, in essence, was a "license... [for]... aggression" for both totalitarian states. The Non-Aggression Pact: specifically, the part for divvying up Europe was to be kept secret. In short, this portion of the agreement was a secret treaty.

Germany and the USSR would both attack Poland. Germany got roughly two-thirds of Poland, and the Soviets got the other third. Germany would also have free rein to make war on Western Europe, while conceding that the Soviet Union could annex the Baltic States, of Lithuania, Latvia, and Estonia.

A marriage made in Hell.

Political cartoonists of the day mocked the Non-Aggression Pact. In one cartoon, it showed Hitler and Stalin standing over a corpse, bowing politely to each other, as they exchanged nasty remarks to each other. Other cartoons show them shaking hands, or strolling along, arm and arm. Probably the best lampoon was the two dictators depicted as a newlywedded couple. It shows Hitler as the groom, and Stalin the blushing bride, with the mocking tag line of, "wonder how long the honeymoon will last?" The joke was quite prophetic, for it was a marriage made in Hell, and it would last less than two years.

Points to Ponder: Soviet hypocrisy over secret treaties.

After the Bolshevik coup in 1917, secret treaties were discovered amongst the Russian state papers, and Leon Trotsky, the Soviet Commissar of Foreign Affairs, had these documents published. These secret treaties indicated how Russia and the other European powers anticipated dividing up the territory they expected to annex after the outbreak of a potential conflict, which turned out to be the First World War. After the discovery of the secret treaty documents, Trotsky wrote that, "Secret Diplomacy is a necessary weapon...of the propertied minority...to deceive the majority...[and]...serve its interests. Imperialism, with its worldwide plans of annexations..." His words drip with self-righteous indignation, while being totally devoid of consistency and truthfulness. Hypocrisy never really bothered the Soviets. Fast-forward almost 22 years, when Nazi Germany's Foreign Minister, Joachim von Ribbentrop, and the Soviet Union's Foreign Minister, Vyacheslav Molotov, signed a Non-Aggression Pact which contained secret provisions. There is a photograph of these gangsters signing the treaty with the head thug, Joseph Stalin, standing next to the German foreign minister. After the defeat of Nazi Germany in 1945, the Allies discovered the German copy of the secret treaty exposing Stalin's dirty deal with Hitler. Soviets denied their complicity in the Non-Aggression Pact for nearly a half-century, until they finally admitted the truth in 1989.

More points to ponder: The Non-Aggression Pact had two signers, but only one is hung?

After WWII, the victorious Allies convened war crimes trials in Nuremberg, Germany. Leading Nazis leaders would be tried for the atrocities committed during the war. Known as the Nuremberg Trials, these tribunals were held from November 1945 through October 1946, and double standards marked them. The laws declared that any country that planned or conspired to wage a war of aggression against peace, wage a war of aggression, participate in war crimes, or commit crimes against humanity, could be held guilty of war crimes. The Nuremberg Trials found only one of the signatories of the 1939 Non-Aggression Pact between the Soviet Union and Nazi Germany accountable. Joachim von Ribbentrop, the Nazi signer of the Non-Aggression Pact, was tried, convicted, and sentenced to death for his role in the war. The other signatory, Soviet Minister Vyacheslav Molotov, never saw the inside of the courtroom, probably because he was on the winning side. Was the Soviet Union as culpable as Nazi Germany? Initially, it could be said that Germany was the more aggressive of the two dictatorships, but the Soviets were still culpable. Furthermore:

-The Soviets had also attacked Poland and annexed the eastern part of the country. The Soviets massacred over 20,000 Polish officers and citizens in the Katyn Forrest, along with many other killings within Poland.

Murderous Marxism

-The Soviets attacked Finland and eventually forced the Nordic country to cede territory.

-Moldova, a small country between Romania

Soviet Union? It seems that since Germany attacked the USSR, and the USSR, was annexed by the USSR.

-Romania was also forced to cede territory to the Soviets.

-In 1940, the Soviets annexed the Baltic States and started deportations of the population. At the end of World War II, the Soviets reoccupied these states.

-Bulgaria never declared war or instigated any hostile action against the USSR, yet it was occupied, towards the end of the war, and forced into the Soviet system.

(Note* *The Black Book of Communism* pointed out that Joseph Stalin, Mao Zedong and Kim Il Sung were all responsible for planning the attack on South Korea, yet none of these communist aggressors were charged or saw the inside of a courtroom; few historians point this out.)

Alexander Solzhenitsyn railed at the fact that none of the Soviets were held responsible for their crimes committed during the war. The writer was incredulous that there were no denunciations of Soviet actions either. Why do historians fail to condemn the Soviets? The communists had territorial ambitions and committed atrocities during the war. Surely, seventy years after Stalin's death, historians could muster the moral courage to condemn this brutal dictator in the pages of a history textbook. This rarely occurs. More history down a black hole?

Poland is sacrificed to the Nazis and the Soviets: WWII begins.

On September 1, 1939, Nazi Germany attacked Poland and gobbled up the portion of territory agreed upon in the Non-Aggression Pact. A little over two weeks later, the Soviet Union moved in and conquered the remaining portion of eastern Poland. **Poland fell in less than four weeks, and the Nazis and the Soviet Union held a joint victory parade in Brest-Litovsk. The Soviets, under Stalin, would be the only primary combatants of WWII to march in a victory parade with the Axis and later be on the side of the victorious Allies**. YouTube has videos of the joint German-Soviet victory parade after the conquest of Poland.

Western leaders could not come to grips with the reality that Poland had fallen so quickly. When Hitler did not immediately attack any other country, British Prime Minister Neville Chamberlain developed a false narrative about the Soviet-Nazi conquest of Poland. The outbreak of hostilities was labeled a "Phony War" because Hitler did not immediately attack other countries. The Poles knew different; they suffered the brunt of Nazi and Soviet brutality during the Second World War. Between 5,675,000 to 7 million Polish citizens were killed, of whom 2,350,000 to 3 millions of those murdered were Jewish people. No doubt, Germany was responsible for the majority of the deaths, but the Soviet Union participated in the slaughter. On the orders of Stalin, over 20,000 Polish military reserve officers, intellectuals, government officials, and clergy were murdered in cold blood and concealed in mass graves, which became known as the Katyn Massacre. Ironically, it was the Nazis who discovered the burial pits and revealed them to the world. The Soviet Union denied its guilt in the massacre until it finally admitted the truth in the late 1980s.

This one incident best illustrates the choice faced by the Poles. "On... [a]... frontier bridge over the Bug... [River]... at Brest, people entering the USSR met others, including Jews, who were seeking haven in the Reich. A Nazi SS officer, seeing the Jews approaching his lines, started screaming, "Where on earth are you going? We are going to kill you." It can truly be said that it is a horrific situation when one must decide who will ultimately murder them. This is more history that went down a metaphorical black hole.

France and Great Britain, what to do?

<u>France and Great Britain declared war on Nazi Germany, but not the Soviet Union, for their role in attacking Poland.</u> While Nazi Germany was planning future military operations, Western Europeans deluded themselves into thinking that Hitler would be satisfied with part of Poland. The Allies had not seriously prepared for warfare; planning and preparing for such a large conflict would be a lengthy process, which took time and resources. When Germany did not immediately attack other countries, the false narrative of a "phony war" began to circulate in Europe and the West. The Allies would soon be dead wrong.

German Blitzkrieg.

Over six months later, Hitler unleashed his forces on Europe. By April of 1940, German forces had captured Denmark, Norway, Greece, and Yugoslavia in what amounted to several weeks of fighting. On May 10th, the Germans attacked France and the European lowlands of Holland, Luxembourg, and Belgium. By May 27th, all three Lowland countries had surrendered, and France capitulated on June 25th, 1940, surrendering roughly two-thirds of the country without firing a shot. Stalin was stunned (as the rest of the world) at the string of German victories, eight countries in 10 months, and the Luftwaffe was bombing English cities, while German submarines were sinking millions of tons of British shipping.

Stalin wants to conquer to expand communism.

Stalin had his own territorial ambitions. At the end of 1939, the Soviets attempted to force Finland to cede an eastern portion of its territory to the USSR. When Finland refused the Soviet demands, the "Boss" ordered the Red Army to attack, in what would be known as the Winter War of 1939-1940. With almost no heavy weaponry, navy, or air force to speak of, the small Finnish Army was able to drive back a huge, but poorly led Red Army, inflicting heavy losses on the communist aggressor. A second offensive, which encompassed hundreds of thousands of Soviet soldiers, forced the Finns to cede a slice of eastern Finland. Soviet forces also moved into Estonia, Latvia, and Lithuania and occupied these Baltic nations. The Soviet secret police moved in and started deporting portions of the population to the USSR. Stalin was not finished. Moldova, a small country between the USSR and Romania, was snatched up by the Soviets. Furthermore, Stalin was then able to pressure Romania into ceding territory to the USSR.

Hitler sees his chance to take out the USSR.

Hitler drew several conclusions from the dismal performance of the Soviets in the Winter War of 1939-1940. First, Stalin's decimation of the Red Army in the 1930s had tangible negative consequences, as demonstrated by the initial success of the small Finnish Army. Second, it would take years to rebuild the Red Army. Third, Stalin had his own territorial ambitions, which Hitler and the German high command believed would bring the Soviets into conflict with Germany. Fourth, Hitler always had territorial ambitions to the east, which he had made clear in his book, *Mein Kampf*. With his quick victories in Europe, Hitler seemed to take on a gambler's mindset, calculating the odds. Better to attack the USSR now than later when the Soviets would probably be stronger militarily. The Führer now planned to attack his former ally, in what would be known as Operation Barbarossa, the invasion of the Soviet Union. Hitler compared the USSR to a rotten door; kick it open, and the Soviets would quickly fall apart. The Second World War was about to enter a phase of unprecedented bloodshed and destruction.

Operation Barbarossa.

Note. Hitler seemed to be a poor student of history. Operation Barbarossa was named after a medieval Holy Roman Emperor, who drowned while crossing a river on the way to a crusade. Drowning before a crusade was surely not a good omen. In 1812, Napoleon's Le Grand Army invaded Russia, and it proved to be a graveyard for the French army. In 1941, Hitler did not seem to fathom how Germany, a country with a population of roughly 80 million people, was somehow going to subdue a vast country, such as the USSR, with a population of approximately 190 million. Yes, the Nazis had dominated Europe with a string of stunning military victories, but a dictator far more barbaric than the Führer ruled the USSR. Soon it would be Hitler's turn to be dead wrong.

The Nazi campaign against the USSR: the numbers.

The death toll for the Soviet Union during WWII has been estimated to be 27 million dead, with 8.668 million military personnel killed, along with 18.332 million civilians who perished. It was not just Russians who were killed, but also Balts, Byelorussians, Ukrainians, Jews, Poles, Central Asian Muslims, along with other minority groups. Note, part of the Soviet war dead was killed in Finland, or fighting the

Japanese at the beginning of the war and the end of WWII. The number is quite small in comparison to those killed by the Germans, but they are still part of the Soviet war dead. Roughly 67 million people died during the Second World War, so the Soviet dead amounted to roughly a little over 40% of the WWII deaths, **or almost one out of every three people killed**. The initial military disaster and the tremendous death toll clearly demonstrate Stalin's abject failure to safeguard the USSR and its citizenry. Once the Soviets turned the tide in the war, Stalin saw an opportunity to use the death and destruction of the USSR to his advantage, which entailed the eventual domination of Eastern Europe.

The percentage of manpower engaged in combat during Operation Barbarossa dwarfed all other theaters of operations combined during the Second World War. Roughly "410 divisions fought from June 22, 1941, until May 8^{th,} 1945... 46 months of nonstop warfare." The Germans initially attacked the USSR with 3.5 million men, and thousands of tanks and artillery pieces. At the beginning of the war, the Soviets had 2.3 million soldiers facing west towards Europe. Later, the number of soldiers in the Soviet Army would swell to millions more military personnel. It must be noted that the Eastern Front tied down millions of German soldiers that otherwise could have been facing the Canadians, British, French and Americans on the Western Front.

Points to Ponder: Did the Soviet desecration of Tamerlane's grave release his curse?

Tamerlane was the scourge of central Asia, a steppe warlord, not unlike Genghis Khan. His mounted warriors probably killed some 17 million people throughout Persia, the Middle East, and parts of India from 1370 through 1405. Tamerlane's raiders wreaked havoc and slaughtered innocent people. His fighters buried people alive and built towers of human heads. On June 20th, 1941, Soviet archeologists opened Tamerlane's mausoleum, located in the central Asian city of Samarkand, which lay within the borders of the former USSR. When Soviet scientists opened his tomb, they ignored the supposed curse of the infamous steppe warlord, which said that whoever violated his grave would suffer an invader worse than Tamerlane. On June 22, 1941, the Germans invaded the Soviet Union, and 27 million Soviets died. It was probably just a coincidence.

Reasons for the initial Nazi success with Barbarossa.

On June 22nd, 1941, Operation Barbarossa began, and the German surprise was complete; the Red Army was completely routed. How did Germany catch Stalin so off guard? There were multiple reasons.

Stalin operated on the premise that he was infallible, and only his opinion mattered. His theories were the only basis for reality. To offer an opposing theory was to risk one's life. The "Boss" was his own worst enemy. As one historian noted, "Stalin's refusal to believe... [that the German invasion was] ... imminent... was the result of herculean self-hypnosis. He staked his being on it, and he lost." Stalin considered himself the all-wise supreme leader, whose orders were considered an iron law. The "Boss" believed that "reality was obedient to his will..." Hitler had other ideas that would initially prevail.

The second reason was connected to the first. Stalin's failure to heed the warning from his intelligence sources about the impending German invasion. The Soviets had an extensive network of spies that gathered vast amounts of information, especially on Nazi Germany. Stalin received information, yet he never heeded these reports. German reconnaissance aircraft made hundreds of observed flights into Soviet airspace, but these tactical warnings were also ignored. He also disregarded a warning from Winston Churchill. When the Soviet ambassador to Germany kept sending messages about a looming German attack, Stalin's secret police chief Beria threatened to "grind... [him]... to dust," if he persisted. In early June, General Zhukov, one of Stalin's highest-ranking generals, asked to put the Red Army on alert, but the "Boss" refused the request. Even the German ambassador informed the Soviet ambassador of the exact day on which the attack would occur. Once again, the warning was ignored. An Axis deserter gave the Soviets the exact hour of the attack but was shot. Soviet frontier soldiers had been alerted to the presence of the German military by the roaring of tank engines, but by that point, it was too late. The Soviet peoples paid a steep price for the Boss's underestimation of Hitler's intentions.

    Much has been written about Operation Barbarossa, and all the military details will not be covered in this book. A week into the invasion, Stalin met with his military advisers and was shocked at the extent of the German advance and the unpreparedness of the Soviet forces. The fault lay with Stalin, yet he never accepted any responsibility. It was he who created the atmosphere of terror that paralyzed military commanders from speaking up and organizing the Soviet forces on high alert. He ignored reports that an imminent German invasion was in the offing. His positioning of military forces, with little or no defensive terrain, also undermined the Soviet military's ability to mount an effective defense. The mechanized German army bypassed, surrounded, and destroyed whole Soviet armies. During the first week of the Barbarossa, a meeting was held, and Stalin was purported to have said something to the effect of... "Lenin left us a great inheritance and we, his heirs... have f__ked it all up!"

OK, it's cool to believe in God again.

During WWII, almost every person in the USSR lost a loved one or a friend killed. To the people of the former Soviet Union, the Second World War would be known as the "Great Patriotic War." This type of death and destruction tends to cause people to become introspective; seek faith in a higher power. One historian noted that prior to WWII, religious worship in the Soviet Union was close to "total extinction." In a bizarre twist, the Nazi attack had the effect of putting religious worship on life support in the USSR. Stalin made radio broadcasts in which he called on the people of the USSR to protect "Holy Mother Russia." He also allowed the opening of some churches, which was a total repudiation of atheistic communism, but the "Boss" understood that people are more apt to follow faith than the ranting and ravings of Marx. [29]

---

29 Trotsky, Leon. "Publication of Secret Treaties," Izvestiia, No. 221, Nov. 23, 1917. P.4. The Great Big Book of Horrible Things put the entire death toll for the Second World War at 66 million; while Norman Davies' book, Europe, puts the death toll at 68 million. White, Matthew. The Great Big Book of Horrible Things. p. 529, Davies, N. Europe. p. Holy Roman Emperor; 358, Napoleon in Russia; 742,744, Non-Aggression Pact, beginning of WWII; 990-1006, 1054, 1329; List of European dictatorships between 1919-1939; 1320. After being sentenced to death Ribbentrop said, "' I won't be able to write my beautiful memoirs.'" Davies, N. Europe. Pp. 1,048-1055. Stephane Courtois, et al. The Black Book on Communism. p.5, 207-208. Radansky, E. Stalin. p. 312, 434, 439-444, 446,447, 448, 449, 450-459. Fugate, B. Operation Barbarossa P. 55-9, 91,92. Davies, N. No Simple Victory. P.77-86, 88-9,91-92 96, 138-152, 175, 211,212-3, 217, 226-7, 269-270, 312, 365-7, 376. Stokesbury, James. A Short History of World War II. P.153-154. Amis, R. Koba the Dread. P. 153, 173-175, 194-198. Solzhenitsyn, Alexander. The GULAG Archipelago, 1918-1956. p. 176-178, 240. Beevor, A. Stalingrad. 26,27,28,29,30. Katamidze, Slava. Loyal Comrades, Ruthless Killers: The Secret Services of the USSR 1917-1991. Pp. 86-87. 93-96. Kennedy Philip. Project coordinator. "How Punch Magazine Changed Everything." Illustration Chronicles. 2016-2023. Partridge, Bernard-Interwar Cartoons Punch Magazine 1938, 12.21.21.687.tif. Shire, William. The Rise and Fall of the Third Reich. Pp. 1,063, 1,087-9.

USSR: From Axis to Allies.

After June 22nd, 1941, the USSR went from being a signatory of the Nonaggression Pact to becoming one of the Allies. British Prime Minister Winston Churchill, a vehement anti-communist, now embraced the Soviet Union as a new ally. As the old saying goes, the enemy of my enemy is my friend. Stalin was now Churchill's new friend.

Although the USA had held meetings and contributed some aid to the British and Soviets, they were not directly involved in the war. That changed after December 7th, 1941. The Japanese sneak attack on the American naval base at Pearl Harbor, Hawaii, brought the United States into the Second World War on the side of the Allies. Four days later, Germany declared war on the Americans, and the grand coalition against the Axis took shape. Winston Churchill of Great Britain, Franklin Delano Roosevelt of the USA, and Joseph Stalin of the USSR became known as the Big Three. The Allies set aside the USSR's prior unprovoked aggression against other countries. The Soviets were now in the Allied camp against Germany and Italy. An American cartoon of the time seized upon this irony. It shows a grubby, dirty Stalin falling through a ceiling, and landing in bed with a caricature of John Bull (Great Britain) and Uncle Sam of the United States.

The "Big Three" would only meet in person twice: in 1943 at Tehran, in Iran, and at Yalta, which was in the USSR. They discussed war objectives, military goals, and a host of other topics. It was a friendship fraught with tensions over wartime goals and geopolitical issues. The reality was that Great Britain's contribution was its ability to hold out against the Germans and become a future base to attack the Axis forces in Europe. The United States would be the purse that provided supplies, weaponry, men, and logistics. The Americans and the British both understood that the USSR would bear the full brunt of the German army. The Soviets would shed the blood of their people, and the vastness of the USSR would tie down the Nazis. In the end, the British and the Americans, along with the other Allies, needed the Soviet Union to defeat Germany. As one historian realistically noted, "the Allies used a thug to get a thug."

The Soviets' brutal war against their soldiers.

When it came to fighting the war against Germany, Stalin was adamant, Soviet commanders were to attack; limiting casualties was not to be considered. The Boss's total lack of regard for the lives of the Soviet soldiers filtered down to the battlefield commanders. The "Boss" knew this would be a war of attrition, and he had numbers on his side. As one historian noted, the Nazis did not have a monopoly on barbarism, for "Stalin yielded nothing to Hitler in his appetite for mass murder." Wave after wave of Soviets were mowed down in attacks on German defensive positions. Battlefields were literally covered with Soviet dead. The "Boss" understood that the Germans could not readily replace the soldiers and equipment they lost. The Soviet leader was also sending a message: he would trade lives and space to keep the USSR in the fight. It was the soldiers and the citizens who paid Stalin's butcher bill.

The military performance of the Russian army was mixed. Initially, many Red Army soldiers fought ferociously, many times to the last man. In some instances, during the beginning of the war, Soviet soldiers, seeing the hopelessness of certain military situations, surrendered. (It did not help Stalin's positioning of the Red Army in untenable locations, and his purging of the Soviet officer corps years earlier.) It is estimated that between 5.1 million to 5.5 million Soviet soldiers surrendered to the Germans during the war, and 3.7 million perished in German captivity.

Make our own soldiers fear us more than the Nazis.

When the outcome of the war with Germany seemed in doubt, Stalin ordered the Red Army commanders to use savagery to stave off defeat. For years, historians have made excuses for the brutality by claiming the Soviets needed to "instill discipline," to stop the German advance. The KGB (known as the NKVD military version of the Soviet secret police) spread terror amongst the ranks of the military. Initially, they had just as much to fear from their own side as the Nazis. Soviet General Chuikov declared that "we did not suffer cowards, we had no room for them." He quoted Lenin: "Those who do not assist the Red Army in every way... are traitors and must be killed without pity." By the end of 1942, Soviet authorities had <u>shot close to two hundred thousand soldiers</u> across the Eastern Front. Special KGB detachments used "blocking units" to shoot soldiers if they hesitated during combat; many thousands died. Soldiers accused of any petty infringements of the Soviet military code, or fabricated accusations, were put in a penal battalion. They were tasked with the most dangerous jobs on the front, such as clearing minefields. The prospect of surviving a punishment battalion was slim at best. (The Germans had punishment battalions also.)

The famous Russian writer and critic of the USSR, Alexander Solzhenitsyn, had been an officer in the Red Army, but he wrote a less-than-flattering letter, which mentioned Stalin. He was arrested and imprisoned. He was lucky most would have been shot or assigned to a punishment battalion. Solzhenitsyn pulled no punches; he witnessed the Soviets throw their soldiers' lives away, and it enraged him. The following are examples of futile attacks that were ordered.

-In one instance, a drunken Soviet commander ordered roughly a 1000 unarmed trainee officers to attack German positions along the Don River. The commander protested that his men would be wiped out, but the attack was carried out, and the trainees were slaughtered.

-In October of 1941, Mongolian cavalrymen (of the Red Army) were ordered to attack fixed German positions. The Germans suffered no casualties, but 2,000 cavalrymen were killed and wounded.

-The Soviets carried out these types of fruitless attacks at the beginning of the war. One could easily deduce that a prudent national leader would have been careful about wasting soldiers' lives, but then Stalin had allowed this catastrophe to happen, and as far as he was concerned, someone else had to pay for his mistake.

Order 270 & 277; proclamations drenched in blood.

To make the Red Army stand firm, Stalin ratcheted up the brutality he inflicted on his armed forces. He signed two proclamations, which doomed even more soldiers and subjected their families to misery. He signed Order 270 in 1941, which stipulated that family members of soldiers who surrendered were not to receive state assistance, and family members could be arrested and imprisoned. Soldiers who surrendered were "subject to being shot on the spot." Order 277 signed the next year, in essence, disallowed retreats. Those who retreated would be shot.

In contrast, military commanders throughout the ages have used strategic retreats as a tactic to preserve their forces. They could fall back, regroup, attack again, or retreat from the area and live to fight another day. In one stroke, Stalin took away this tactic, which meant the death of more Soviet soldiers. A prudent commander would use this tactic to preserve his armed forces, improve morale and contribute to victory, but Stalin's murderous vanity would never allow that. The following are examples of this brutality.

-Red soldiers could be arrested or shot if they did not shoot comrades who ran away during a battle.

-Commanders, who had no idea that soldiers had deserted during combat, could be shot if the soldiers could not be accounted for at the end of a battle.

-In one battle, a German tank pulled in front of a group of surrendering Soviet soldiers to protect them from being shot by their own side.

-Red soldiers wounded in the foot or the hand could be executed for supposedly self-inflicting a wound.

-One Red pilot had to bail out of his plane when the aircraft was damaged in combat. When he made his way back to his base, he was arrested on Order 270 for desertion.

-Then there was the story of Mikhail Devyatayev, a Soviet pilot, shot down while in aerial combat with two German fighter planes. Devyataev broke his leg and was captured and sent to a German POW camp. He was later shipped to Peenemunde, a "rocket testing center," which has been described as a German manufacturing facility for ballistic missiles and a death trap for slave laborers. When the British and Americans discovered that Peenemünde was building ballistic missiles, the Allies subjected the facility to intense bombing operations. By the beginning of 1945, Devyataev weighed less than 100 pounds and was living day by day, hoping not to be killed by Allied bombing raids. With nothing to lose, he and some other prisoners made a daring escape and stole a German bomber. The Soviet pilot flew the plane to the USSR, dodging friendly anti-aircraft fire and crash-landing. The KGB promptly arrested him. Despite his heroism and the information, he was able to bring back about the German missile program, he was charged with violating Order 270. He remained in prison until 1947 and was not able to work in the USSR because he had been a POW. If Devyataev had been an American flyer who had carried out these daring acts of valor, he probably would have received a ticker-tape parade, medals, and Ronald Reagan would have played him in a movie. In the USSR, under Stalin's barbaric rule, he was a villain as far as the other Soviets were concerned.

Points to Ponder: The sad death of Stalin's first son.

Stalin's son from his first marriage, Yakov Dzhugashvili, was captured at the beginning of the war. Stalin turned down German requests to exchange his eldest son for some German generals. The "Boss" would not contemplate the swap. Although accounts vary, in late 1943, Yakov approached the electrified fence of the POW camp and was in the process of grabbing the wire when he was shot and killed. His body lay there for a day. His corpse was photographed and then cremated. His wife, Stalin's daughter-in-law, was sentenced to several years in prison.

The children from Stalin's second marriage fared better, to a degree. His son, Vasily Stalin, was a raging alcoholic, a womanizer, and a constant source of disappointment for the Boss. Given Stalin's murderous deeds, Vasily feared that when his father was no longer around to protect him, he would be killed by the Soviet authorities. After the Boss died, Vasily crawled into a bottle and died of alcoholism in 1961. He was forty years old.

Stalin's only daughter, Svetlana Alliluyeva, was born in 1926. Given her father's legacy, she opted to take her mother's maiden name. Unfortunately for Svetlana, she "could never escape Stalin's shadow." Her personal life was turbulent. Who wouldn't have had psychological problems knowing her father's murderous past? She married several times and had numerous romances. In 1967, Svetlana defected from the USSR, abandoning her children. She lived in Europe and the United States, coauthored several books, but had persistent financial problems, and at times, she was prone to depression. Disillusioned with the West, Svetlana returned to the Soviet Union with her third child in 1984. After squabbling with Soviet authorities, she left the USSR and returned to the United States and died of complications from colon cancer in 2011.

Stalingrad.

The battle for Stalingrad epitomized the brutality of the Nazis and the Soviets; it consumed human life like a furnace. Both dictators fixated on the strategic city. Hitler wanted to take the city named for his nemesis, and Stalin wanted it held at all costs. The slaughter of soldiers on both sides is difficult to fathom. Fighting was ferocious, and soldiers battled for every inch of territory in the burned-out rubble. Trenches were full of dead; body parts were strewn across the battlefield. For the soldiers, it was a whirling vortex of death, sweeping away all. On numerous occasions, certain positions changed hands several times on the same day.

As for the civilians, both sides had treated them with brutal indifference. Bombing raids and fighting killed tens of thousands. It was over a year before the fighting reached Stalingrad, but the evacuation of civilians was limited because the "Boss" figured soldiers would fight harder with noncombatants in the city. When authorities did allow the evacuation of women and children, steamboats ferried them across the Volga River, but the Germans sank the ships with artillery and dive-bombers. Corpses floated down the river, charred and covered in oil. As one civilian noted, "No one bothered about human beings... we were just meat for the guns."

Bombing raids and artillery reduced most parts of the city to rubble, killing more civilians. As the harsh Russian winter set in, conditions worsened. When there were lulls in the fighting, civilians would emerge from the bombed-out buildings and scurry about looking for dead horses to scavenge rotting flesh to eat. When gunfire erupted, they would dash back to their hiding places. Orphaned children looking for food would take crusts of bread from German soldiers, in exchange for filling their canteens in the Volga River. When the Soviets found out, their snipers shot the children as they kneeled at the river's edge. The Germans also forced civilians, at gunpoint, to dig graves for their dead; so Soviet snipers shot them too. The delay of evacuating many of the noncombatants was the primary reason civilians had to choose between being murdered by the Nazis or being killed by their own side. Not much of a choice.

To stiffen the resolve of the soldier to fight on, no matter the hopelessness, the Soviet military authorities resorted to terror. Some 13,500 soldiers were executed at Stalingrad. The "Boss" was not going to have any soldiers wavering in the ranks. Soldiers were marched to the front, and informers would immediately denounce anybody who expressed the slightest doubt about the war. The doomed were led away, stripped of their uniforms and boots, then shot. Blocking units also shot soldiers who hesitated or tried to retreat during combat. At night, Soviet soldiers were ordered to crawl into the battlefield and retrieve the boots and clothes from their dead comrades. Eventually, the Soviets, with superior numbers of men and material, were able to overwhelm the Germans, lifting the siege of Stalingrad. It is estimated that "750,000... [German and Soviet] ... soldiers and 140,000 civilians died at Stalingrad," but the "Boss" kept his namesake city.

Ukraine: death and destruction.

Ukraine has a long history of conflict with Russia, starting with Catherine the Great, who conquered the region in the eighteenth century. The region saw brutal fighting during World War I. Millions died from Soviet brutality during the Civil War, the Ukrainian Terror Famine, and the Great Terror. Decades of atrocities fueled a burning hatred of the Soviets by the Ukrainians. When the Nazis entered Ukraine, they were welcomed as liberators, but German savagery soon alienated the very people who loathed Stalin and the communists. The German General Reinhard Gehlen wrote in his memoirs that Adolf Hitler made a monumental error in brutalizing the Soviet populace. The general pointed out that they had been welcomed when they invaded, but the Führer squandered the possibility of harnessing their hatred of the USSR. Yet, even with Nazi atrocities, the Germans were still able to raise and field two military divisions of Western Ukrainians, which served on the Eastern Front. The historian Norman Davies opined that if Hitler had treated the Ukrainians like a "benevolent liberator", the outcome on the Eastern Front could have been quite different.

Ukraine was not spared the devastation of the war; cities and the countryside were ravaged. The Nazis massacred civilians and targeted Jews for extermination. When the Soviets reoccupied the region, the Ukrainians experienced another wave of retribution from the communists. Norman Davie's *No Simple Victory* listed a few of the sadistic methods used to murder clergy in the region.

-One priest was "boiled alive..."

-One died "during a mock crucifixion..."

-A nun "shot at the door of her convent..."

-Another was "walled up... alive..."

To be clear, the Nazis committed unspeakable acts of barbarism, but far too many times, historians fail to point out the savage actions of the Soviets. When the atheistic officials of the Soviet Union were not sure they could defeat the Germans, the "Boss" turned to religion and Mother Russia to inspire the masses to resist. When victory seemed assured, all bets were off. One can only imagine the horrific acts inflicted on the general civilian population once the Soviets regained control of Ukraine. More history down the black hole.

Points to Ponder: Ukraine: Potemkin's Village, the "byword for... deception."

Disinformation has been used for centuries to mislead adversaries or deceive the general populace with propaganda. The Soviets had developed a special department that produced expert forgeries to facilitate their disinformation campaigns, which were known by the euphemism, "active measures." Prior to the Soviets, the Russian Empire had engaged in disinformation. It is believed that the Czarist secret police penned the anti-Semitic screed, the *Protocols of the Elders of Zion,* to whip up hatred against Jews in Russia.

In the late eighteenth century, the Russian Empire forcibly annexed this large region. Czarina Catherine the Great wanted to sway the opinions of European states, which took a dim view of the massive land grab. Catherine had Field Marshal Prince Gregory Potemkin develop a grand ruse to deceive European diplomats who were uneasy about the annexation, which upset the balance of power in Europe.

Potemkin organized a river tour for the diplomats aboard an "imperial barge," which sailed down the Dnieper River. The diplomats saw ships, fortresses and villages with enthusiastic peasants cheering; it was pure deception. What they saw was Potemkin's soldiers dressed as Ukrainian villagers; the ships and the fortresses were crude mockups that fell apart after the tour. Once the barge sailed past, the soldiers changed, "broke down the sets," and repeated the charade "further downstream." It seems to have worked; the diplomats never urged their respective governments to take any actions against Russia. It is from this elaborate fraud that we get the phrase, "Potemkin's Village," a term which is now associated with "deception and disinformation." The Soviets simply built upon the Russian tradition of elaborate fraud.

Vasily Mitrokhin had numerous files on KGB "active measures" and disinformation campaigns. The KGB had a department that specialized in creating forgeries of diplomatic papers, documents, and other intelligence data. Agents posing as Soviet diplomats and government officials would arrange to have these expert forgeries surreptitiously passed into the hands of government leaders and newspaper reporters. These "active measures" were created for the specific purpose of swaying the opinions of world leaders. The KGB would also have stories planted in newspapers to influence public opinion. Specifically, these "active measures" were used to undermine the credibility of the United States or other Western nations. It would be one of these fake stories, which claimed that the US weapons laboratory developed AIDS as a bioweapon. The story was planted in an Indian newspaper in 1984, and after several years, over forty newspapers picked up the fake news in the Third World. Only a storm of protests from the Western scientific community brought the Soviet hoax to a halt. Only then did the USSR acknowledge that the KGB fabricated the story.[30]

Point to Ponder: Why did people, conquered by the Germans, end up fighting for the Nazis?

During the war, Germany was still able to raise foreign Waffen SS infantry divisions from countries it had subjugated. The reasons for joining the German Waffen SS varied, fear of being pressed into slave labor in Germany, but also the looming specter of Soviet domination played a major factor. Fascist propaganda posters played to these fears in defeated countries. It was an effective recruiting tool. At the beginning of the war, the early Waffen SS divisions were predominately German, but others would be raised throughout Western Europe. By 1943, volunteers from Norway, Denmark, Holland, Belgium, Yugoslavia and France, all countries conquered by the Nazis, volunteered to join the Waffen SS. Units from the French Division (XXXIII) Charlemagne, Legion Volontaire Francaise, were one of the last Waffen SS soldiers to surrender to the Soviets during the battle for Berlin.

The appendix of Norman Davies's book, *Europe,* in pages 1,326-1,327, contains information on almost 30 Waffen SS divisions,

---

30Fugate, Bryan. Operation Barbarossa. 292,293. Katamidze, Slava. Loyal Comrades, Ruthless Killers: The Secret Services of the USSR 1917-1991. Pp.96-98. Davies, N. No Simple Victory. 105-6, 160-5, 194, 231, 232, 233, 235, 245, 258, 259, 260, 265, 269, 272, 273, 302, 415. Beevor, Anthony, Stalingrad. 26, 59, 67, 88-9, 90, 91,104,105,106, 109, 111, 128, 129,148, 149,162, 166-177, 179, Radansky, E. Stalin. p. 487. White, M. The Great Big Book of Horrible Things. p. 404, 605. Davies, N. Europe. P. 658, 1013, 1015. Amis, Martin. Koba the Dread. pp. 218-219. Gehlen, Reinhard, The Service: The Memoirs of General Reinhard Gehlen. Pp. 73-92. Vronskaya, Jeanne, Chuguev, Vladimir. A Biographical Dictionary of the Soviet Union 1917-1988. Stalin wife and daughter. Pp. 11. Vasily pp. 418. Sullivan, Rosemary. Stalin's Daughter. Pp. xv, xvi, 1-7, 121, 31, 97, 103, 100-105, 193, 194-98, 201-203, 249, 258-64, 289-92, 303-8, 345-8, 352, 481, 523-525.

identified by name, country of origin, and identification numbers. They were from western and eastern Europe, two were made up of Soviet POWs, one Albanian and a Croat/ Bosnian Muslim from Yugoslavia. There was also an Italian division, along with a division of Spanish volunteers known as the Blue Division. There were numerous other groups of foreign fighters that joined the Waffen SS, but the numbers were quite small. Rarely do historians mention these facts.

The Baltic States: OK, guess we need to join the Waffen SS.

Estonia, Latvia, and Lithuania had, in part, compelling motivations for volunteering for the Waffen SS divisions. As Germany moved against France and the Lowland countries, the Soviets built up their military forces around the three Baltic States. After making territorial demands, the USSR occupied the Baltic States on the pretext of coming to the aid of communist groups that pleaded for Soviet protection. After the Soviets were driven out of the Baltic States during Operation Barbarossa, it is easy to see why the Baltic peoples joined the German forces. The Germans raised three Latvian divisions (one being from Courland) and one Estonian division. For the Baltic peoples, it boiled down to either being killed in battle, murdered, imprisoned, or deported. Not much of a choice. More history down a memory black hole.

Eastern Europe and Finland in the Nazi camp?

Punch magazine was a British satirical magazine, which was published from the mid-nineteenth century through the twentieth century. The writers and cartoonists of this magazine poked fun at everyone. Just before the outbreak of the war in Europe, the magazine ran a cartoon portraying Hitler as Snow White and the Eastern Europeans as the Seven Dwarves. The implication was clear; Hitler was trying to coax the dwarves to align themselves with the Axis. These "dwarves" probably watched anxiously as Stalin consolidated power in the USSR and Hitler took control of Germany. They witnessed as Austria willingly allowed itself to be annexed by Germany.

Furthermore, they stood on the sidelines as Hitler demanded the eastern part of Czechoslovakia in 1938. France and Great Britain did not have the stomach to stand up to the Nazis, so they midwifed the annexation of the eastern part of Czechoslovakia. Snow White, now the cannibal, annexed the rest of the country roughly a year later. The Nazi strong-arm geopolitical annexation of Czechoslovakia and the weak-kneed response of Western Europeans made it clear. You're on your own, and no one is coming to your aid.

Romania, Hungary, and Bulgaria probably threw their lot in with Germany out of necessity, certainly not willingly. They became client-states, allies of Nazi Germany. To varying degrees, they followed Germany's foreign policy; they allowed the stationing and the transit of the German soldiers through their territory. The Romanians had several divisions under German command when the Nazis attacked the USSR. The Nazis were also able to raise almost five Waffen SS divisions in Hungary. Czechoslovakia, another victim of Nazi aggression, fielded a Bohemian and Moravian Waffen SS division. Although a client state, Bulgaria kept Germany at arm's length; cooperation was limited. Finland, a Nordic country, was clearly an early victim of Soviet aggression during the Winter War. The Finns fought with the Nazis, not as an ally or client state, but as two countries that viewed the USSR as a common enemy.

The actions of the Eastern Europeans and Finland were summed up by one historian, who said they were "not Pro-German, but anti-Soviet." Germany was the more immediate threat, but the USSR could be the greater threat somewhere over the horizon. The thread that binds these nations together is that they feared the Soviets far more than the Germans.

By 1943, the Soviets get the act together, or someone gets shot.

From 1941 to mid-1942, the war had been a disaster for the USSR. By the summer of 1942, the ferocious tactics used against their own armed forces worked. The German steamroller had been stopped, for the moment, but the Nazis still posed a grave threat to the Soviets. Stalin changed tactics and allowed competent Soviet military leaders, who were better at organizing the Red Army for defense and counteroffensive operations. The vastness of the USSR slowed down the German army, and the Soviets moved military manufacturing to areas beyond the reach of the Nazis. War production increased, and the Soviets developed new, highly effective weapon systems. The USSR was also augmented by American Lend-Lease aid.

By 1943, the Soviets were able to marshal their forces to counterattack, and their greatest advantage, in part, lay in their population. Furthermore, Nazi atrocities also fired up the Soviet people to defeat the invaders. In 1942, a young Russian partisan, Zoya Kosmodemyanskaya, was captured while attempting to sabotage German facilities. She was brutally tortured, then hung. As Zoya was being led to her execution, she "fought the hangman who finally managed to slip the noose around her… neck." Before dying, she supposedly yelled, "There are two hundred million of us. You won't hang everybody. I shall be avenged." A German officer took several photographs of the struggle to hang the young woman. The last image shows Zoya's lifeless body swaying as German soldiers looked on. The photographs were recovered from the body of a German officer. The Soviets had **well over 100 million more people than Germany**, and Stalin willingly sacrificed soldiers and the populace. German savagery only served the purposes of the "Boss." The propaganda wrote itself. (See notes.)

Operation Citadel: Stalin finally listens to his intelligence sources.

The summer of 1943 would be the military showdown between the Germans and the Soviets. Operation Citadel was the all-out German offensive against the small town of Kursk near the Ukrainian border. The Germans assembled a huge force of men, tanks, planes, and artillery to swamp the Red Army defenses, but the KGB had forewarned Stalin. Ironically, prior to Barbarossa, the Soviets had collected military intelligence, which warned of an impending German attack. Stalin ignored the warnings because the "Boss" was infallible. This time, Stalin listened and acted upon his Soviet espionage sources, which accurately identified the pending German offensive. (Great Britain also provided information discovered by Project Ultra and their code breakers.)

Kursk would have the distinction of being the largest tank battle of the war. The Soviets ringed Kursk with a vast, in-depth defensive perimeter, bristling with soldiers and weaponry. The Germans attacked but could not break the Soviet defenses. Once the German offensive stalled, thousands of Soviet tanks that were held in reserve counterattacked. It worked, and over several weeks, the Germans were decisively defeated. Casualties on both sides were tremendous. The Soviet arithmetic was simple; they could afford to lose the men and material; the Germans could not replace their losses. As the battle of

Kursk wound down, and the smoke cleared, Operation Citadel was the beginning of the end for the Germans. They would be on defense until they were finally defeated. It could be argued that if Stalin had listened to his intelligence sources (and all the other indicators) in the summer of 1941, and set up a Kursk-like trap, maybe, just maybe, the Soviet Union would not have suffered the cataclysmic losses of the Second World War.

Monster.

In 1944, the Free French leader, General Charles De Gaulle, visited Moscow to meet with the Soviet leader. De Gaulle's hotel room was probably bugged, and the General probably spoke a little too candidly about his opinion of Stalin. Although we are unsure of the general's exact words, it was probably not very flattering of the Soviet leader. Later, during a banquet for the French leader, Stalin toyed with De Gaulle while giving a toast. The "Boss" focused his remarks on one of his Soviet subordinates. At first, he spoke fondly of the man, and then Stalin remarked that if the subordinate failed in a certain task, "we will shoot him." Not missing a beat, Stalin turned toward a Soviet Marshal, and while smiling, commented that if he fails to carry out an order on time, "we will hang him." Chuckling, Stalin said, "People call me a monster, but as you see, I make a joke of it. Maybe I'm not so horrible after all."

Rape of Germany.

Rape is a scourge that is ever present in the world, past and present, but during war, it becomes it can become more prevalent. All the armies that fought in the Second World War had soldiers who sexually assaulted the populace. As Soviet forces fought their way into Germany, the Soviet Army took its revenge on the German populace.

Murderous Marxism

The Soviet Army committed mass rape on a scale that went far beyond anything committed by the soldiers of other countries combined. Fearing Soviet retribution, German civilians and soldiers fled towards the British and American lines to surrender. They had good reason. As the Soviet Army entered Germany, the Soviets carried out wanton acts of violence, killing civilians, along with the rape of hundreds of thousands of women. There were instances of German women being raped and crucified. All women were targeted. Young girls to grandmothers were gang raped; many perished. Russian women taken to Germany against their will were also sexually assaulted. The Nazis had committed unspeakable acts in the USSR, destroying tens of millions of lives and destroying large swathes of the country. Soviet retaliation would have been difficult to stop. It should be noted that Soviet authorities did encourage acts of widespread sexual assault.

In 1944, Stalin's territorial ambitions were soon to be realized. Poland was stabbed in the back, again.

By 1944, the Red Army had driven the Germans from the Soviet Union. The Red Army, now renamed the Soviet Army, moved into Poland. As they approached the capital of Warsaw, Polish resistance fighters, numbering in the thousands, rose against the German forces in the city. The Soviet Army, which had been seemingly unstoppable, just stopped. The Poles fought heroically, expecting relief, which never arrived. The Poles drove off multiple attacks, and finally, the Führer ordered an all-out assault, and the uprising was crushed. Most of Warsaw was reduced to rubble, and Hitler had the city almost completely razed. The Germans suffered 15,000 casualties, while they killed roughly 50,000 resistance fighters and civilians. The German bombardment killed another 100,000 Poles. Historians have opined that Stalin could have easily relieved the city, but chose not to, allowing the Germans to do his dirty work. After Warsaw was crushed, the Soviets resumed their offensive, capturing the rest of Poland.

From the middle of 1944 through 1945, the Soviets rolled through Eastern Europe. Soviet forces captured Romania, Bulgaria, Hungary, and Czechoslovakia. Each one of these nations became a satellite of the USSR; in other words, these countries were now communist. Complete communist control was not immediate. Over several years, the Soviet Union ratcheted up its control of these countries. Within several years, the Eastern Europeans were taking their orders from Moscow. The "Boss" was in charge.

The Soviet Army aided Tito (Josip Broz) in clinching victory in Yugoslavia. Albania would also fall under communist control. The Baltic states of Lithuania, Latvia, and Estonia would once again come under Soviet control and were annexed into the USSR. These countries would be under communist control for the next four decades. Only Finland and Greece avoided communist rule at the end of the Second World War. (The fate of Eastern European countries and the Baltic States under Soviet control will be covered later.) By 1945, the Soviet Army had driven into eastern Germany, while the Allies had captured the western part of the Third Reich. By the middle of May, Hitler was dead, and Germany had surrendered.

Did Eastern Europe have to become communist?

Did Eastern Europe and the Baltic have to become states become communist states? Certainly, the Americans and the British would have preferred these countries to be democratic, but there was little Roosevelt and Churchill could do. No amount of diplomacy could persuade Stalin, and they could not risk alienating the Soviet dictator, so they had to accommodate the "Boss." Also, the Americans and the

British had to save manpower for the final push to beat Japan. China's lackluster performance against the Japanese on the mainland meant the Soviet Army might be needed to finish off the Imperial Army of Japan.

Soviet POWs, are you ready to be persecuted by your own side?

At the end of the war, American and other Allied prisoners of war (POWs) were welcomed home. There was no stigma attached to their capture. For Soviet POWs, it was the exact opposite. By the end of the war, they became a new fictitious enemy to be scapegoated by the state. They were brutally treated, and many were killed. At a minimum, tens of thousands were tortured and imprisoned in the GULAG. The Soviets wanted to squeeze as much labor out of these former POWs before they died. Solzhenitsyn railed against the betrayal of Soviet POWs, and he saved most of his venom for Stalin. The writer had a point. The Soviet propaganda labeled these prisoners as traitors. No one dared to speak up on their behalf; it could cost you your life. Solzhenitsyn wrote that Soviet military personal was "the only soldiers in the world who couldn't surrender... Go and die; we will go on living... lose your legs, yet manage to return from captivity on crutches, we will convict you..."

The story of Soviet POWs in German captivity is a wretched, sad story. The Third Reich deemed Slavic peoples as sub-human, and being a communist only made things worse for the prisoners. The captivity of American, British, and French POWs stood in stark contrast to the millions of Soviet prisoners who died in German captivity. Although there were shortcomings, the Germans provided Western Allied prisoners with the basics. They had barracks, supplies, and just enough food and were visited by the Red Cross. The treatment of Soviet POWs was horrible. The Germans captured between 5.1 to 5.5 million Soviet soldiers, and roughly 3.7 million died from the harsh treatment. Their camps were a little more than barbed wire enclosures, no barracks, blankets, clothes, or latrines. They were deprived of food, water, medicine, and other necessities. They froze in the winter and suffered in the summer heat. Prisoners cannibalized their dead, anything to survive. Out of desperation, prisoners volunteered to fight for the Germans and escape the captivity hell hole and survive. Many Soviet POWs saw very little choice, so they joined the Waffen SS or became Hiwi(s), who were support soldiers for the German army. The Nazis were able to raise two divisions of Soviet POWs.

Solzhenitsyn described the terrible fate of several Soviet POWs who were recaptured by the Soviet Army. In one instance, He witnessed a Soviet prisoner being marched to the rear for probable execution. As a Soviet tank passed by the prisoner, the man dove under the tracks. Solzhenitsyn watched in horror as the man died, "foam flowing from his mouth." The doomed prisoner preferred to be crushed to death then die at the hands of the Soviet secret military police. In another instance, the writer described another Soviet prisoner being brutally whipped by a "security man" on a horse. The soldier, being beaten, pleaded for help from Solzhenitsyn, who at that time was a captain in the Soviet Army. Fearing arrest, he ignored the man being viciously lashed and walked by, as if nothing had happened.

No matter the gallantry of a Soviet soldier, if captured, punishment would be followed. One officer, a volunteer, attempted escape three times but was recaptured every time. After being liberated during the war, he was sentenced to a penal battalion. He participated in the capture of Berlin, was awarded the Order of the Red Star, but was later sentenced to prison.

Soviet soldiers are returned to the USSR for death sentences or imprisonment.

The British or Americans yielded to Soviet demands when it came to Soviet POWs. The Soviets wanted their captured soldiers and civilians returned. The British feared that the USSR might not return their POWs, whom the Germans had held, unless they complied with Soviet demands. All Soviet POWs who fought for the Nazis, or prisoners that languished in German prison camps, which also included civilians forcibly taken to the Reich, had to be returned to the USSR.

-When British authorities informed a group of Russian internees and Soviet prisoners that they were being returned to the USSR, many tried to flee, and others killed themselves.

-In Austria, the British oversaw a large POW camp that had Soviet (Cossack) prisoners, who had fought for the Germans. When prisoners were made aware that they would be returned to the USSR, a riot occurred, and many prisoners committed suicide. British soldiers had to beat the doomed Cossacks and force them into the hands of Stalin's thugs, who probably murdered many of them and imprisoned the rest.

A report written British officer, Major Dennis Hills, shines an unflattering light on the fate of Soviet POWs.

-Hills oversaw a POW camp, which included many Soviet soldiers. He accompanied a group of Soviet prisoners who were returned by ship to the USSR. After disembarking the prisoners and getting the ship underway, the Major heard gunfire. Hills was sure that, if not all, most of the prisoners were shot.

-In another instance, Hills was involved in returning another batch of POWs, numbering just under 500 prisoners. Knowing that they would be killed, Hills used every loophole to exclude prisoners from being turned over to the Soviets. He was able to save over 300 former Soviet soldiers. One of the doomed soldiers, for whom Hills could find no premise for excluding, reproached the British officer, saying, "So you are sending us to our deaths... Democracy has failed us. You are the sacrifice," Hills replied, "The others will now be safe." I doubt the doomed soldier found little comfort in the officer's words.

- In yet another instance, he was part of a group of British officers who refused to turn over "Ukrainians from a Waffen-SS Galicia Division." Since these POWs were "Polish, not Soviet citizens," they were not turned over.

Major Hills had written official reports concerning the fate of Soviet POWs. He documented the whole sad affair, but this information was buried in an archive until it was rediscovered in 1973. Yet over the decades, few historical texts acknowledge these dastardly acts. More history down the memory black hole.

Points to ponder: Should I allow myself to be murdered, or should I commit suicide?

One must contemplate the abject blind fear that would drive a human to commit suicide. Not sadness, or depression, but the fear and the certainty of a horrific death or a terrible fate that was beyond their control. On September 11, 2001, people who survived the initial terrorist attacks faced this terrible choice. After the two jets crashed into the Twin Towers in New York City, people were trapped on the upper floors of the buildings, by raging infernos. They had to decide if they wanted to be incinerated alive or jump to their deaths. Many chose the latter. Now consider the probable fate of the Soviet POWs and civilians when they found out that they were being turned over to

Stalin's pack of killers. Some POWs jumped to their own deaths, purposely smashing their skulls against the ground. Some slit their own throats or dove under the tracks of a tank, rather than face the wrath of Soviet communism. With no court of final appeal, their fate was sealed. Is it better to be murdered or commit suicide? It was not uncommon for Western supporters of communism to say, "You have to break a few eggs to make an omelet." This blithe brush off, of Soviet atrocities, illustrates that they have no answers, and they are trying to deflect the question with empty philosophical hogwash. Would you partake of such an omelet?

Points to ponder: Code names and Operation Keelhaul.

During modern times, military operations and secret government projects have been given code names. The Normandy Invasion was codenamed "Overlord"; the Nazi invasion of the Soviet Union was "Operation Barbarossa," and the American project to develop the atomic bomb was the "Manhattan Project." The British repatriation of Soviet POWs was codenamed "Keelhaul." To keelhaul someone involved a sadistic punishment, used by mariners of old, to punish insubordinate sailors. Rope was looped around the sailor's hands, while another length of rope was tied around the feet and ran beneath the bottom of the ship, while at sea. The doomed sailor would then be hauled along the bottom of the ship, the keel. Drowning (although not certain), while being de-fleshed by barnacles, usually made for a horrible death for the unfortunate sailor. It begs the question. How did British planners choose such a codename? Did British authorities know what was going to happen to the Soviet POWs, or did they just haphazardly pick a ghastly codename, which foreshadowed the horrible fate that awaited these repatriated soldiers and citizens? You decide. [31]

Points to Ponder: Some Red Generals live, some die.

They say karma is a beast, and Mikhail Tukhachevsky blood-spattered confession seems to support that contention. Tukhachevsky was the "famous" Soviet General who waged total war on the Tambov region during the Russian Civil War. He had hostages shot and ordered the use of poisonous gas and planes to bomb civilians, which had few weapons. When the Soviet Union attacked Poland (1920-1921), he was a leading general who supposedly uttered the command, "over the corpse of White Poland lays the path to world conflagration." Luckily, the Soviets were defeated at the Battle of Warsaw. In 1937, Tukhachevsky was arrested, tortured, and executed, as was most of his family. During the purge of the Soviet military, many officers, including generals, lost their lives. In Stalin's Soviet Union, you could always get more generals. During WWII, one Air Force General, outraged at the

---

31 Andrew, Christopher, & Mitrokhin, Vasili. The World Was Going Our Way, The KGB and the Battle for The Third World. P. for the information on AIDS see page 340, 466, 483. Mitrokhin has a great deal of information about active measures. pp. See page 623 of the index; it contains dozens of misinformation campaigns. Beevor, A. Stalingrad. pp. 26, Davies, N. No Simple Victory. Pp.18, 19, 57,58,85,88,89,110-112,119-122,123-5, 128-9,194, 209, 210, 269, 271, 290-291, 292, 293,294, 338-9, 340-342; Dennis Hills wrote a book about Operation Keelhaul, detailing Soviet treachery. Davies, N. Europe. pp. 990-991, 1017, 1046-1047, footnotes,1188, 1326-1327. Solzhenitsyn, Alexander. GULAG Archipelago. p.239-262. Radanzinky, E. Stalin. pp. 500, 506-507, 510-511. Young, Peter. ED. The Atlas of the Second World War. pp. 204, 211. Amis, Martin. Koba the Dread. P. 135,199-200, 207, 211. Ambrose, Stephen & Sulzberger, C.L. American Heritage: World War II. P. 222-223. This book has other photographs of Nazi atrocities, yet the authentication of these images has never been verified. It was not beyond the Soviets to fabricate photographs, but such forgeries would have been based on reality. Matanle, Ivor. World War II. Pp. 164-165. Heroes: Kosmodemyanskaya. Times: Online. March 2, 1942. Kennedy Philip. Project coordinator. "How Punch Magazine Changed Everything." Illustration Chronicles. 2016-2023. Partridge, Bernard-Interwar Cartoons Punch Magazine 1938, 12.21.21.687.tif.

use of subpar aircraft, accused Stalin of sending pilots up in "flying coffins." Shortly after making the comment, the general was shot. One lackluster Soviet General, Grigori Kulik, resisted the development of the new weaponry that contributed to Soviet victory during WWII; yet he still became a Marshall. In 1940, on Stalin's orders, Kulik's wife was kidnapped, raped, and murdered by the Soviet secret police chief, Beria. Later in 1950, Kulik was arrested and shot. Georgy Zhukov, the Soviet General, who was critical in the defeat of the Nazi Germany, was not immune from being persecuted by the Boss. He had been demoted and accused of improprieties. In the end, Zhukov outlived Stalin. The general did get a measure of revenge; he aided in the arrest of Beria, who was later executed. You could say that General Zhukov had the last laugh. [32]

Deportations.

On February 19, 1942, President Franklin D. Roosevelt signed Executive Order 9066, ordering the forced evacuation of Japanese immigrants and citizens from the West Coast of the United States. Approximately 120,000 Japanese were forcibly relocated to internment centers after the attack on Pearl Harbor. It was a red-letter day for the United States, but the Americans were far from being the only country to carry out such acts.

State-sponsored forced evacuations have been referred to as deportations, and were used by both Nazi Germany and the Soviet Union. The Nazis rounded up the Jews and put them into ghettoes like

---

32 Amis, Martin. Koba the Dread. pp. endnote 30n. Radzinsky, Edvard. Stalin. 168,169,172, 173. 371-373, 580. Davies, Norman. No Simple Victory. Pp. 89-90. 175, 227, 243, 244. Hingley, R. Joseph Stalin. Man & Legend. Pp.426. Montefiore, Simon. Stalin. pp. 652. Information on Kulikov. Vronskaya, Jeanne & Chuguev, Vladimir. A Biographical Dictionary of the Soviet Union 1917-1988. Pp. 215.

that of Warsaw in Poland, so that they could be easily transported to labor or death camps. The scope of deportments carried out by the Soviet Union, which occurred before, during and after WWII, dwarfs all other forced relocations in comparison to other states.

The Russian Czars exiled political rabble-rousers and criminals to Siberia, but Stalin went far beyond that, uprooting whole communities. These groups were considered enemies of the state, and in a little over a decade, millions were deported to inhospitable regions within the Soviet Union. They were exiled thousands of miles from their home, and most never returned.

Why have we not heard of Soviet Deportations?

It must be noted that deportations, especially Soviet deportations, are a neglected historical subject matter. Many have heard of what happened to the Japanese civilians and immigrants after the attack on Pearl Harbor, but few have read of the Soviet deportations of their minority peoples during the war. Whether on purpose or a lack of academic attention to detail, the sad history of Soviet deportations is absent from many historical texts, which makes for a strong case that communist history is being tossed into a figurative blackhole. Norman Davies' book, *No Simple Victory,* paints a grim picture of Soviet actions.

-Before the war broke out in 1939, half a million Poles, living within the USSR, were deported to regions in central Asia.

-After hostilities broke out, two and a half million Volga Germans, who had lived in Russia for almost two centuries, were uprooted from their homes. These Germans, alongside Poles who lived in the USSR, were sent to Kazakhstan, while some of the Germans were sent to forced labor camps. Davies noted, that over half of the Poles and the

Murderous Marxism

Volga Germans would die by the early 1950s. That would be a million and a half people, who lost their lives on Stalin's orders.

-In 1940, the Soviets annexed Latvia, Lithuania, and Estonia, on the pretext of coming to the aid of communists living within these Baltic countries. Deportations were quickly instituted. Forced evacuations only stopped after the Germans launched Operation Barbarossa in the summer of 1941. By 1945, the Soviet Army reoccupied the Baltic States. Once again, deportations were reinstated. Roughly 1 out of 4 persons in the Baltic States was said to have been "lost."

-During the war, Muslim groups were targeted and forcibly removed. The Soviets deported "Chechens, Ingush, Balkars, Karachays and Kalmyks." Under a quarter million of these deportees died. (See Communist comparisons. Communist brutality against Muslims.)

-In the spring of 1944, the Soviet secret police deported approximately one million Crimean Tartars; probably half died.

-After the war, Germans who lived within Soviet controlled Poland and Czechoslovakia were deported to the west side of the Oder River. In fairness, all the blame cannot be placed on the Soviets; the Czechs and Poles wanted the deportation of the Germans in these areas for obvious reasons. Between 1945-1947, over two million perished.

-Other groups were also deported: Koreans, Greeks, Bulgars, Moldavians, Balts and Meskhetians. Stalin left no stone unturned.

Victims were crammed into trains and sent to desolate regions in the USSR. It was not uncommon during the summer months for many of the deportees to die from heat exposure, while others froze to death in the winter. One could argue that the Soviets were just as terrible as the Nazis.

Communist comparisons. Communist brutality against Muslims.

The Communist Party USA (CPUSA) has become a vocal supporter of the Hamas terrorist group, which attacked Israel on October 7, 2023. For the past year, the CPUSA has denounced Israel's self-defense military operations against Hamas, in the Gaza Strip, as genocidal. CPUSA hypocrisy knows no bounds. Critics refuse to acknowledge the hundreds of terrorist attacks perpetrated by Hamas on Israel over the decades. There are other glaring memory lapses. They have conveniently forgotten that communists have carried out acts of mass murder against Islamic groups. The Crimean Tatars are a Turkic Muslim ethnic group, which had resided in the Crimean Peninsula, within the former Soviet Union. During the Russian Revolution and the Great Terror, the Soviets had subjected the Crimean Tatars to mass killings, state confiscation of their property and numerous other acts of brutality. During WWII, Stalin ordered the deportations of other Islamic groups, which probably killed 100,000s of thousands within the former Soviet Union. Furthermore, there were numerous other atrocities committed against Islamic peoples by communist regimes. (Please see examples below.)

The 1979 Soviet Invasion of Afghanistan.

The Soviet Union and Afghanistan had diplomatic relations since the 1920s, and by the 1950s, the Soviets had recruited agents within the country. By the 1970s, the Soviets intensified their attempts to influence events in the Central Asian country.

After the assassination of a pro-Soviet president of Afghanistan, the KGB settled upon a plan to initiate regime change within the Central Asian country. Eventually, they settled upon a plan to invade

Afghanistan. The KGB got a green light to carry out the invasion after feeding false intelligence information to the ailing Soviet leader, Leonid Brezhnev. The Soviets invaded on Christmas Day 1979. A special military commando group stormed the Afghan palace, killing all inside, which included murdering the Afghan President, Hafizullah Amin and his entire family. The attack on the palace did not go as planned; guards put up a fierce resistance, killing and wounding some 100 Soviet Special Forces members, which included their commanding officer. The losses of so many Soviet Special Forces soldiers seemed to foreshadow the difficulties the USSR would have in Afghanistan. In early 1980, the United Nations overwhelmingly passed a toothless resolution, condemning the invasion, but the Soviets simply ignored the worthless U.N. Proclamation.

The Soviet resort to barbarism, again.

By 1982, when the Soviets could not subdue the Afghan countryside, they adopted a "scorched earth strategy." Their tactics were reminiscent of the savagery used by the Bolsheviks during the Russian Civil War. Soviet aircraft and helicopters pounded villages to the ground with every type of high explosive and incendiary ordinance. The Afghan guerrillas did receive a boost when the US started supplying them with anti-aircraft, shoulder-fired Stinger missiles. The success of the Stinger missiles kept low-flying Soviet planes and helicopters from bombing villages with impunity.

The Afghans were successful in resisting the Soviets. The invaders were only able to control about twenty percent of the country. In reprisal, Soviet patrols, using armored vehicles, sealed off villages, bombarded them with artillery, and then machine-gunned villagers as they emerged from the ruins. The *Black Book on Communism* noted that the Soviets repeatedly used a wide variety of savage tactics against the Afghans. Villages were looted, and civilians were routinely killed. Women were raped, and in some instances, stripped of their clothing and thrown from helicopters. Afghan children were doused with flammable liquids and set ablaze in front of their parents. Barbarism was routine; nothing was out of bounds.

Although banned after the First World War and later in the 1970s, the Soviets used bioweapons, neurotoxic gases, and various other lethal gases with impunity (just as they had done during the Russian Revolution.) The Soviets poisoned water supplies and planted some twenty million mines, which inflicted what has been estimated to be approximately 700,000 injuries. The Soviets specifically targeted children by deploying booby-trapped toys, which were dropped from aircraft. The Soviets and Afghan communist forces used every conceivable form of torture, from pulling out fingernails, beatings, electronic shock, jamming objects into different orifices of the body, and hacking off limbs. The list of Soviet atrocities outlined in *The Black Book of Communism* was gruesome and quite lengthy. To add insult to injury, the Soviets invoiced the Afghan government for the cost of military operations. In what has been described as "colonial plundering," the USSR forced Afghan authorities to sign over rights to natural gas, cotton, copper, and other commodities.

By the end of the Soviet occupation of Afghanistan in 1989, almost 15,000 Soviet soldiers had been killed, and some 35,000 were wounded. The effects on Afghanistan were catastrophic. It has been estimated that 1.5 to 2 million Afghans had been killed, and between 2 to 4 million were wounded. Roughly 5 million Afghans became refugees in Pakistan and Iran. Afghanistan suffered a "brain-drain" of educated professionals who fled for their lives. Communists aggression erased any small societal gains made in Afghanistan between the 1940s through the early 1960s. The Soviets suffered no international repercussions, save the worldwide boycott of the 1980 Olympics in Moscow. In 1981, the Permanent Peoples Tribunal in Stockholm and London investigated Soviet atrocities in Afghanistan and condemnations were lodged against the USSR. The tribunal achieved nothing, and the international community was never able to alter the unprecedented level of Soviet brutality. It was only when the financial mismanagement and corruption of the USSR became unsustainable that the Soviets ceased operations and pulled out of Afghanistan in 1989. [33]

The Communist Chinese imprison the Uighurs.

Since the early 2010s, China has been accused of committing cultural genocide against the minority Uyghur peoples of the Xinjiang region of western China. Culturally distinct, these Islamic peoples are fighting to keep their faith and ways of life from being destroyed by the communist Chinese authorities. They are fighting a losing battle. While claiming to be fighting a war against terrorism, the Chinese have

---

33 Smith, Charles. Palestine and the Arab-Israeli Conflict: A History with Documents. Hamas terrorist acts, rocket attacks, Pp. 448-9, 501, 515, 524. Andrew, C. & Mitrokhin, V. The World Was Going Our Way: The KGB and the Battle for The Third World. 269, 386-419. Courtois, Stephane, et. al. The Black Book of Communism. Pp. 10, 97, 216,, 219-224, 256, 259, 708-725. Katamidze, Slava. Loyal Comrades, Ruthless Killers: The Secret Services of the USSR 1917-1991. Pp. 196-201. "Stop arming the fascist Netanyahu Regime!" Communist Party USA: http://www.cpusa.org. Deportations. Medvedev, Roy & Zhores. The Unknown Stalin. Pp. 11-12. Davies, N. No Simple Victory. Pp. 178, 309-311, 349. White, Matthew. The Great Big Book of Horrible Things. Pp. 422-424, 389. Radzinsky, Edvard. Stalin. Pp. 502-503. Davies, N. Europe. Pp. 1329. Central Intelligence Agency. "Motivations for the use of Chemical Weapons in Afghanistan and Southeast Asia" An Intelligence Assessment. (SECRET SOV 83-10005x, January 1983. COPY 484.) Approved For Release 2008/04/15. This document was heavily redacted. For the Soviets, chemical weapons were a cost effective tactic to be used against the resilient Afghan fighters.

resorted to mass imprisonment of Uighurs, and in the process, destroying their culture and religion.

Satellite imagery has shown that from 2015 through 2020, there has been a massive buildup of prison camps throughout the region. International civil rights groups estimate that there are over 300 re-education camps and over one million Uighurs have been detained. Besides killings, the communists have used brainwashing and torture. The Chinese are also using the imprisoned Uighurs as slave labor for the manufacturing of consumer goods. There are images of Uyghur people picking cotton for their Chinese overlords, yet there is little outcry by the international community. The Global Slavery Index estimates that over 5 million persons are in involuntary servitude in China, and the Uighurs are a sizable part of this slavery population. (See the Laogai Prison system in Communist Comparisons.)

The Chinese authorities have also been accused of engaging in a deliberate campaign to cut the Uyghur population by forcing their women to have abortions and undergo sterilizations. Uyghur birthrates have dropped dramatically. To further control the Uyghur population, the Chinese communists are pioneering surveillance technology that literally tracks almost all human behavior. Cameras are everywhere, and authorities routinely clone people's phones to track their movements. The list is quite lengthy. The Uyghurs have become guinea pigs for the communists to perfect their ability to spy on the population of China, and they are honing their skills in Xinjiang.

"Dr. Erkin Sidick, President of the Uyghur Projects Foundation," wrote that "the situation is much, much worse than what is being reported... Death is everywhere right now." An Internet search provides ample sources of Chinese atrocities against these people, but given the economic clout of China, there is little appetite to take decisive action against the communists.

The Khmer Rouge killed half of the Cham people in Cambodia.

The communist Khmer Rouge not only committed mass murder against Cambodians and native Vietnamese in their country, but they also targeted the Cham people. For centuries, this small Muslim group has lived within modern-day Cambodia. At the time of the takeover, the Cham probably had a population of roughly a quarter million. Fiercely independent, they had for the most part, peacefully coexisted with other groups within Cambodia. Unfortunately, for the Cham, independence and non-assimilation are traits not tolerated by communists. The Khmer Rouge destroyed their mosques, burned Korans, and made attempts to force the Cham to eat pork, which is prohibited by many within the Islamic faith. The atheistic Khmers tried to coerce them to renounce their beliefs, but the Cham resisted. It is estimated that the communists have killed between 100,000 to 125,000 of the Cham, which was roughly half of the population.

It is mind-boggling to read the sheer audacity of the CPUSA to accuse Israel of genocide while they are fighting a war of survival. Since the founding of this Jewish state in 1948, it has been attacked by several Arab countries over the past several decades. Terrorist groups operating as proxies for rogue states such as Iran have also been waging a war against Israel for years.

As I wrote at the beginning of this book, true Marxist believers have an unlimited capacity to block out communist mass murder and atrocities, while fixating on the shortcomings of people they consider opponents. It should come as no surprise that the CPUSA has turned a blind eye to the barbarity of the Soviet Union, communist China, and the Cambodian Khmer Rouge, which have killed millions of Muslims. They will never deny their faith in Marxism. [34]

Post-War: Friction between the Soviets and the Allies.

By the fall of 1945, the primary Axis combatants, Germany and Japan, had surrendered. Although the Second World War had ended, a new low-level conflict was brewing between the Soviet Union and the United States of America, the Cold War.

In general, some liberal historians seem to fixate on finding fault with American postwar foreign policy in relation to the Soviet Union. The critiques run the gambit. Either American policy was insufficient, inflexible, or we did not understand what the Soviets had gone through during the war. Quite the contrary, the Americans and the West had the right to be wary of the Soviets. The Soviets and the Germans had signed the Non-Aggression Pact in 1939. This diplomatic agreement contained secret protocols which outlined how these two totalitarian regimes would divide and conqueror countries in Europe. It was only when the

---

[34] Courtois, Stephane, et. al. The Black Book of Communism. p.498-513, the Cham, 592, 594-5. Brotherton-Bunch, Elizabeth. "Despite Accusations That It Benefits from Forced Labor in Xinjiang, Nike Remains Committed to China," Alliance For American Manufacturing. Aug. 9th, China Forbes. Mistreanu, Simina. "Study Links Nike, Addias and Apple to Forced Uighur Labor. Editors' Pick. March 2, 2020.Werleman, CJ. "'Death is Everywhere' Millions More Uyghurs Missing" Byline Times. Aug. 24, 2020. Xiuzhong Xu, Vicky, et. al. "Uyghurs for Sale: 'Re-Education', Forced Labor, and Surveillance" Australian Strategic Policy Institute. March 1, 2020. "Who are the Uighurs and why is China being accused of Genocide." BBC. May 24th, 2020. Andrews, C. & Mitrokhin, V. The World was Going our Way: The KGB and the Battle for the Third World. pp. 278, 279. U.S Department of Labor. Bureau of International Labor Affairs; Against Their Will, The Situation in Xinjiang. Sept. 4th, 2018. For Israeli wars of survival, and Lebanon terror bases that operated against Israel. Laffin, John. Brassey's Dictionary of Battles. Pp. 205,207, 240, 241.

Nazis turned on the Soviets did the communists aligned themselves with the Allies.

Rosemary Sullivan's biography of Joseph Stalin's daughter details how she was painfully aware that her father had virtually no compassion for other human beings. So much so, that Svetlana took her mother's maiden name (Alliluyeva), rather than her father's last name. During her grade school years, Svetlana became alarmed when her own family members started disappearing in the 1930s. Her father was the leader of the Soviet Union; surely, he would never allow her relatives to vanish? As Svetlana entered her late teens, she realized that her father was a ruthless dictator. She remembered conversations with her father about the Non-Aggression Pact and his dirty deal with the Nazis. Svetlana stated that "after the war was over, **she recalled his habit of repeatedly saying 'Ech, together with the Germans we would have been invincible.'** Moreover, her interaction with her father gives historians a glimpse into the diabolical nature of Joseph Stalin.

Yet there is further evidence of Soviet treachery that was uncovered after the war. During the Second World War, US military intelligence officials became suspicious of the Soviets' wartime intentions. Some believed that Stalin might try and broker a backroom deal with the Germans for a separate peace agreement. American officials were so alarmed that in 1943, they secretly gathered a special unit of crack cryptologists to investigate coded Soviet diplomatic messages. What they discovered in the mid-1940s was a diplomatic bombshell, which was kept a secret until the 1990s. Information gathered by the code breakers revealed that the Soviets had been operating several extensive espionage rings in the US during the 1940s. Soviet spies, foreign agents and other American turncoats had made inroads into the highest level of the US government. (See Venona)

Furthermore, in Eastern Europe, the Soviets, by force of arms, installed communist regimes that were subservient to Moscow's wishes. These Soviet backed thugs used mass killings, imprisonment, and terror to get a parasitic hold on Eastern Europe. The USSR also supported the Greek communists' bid to take over this Mediterranean country. Furthermore, Stalin also demanded "some control" of the Dardanelles Straits, which was a strategic waterway that connects the Black Sea to the Mediterranean Sea. The Soviets were also active in trying to expand their influence in Iran. (See the Domino Theory and Greece). Yet the first potential flash point between the two superpowers would take place in post-war Germany.

The Berlin Blockade: Stalin loses this round.

At the end of the war, Germany was split into zones of occupation: American, British, French and Soviet. By 1948, a rift developed between the Soviets and the other three allies over post-war Germany's future. Germany's currency was dropping in value, and black-market activity was roiling its economy. Money is the lifeblood of an economy, and currency without value will create social unrest. The Americans surmised that the Soviets would take advantage of the economic chaos. The US countered the monetary problems by creating a new occupation currency. The Soviets responded by cutting off roads and rail lines to Berlin, thus precipitating the Berlin Blockade Crisis in the summer of 1948.

Instead of trying to break the blockade by force, the US and Britain used air power in a non-confrontational way to beat the Soviets. The Americans and the British started flying large cargo planes, almost around the clock, delivering thousands of tons of food and supplies into Berlin. After a year of flying in supplies, the Soviets gave up, and the

Americans and the British chalked up a victory against the USSR, but that would not last for long.

Communist victories and near misses between 1948-1950.

-The Soviets stole the secrets for the development of nuclear weaponry and detonated an atomic bomb. (See Venona)

-The communist forces of Mao Zedong defeated the Chinese Nationalists and took over China in 1949.

-Communist North Korea, with the backing of communist China and the Soviet Union, attacked South Korea, but the United Nations, led by the United States military forces, beat back the attack.

Venona: American code breakers catch Soviet Spies red-handed.

After a half-century of secrecy, the United States government revealed the existence of Project Venona in 1995. Venona was the code name given to the operation, which entailed a group of Army code breakers that cracked Soviet diplomatic codes. What they found was explosive. The code breakers uncovered several massive communist spy rings, which operated in the United States during the Second World War.

In 1943, the US Army's Military Intelligence became concerned that Germany and the Soviet Union might make a separate peace deal, which would have left the Allies to face the whole German Army. The Signal Intelligence Service tasked an "elite" group of cryptanalysts to break encrypted Soviet telegrams and try and discover Stalin's intentions. Two years before the American entry into the war, the US government had started collecting copies of all international telegrams.

From these copies, the code breakers tried to decipher the encrypted Soviet telegrams. By 1946, the Americans were able to crack the codes, and what they discovered alarmed them. Venona code breakers were able to decipher coded telegrams from 1948 through 1952. They uncovered a massive Soviet spy ring(s) that had thoroughly infiltrated the United States government and military.

The Venona Project revealed an astonishing number of individuals had spied for the Soviets. Some 349 citizens and immigrants had "covert relationships" with Soviet espionage rings. A little less than half of these spies were known by their actual names; the rest were only known by aliases and code names. Further investigation revealed another 139 spies and handlers, which had not been uncovered by Venona code breakers. The Americans spies included the Assistant Secretary of the Treasury, Harry Dexter White, numerous State Department officials, people associated with the development of the atomic bomb, and members of President Franklin D. Roosevelt's staff. And that was just the tip of the iceberg. Venona was the secret intelligence source (along with other sources), which exposed Julius Rosenberg's complicity in handing over US atomic secrets to the USSR. Furthermore, not only did Venona expose Soviet espionage in the United States but led to the eventual exposure of a renegade spy ring in Great Britain. All in all, American turncoats and Soviet spies were able to steal a treasure trove of intelligence secrets involving government policy, strategy, military hardware, and communications.

The cables also identified over 30 foreigners who had been temporarily engaged in espionage activity in the USA. One of these spies, although unknown at the time, alerted the USSR to the Venona Project. This Soviet spy was a British turncoat, Kim Philby, a long-serving intelligence officer in the British Secret Intelligence Service. He feared that Venona had exposed him and his clandestine activities. Although undetected, British officials were starting to become suspicious of him, so he fled the United Kingdom and defected to the USSR. The Soviets considered him such a valuable espionage asset that in 1990, they issued a stamp commemorating him.

The British Cambridge Five.

Destiny is a fickle creature. When Philby informed the Soviets about the Venona Project, it indirectly led to the exposure of the Cambridge Five spy ring. These British traitors were extremely intelligent and had either been students or associated with the prestigious University of Cambridge. Almost all were from privileged upbringings, and four had worked within the British governmental intelligence services. The other spies were Guy Burgess, a diplomat who also worked in British intelligence, and Donald Maclean, a diplomat. John Cairncross was a civil servant who also worked in British intelligence. Anthony Blunt was a notable British art historian and advised the monarchy on artwork. He was knighted, but when his traitorous past was revealed, his knighthood was rescinded.

Venona exposed that the Soviets were our mortal enemies, and they used espionage to gain an advantage over the United States. The Venona Project was so secret that its existence was not revealed until several years after the fall of the USSR in 1991. History books devote very few pages to Soviet spying being exposed by the Venona Project. More history down the memory black hole.

The British code breaker and communist spy: John Cairncross, and the Battle of Kursk.

John Cairncross was the British code breaker and communist spy who passed decrypted German messages to the Soviets. Besides passing information about the US nuclear bomb program, he also alerted the Soviets to Operation Citadel, the German military offensive against the Kursk pocket. After the resounding Soviet victory, Cairncross was secretly awarded the "highest of Soviet decorations, the Order of the Red Banner." Of course, he could never acknowledge it without revealing his traitorous role in the Soviet espionage ring.

Ironically, Stalin detested the British spies, which made up the Cambridge Five. In the Boss's paranoid, conspiratorial mind, the British turncoats should have uncovered an extensive English spy ring operating in the Soviet Union. Ironically, the English had decreased their intelligence-gathering operations against the USSR during the war years.

Richard Sorge, master Soviet Spy.

It is said that no one fights harder for a cause than a true believer. Richard Sorge was an ardent communist, devoted to the Soviet Union, and he was also one of their best spies. In 1941, while working undercover as a correspondent in Tokyo, he supplied information about the impending German attack on the Soviet Union, Operation Barbarossa.

Sorge was born to Russian German parents, and one of his relatives worked with Karl Marx. He was brilliant, debonair, while also being a functioning alcoholic and a womanizer. He lived in Germany and after the First World War, immersed himself in Marxism and socialism. After receiving a university degree, Sorge became a communist. He wrote for a communist paper and taught at a German university until he was dismissed for trying to indoctrinate students. After a stint in the Soviet Union, Sorge spent time in London and later Los Angeles. He was a communist recruiter, and he carried out espionage activity. He returned to the USSR for more espionage training, then returned to Germany, which was controlled by the Nazis.

The communist spy joined the Nazi Party and established himself as a journalist, in which he was quite successful. Later, Sorge was stationed in Tokyo, Japan, and he used his contacts within the German embassy to gather information for the USSR. It was at this point; he discovered the date for the beginning of Operation Barbarossa. Stalin contemptuously dismissed his report and referred to Sorge as a "brothel keeper..." After the initial German success during Barbarossa, Sorge was able to gather information indicating Germany's Axis partner, the Empire of Japan, had no intention of attacking the USSR. This allowed the Soviets to transfer hundreds of thousands of soldiers that were tied down in the east to the Russian front against the Nazis. Thanks to Sorge, these Soviet reinforcements were able to blunt the German attack.

Given the risk of being a Soviet spy in an Axis country during WWII, Sorge's days were numbered. Moscow recalled the spy, but he declined to return because he was aware of what happened to those summoned back to the Soviet Union. Furthermore, Sorge's scandalous behavior and his dodgy contacts in Tokyo drew the attention of the Japanese secret police. Japanese counterintelligence agents used a dancer to set up Sorge, and he was arrested in the fall of 1941. One Russian source indicated that Soviet agents supposedly shot the dancer on the streets of Tokyo. The Soviets declined an offer to exchange the spy for several Japanese agents, and Sorge was executed in 1944. Sorge's wife was arrested in the Soviet Union and "perished" in captivity.

In the 1960s, he was made a posthumous hero of the Soviet Union. Years after his execution, Sorge's exploits made him quite popular. Several books, a movie and a mini-series were made about the famous spy. Many fail to realize Sorge was just the tip of the iceberg of a massive Soviet worldwide espionage network, which exposed the true murderous nature of the USSR.

Stalin's last despicable act: the Jewish Doctors' plot.

Historian Edvard Radzinsky opined that Stalin was busy identifying new enemies so he could justify starting new purges of Soviet society. Radzinsky believed the "Boss" wanted to ready the Soviet people for a grand new conflict. The Jewish people within the Soviet Union would be Stalin's new enemy of the state. By early 1949, he began concocting a plot to accuse Jewish groups of trying to sabotage the Soviet Union

Was Stalin Anti-Semitic?

Was Stalin anti-Semitic? The short answer is yes, but it never approached the supposedly "science-based" street gutter anti-Semitism espoused by the Nazis. It must be noted that anti-Semitism had been prevalent in the Russian Empire prior to the Russian Revolution. Supposedly, the Tsarist secret police had anonymously penned *The Protocols of the Elders of Zion*, an anti-Semitic publication, which claimed that there was a Jewish plot to govern the world. Ironically, the Bolsheviks had many Jewish persons within their ranks, and that included Stalin's inner circle. Lenin had Jewish ancestry, and Trotsky came from a religious Jewish family, of which several were rabbis. Nonetheless, Khrushchev described Stalin as being anti-Semitic, calling him "dyed in the wool." Historian Simon Montefiore wrote that, as the Soviets and the Nazis were negotiating the Non-Aggression Pact, the Boss played up to the German diplomats by making anti-Semitic remarks. "Purge the ministry of Jews...[and]...Clean out the Synagogue..." were a few of his terrible comments.

The strange case of Stalin's hairdresser-bodyguard, Karl Pauker.

Probably one of the most bizarre examples of anti-Semitism connected to Stalin involved one of his personal bodyguards, Karl Pauker. Originally, he was a Hungarian Jew who worked as a hairdresser at an opera house. Being from the Austro-Hungarian Empire, Pauker had been drafted into the Austrian Army after the outbreak of the First World War. He was captured by the Russians Army, and with the outbreak of the Russian Revolution, Pauker became a Bolshevik and began working for the KGB (known as the Cheka at the time). From that point, he was able to become assigned to Stalin's security detail and later became one of the Boss's personal bodyguards. Pauker was bald, reeked of cologne, wore shoes that made him look taller, and used a girdle to hold in his gut.

Although open religious worship was still prohibited in the USSR during the 1930s, Stalin allowed Pauker to dress as Santa Claus and hand out presents and engage in Christmas festivities with members of the communist elites. As one historian noted, it was bizarre that in a self-professed atheist-communist state, a Jewish man, who worked for one of the most ruthless secret police in history, dressed as Santa Claus. Truth is stranger than fiction.

The bodyguard was a natural entertainer. He told jokes, did imitations, and the dictator's children enjoyed having him around. Although Pauker was Jewish, he routinely told anti-Semitic jokes to amuse the "Boss." When Stalin started eliminating the old Bolsheviks, Pauker was involved in killing off some of these early revolutionaries. In late August 1936, two old Bolshevik party leaders, both Jewish, Gregory Zinoviev and Lev Kamenev, were executed for supposedly being involved in a plot against Stalin. While Kamenev was composed before being shot, Zinoviev became hysterical as he was being led to his execution. He called out to Stalin, to God, anyone to save himself. He died begging for his life. Pauker witnessed the killings, and later, with great relish, imitated Zinoviev pleading for his life. It was said that Stalin laughed uncontrollably as Pauker mimicked the old Bolshevik's final moments. The "Boss" laughed all the harder, as the former hairdresser exaggerated a Jewish accent of the old revolutionary. Roughly a year later, it was Pauker's turn. He was arrested and shot. It was never noted if the bodyguard cried out to anyone. Perhaps Pauker ran out of jokes; either way, he knew too much about Stalin, and in the Boss's mind, the hairdresser had to go.

Molotov turns on his own wife to stay alive.

By the late 1940s, Jews were being arrested in the USSR. One of those arrested was Vyacheslav Molotov's wife, Polina. Radzinsky surmised that Molotov was quite aware of Stalin's obsession with having those closest to him killed. Molotov probably figured that it was only a matter of time before he became a target. In 1948, the Boss demanded that Molotov divorce his wife, and in 1949, she was arrested. Scouring the Soviet archives, Radzinsky found a convoluted letter, written by Molotov, denouncing his wife. Radzinsky noted that, "betraying his wife was the price of liberty." She was tortured and imprisoned by the secret police, but she survived. "As always, he... [Molotov]... observed the rules." By 1953, Stalin had set into motion the imaginary Jewish doctors' plot. Radzinsky concluded that Stalin's goal was a "unified society, forged in the white heat of... [a]... purge," which would allow the Boss to instigate the third and final world war. To the Great Dream—the worldwide Soviet republic."

The death of Stalin; some mystery to his demise.

Fate sometimes turns on a dime, and this is what happened to the Soviet Union and the rest of the world when Joseph Stalin died on March 5th, 1953. The Boss's death was shrouded in mystery. It is believed that he was stricken sometime on February 28 or early on March 1. Fearing Stalin's wrath for waking him, nobody dared enter his room until late on March 1st. He was discovered semi-conscious, lying on the floor in a pool of urine. He drifted in and out of consciousness until he died on the 5th of March. It is generally believed that a stroke or a brain aneurism was the cause of his death, but some historians have suggested foul play. Prior to his death, the Boss vomited some blood, and some have loosely speculated that Stalin might have been given a blood-thinner to hasten his demise. Why murder? The thought of another Stalin purge, or maybe another devastating war, might have emboldened someone to take a chance of getting rid of the "Boss." Edvard Radzinsky scoured the former Soviet Archives for material covering the Boss's death, and he pointed out the inconsistencies in the movements of certain Soviet leaders, but never any information pinpointing an assassination. It is generally believed that Soviet leaders, fearing the wrath of Stalin, simply denied him help. They stalled before they summoned medical attention. As Stalin's remains were being transferred, some people were crushed to death when they tried to catch a glimpse of the deceased leader. Even in death, the Boss was able to take some people with him.

Immediately after the Boss's death, most of his secret files were removed from his residence, and it is unclear if these documents were either destroyed or hidden away. One can only imagine the damning material potentially contained in these files, or if these documents still exist. Stalin was embalmed and interred next to Lenin on March 9th, 1953. In the same year, Nikita Khrushchev became the First Secretary of the Communist Party of the Soviet Union.

In 1956, Nikita Khrushchev held a secret meeting in which he denounced Stalin's crimes. (Some historians have suggested that he was trying to distance himself from the mass murder he had participated in.) Khrushchev stunned the party members in attendance when he not only admitted to, but detailed Stalin's bloody transgressions.

In 1955, the plans to build a museum dedicated to Stalin were dropped, and in 1961, the "Boss" was quietly and without fanfare reburied in the wall of the Kremlin. After Khrushchev's rise to power, arrests, executions, and the Gulags still existed, but nowhere near the level of mass murder engaged in by Stalin. The Soviet Union became reluctant to use overt military action to expand the communist regime, but it used utter ruthlessness to maintain its empire. Soviet energies were focused on espionage and supplying Third World communist insurgencies. The KGB also engaged in undermining Western countries by utilizing "active measures" which were designed to weaken a country from within, by poisoning the minds of citizens, with disinformation. [35]

---

[35] Kennedy, Paul. The Rise and Fall of the Great Powers. Pp. 377-378. Acheson, Dean. Present at the Creation. 259-263. LaFeber, Walter. The American Age. 446-461. Kissinger, Henry. Diplomacy. Pp. 451-452, 461, 469, 473-4, 476, 479, 482, 483.

Information on Richard Sorge. Vronskaya, Jeanne & Chuguev, Vladimir. A Biographical Dictionary of the Soviet Union 1917-1988. P.413. Toland, John. The Rising Sun: the Decline and Fall of the Japanese Empire. Pp. 23-24, 90, 139-140.

Radzinsky, Edvard. Stalin. p.511, 513, 517, 518, 529-536. Montefiore, Simon Sebag. Stalin. 66-67, 198-199, 221, 304-306. Information on Richard Sorge pp. 403. Amis, Martin. Koba the Dread. pp. 85,91, 217-222. Solzhenitsyn, Alexander. GULAG Archipelago. p. 92, 157,158, 638. Hingley, Ronald. Joseph Stalin: Man & Legend. Pp. 424. Courtois, Stephane, et. al. The Black Book on Communism. 24-25. Davies, N. No Simple Victory. Pp. 417-419. Haynes, John Earl. & Klehr, Harvey. Venona: Decoding Soviet Espionage in America. pp. 1-14. 52-56. 339, 371, 383-384. Andrew, Christopher, Andrew, Mitrokhin, Vasili. The Sword and the Shield. Pp. 56-67, 92, 126. 143-144, 155, 157,165. Information on Richard Sorge. Pp. 36, 43, 93, 95-6. Medvedev, Roy & Zhores. The Unknown Stalin: His Life, death, and Legacy. Stalin's death, persecutions and the "Doctors plot." Pp. 1-42, the disappearance of Stalin's files, 66-70, espionage, 124, 141. Medvedev, Roy. Let History Judge. Pp. 425. Information on Richard Sorge. Pp. 428-429. Sullivan, Rosmary. Stalin's Daughter. P. 85.

Chapter 3
Post-WWII: Communist actions in Eastern Europe.

The communist Iron Curtain is drawn across Eastern Europe.

By the summer of 1945, Stalin was about to expand the scope of Soviet dominance over Eastern Europe. Nazi aggression during WWII paved the way for decades of Soviet domination. By 1948, the Soviets had solidified their control over the governments of Poland, Romania, Bulgaria, and Hungary. Czechoslovakia, which the Germans had annexed, once again lost its freedom in 1948, when the government was overthrown by communist thugs taking their orders from Moscow. The Baltic states of Estonia, Latvia, and Lithuania, the eastern European country of Moldova and the territory taken from Romania were forcibly annexed by the USSR. Czechoslovakia and Hungary, although occupied by the Soviets, would hold onto local autonomy for several years. By 1948, communist groups with the support of the Soviets, took over these two Eastern European countries.

At the Potsdam Conference of 1945, the Allies (USA, Great Britain, France, and the USSR) agreed Germany would be partitioned, and communist-controlled East Germany was created in 1949, with the line of demarcation running through Berlin. Yugoslavia was able to avoid Soviet control and exercise autonomy over its own country. Although a communist, Tito was detested by Stalin, who tried to have the

Yugoslavian leader assassinated. Albania would also fall under communist control, completing the almost total communist subjugation of Eastern Europe. In a 1947 speech in the United States, Winston Churchill noted that an "Iron Curtain" had been drawn across Europe, and those in the east were under Stalin's control.

Communism gets an iron grip on Eastern Europe: 1945-1949.

After overrunning Eastern Europe in 1944-1945, the Soviets backed communist groups grabbed control of the governments within Poland, Romania, Bulgaria, and East Germany. Although Czechoslovakia and Hungary were occupied by the Soviets, it would take several years before local communists were able to take full control of these nations. All would become Soviet satellites, taking their orders directly from Moscow. Communist toadies throughout Eastern Europe, carried out the orders of the Soviets, and Stalin was the man behind the curtain. These newly subjugated nations experienced killings, mass arrests, and rigged show trials, which ended in executions or imprisonment. The local communists, with the assistance of the Soviets, recreated the dreaded GULAG system throughout Eastern Europe. Anyone perceived as a threat or who resisted communist authority was arrested and imprisoned. This show of power was meant to cow the local population. The perfect communist paradise would be built with terror, fear, and slave labor.

"The destruction of civil society."

The monopolizing of all power within Eastern Europe began immediately. Civil society was counter-revolutionary to the Marxist-communist mindset. They viewed individualism, private property rights, freedom of speech and movement, as tools of capitalism. All facets of capitalism were to be destroyed. As you recall, Marx's Communist Manifesto called for the "abolition of individuality and freedom!" He wrote further that "communism abolishes eternal truths; it abolishes all religion and all morality…" Also mandated in the manifesto was the destruction of the family, private property and eventually the dissolution of all nation-states. Once the communist "Iron Curtain" was drawn across the continent, the Soviets forced Eastern Europeans to accept this new *1984* Orwellian nightmare.

Rigged communist courts.

Communist terror and violence broke early resistance, and a fraudulent court system was just another tool in the Soviet arsenal of domination. Eastern Europeans experienced mass arrests, torture, followed by sham trials that ended with lengthy prison sentences or executions. As in the Soviet Union, trials were a farce, and it was not uncommon for trials to be less than half an hour. In the USSR, some trials were only five minutes. The trials also served as a farcical backdrop in which authorities could claim that the defendants had received a fair trial.

Historically, Czechoslovakia and Hungary had judicial systems based on the rule of law. Jurisprudence was thrown out the window by the communists, which turned the law courts into blunt instruments to terrorize the people. Qualified judges were replaced by communist cronies, who disregarded law books as an impediment to revolutionary fervor. People were arrested on flimsy political accusations, such as posing a threat to the state; almost all would be imprisoned. The dilution of people's civil rights went even further. One historian noted that the secret police and communist law courts did not have to be concerned with the rule of law. Many times, defendants were informed of the charges against them just a few minutes before their court case was to be convened.

Furthermore, it was commonplace for defendants to meet their defense attorney just before the trial. Defendants were threatened that if they tried to defend themselves in court, the consequences would be worse. Defense attorneys were also threatened not to vigorously defend their clients. Civil rights were an impediment to communist domination.

The private sector is destroyed.

The communists wiped out almost all private enterprises. Businesses, large and small, were confiscated by the state. Small shopkeepers who had worked hard to build their businesses stood by helplessly as state goons took away their livelihood. Farmers saw their land collectivized for the greater good of communism. Authorities closed clubs, unions, political parties, guilds, and any other associations. Remember, the Communist Manifesto called for the abolishment of individuality. Any endeavor that did not emanate from the communist state was forbidden. The unspoken goal of the communists was to create a sense of helplessness; all would have to depend upon the state.

Prison and Forced Labor Camps.

Prison and forced labor camps sprang up behind the Iron Curtain. *The Black Book of Communism* noted that prisoners became "modern slaves... [which]... may not have built pyramids, but they did build canals, dams, factories, and buildings in honor of the new pharaohs." The slightest transgression or perceived disloyalty to the communist regime could land you in a forced labor camp; hundreds of thousands were imprisoned across Eastern Europe. Many dozens of camps were established near mining operations and transportation routes to exploit unpaid labor. Marx claimed that communism would create a workers' paradise, but this new Eastern European GULAG system indicated otherwise.

Kill the non-communist heroes; show the people that gallantry is futile.

Raoul Wallenberg.

During the final days of World War II, Raoul Wallenberg, a Swedish diplomat, travelled to Hungary to save Jewish people from being killed by the Nazis. Although he was a diplomat from a neutral country, the Soviet secret police snatched him up and imprisoned him. The Wallenberg family tried in vain to locate Raoul, but Soviet authorities stonewalled their efforts, and authorities gave conflicting accounts of what became of the ambassador. At first, the Soviets claimed the Nazis shot him, and then they admitted that they had detained Raoul. The story changed several times. Supposedly, he died of torture, and then it was suggested that he died from heart failure, or Raoul was somewhere lost within the massive Soviet prison system. Never the truth. His disappearance devastated his family, and his parents died without knowing his exact fate. Decades after his arrest, the Soviets admitted that Raoul died in their custody in 1947, and some of his personal effects were returned. Although it cannot be conclusively verified, Wallenberg was probably killed by the Soviets. The Swedish diplomat was a totally innocent humanitarian, trying to save others in war-torn Hungary, only to be killed. The murder of Raoul Wallenberg demonstrated that at any time, at any place within Eastern Europe, communists would grab an innocent person and kill them with no repercussions. No one was safe.

Eastern European show trials and victims.

Communist show trials in Eastern Europe served several purposes. These farcical law courts gave a fig leaf of legitimacy to these miscarriages of justice. Furthermore, the rigged court system was used to terrorize the populace and showcase the power of the communist state. As far as the Soviets were concerned, past feats of courage and heroism in the face of the Nazis was irrelevant. Brave heroes who stood up against fascists could potentially resist the state. Totally innocent persons would be arrested, falsely accused in a rigged communist court, and "judicially murdered." They wanted to make people think twice before being valiant. The Soviets wanted obedient sheep that obeyed their orders.

Witold Pilecki.

-Witold Pilecki, a Polish freedom fighter, was a bona fide hero who was "judicially murdered" by the Soviets on ludicrous charges after WWII. This is a fact: Pilecki was a man of immense courage. In 1920, he had fought the Bolsheviks when they attacked Lithuania. Fast-forward almost twenty years; he served in the Polish Army, fighting the Germans when they invaded his country in 1939. After the fall of Poland, Witold assisted several resistance groups that fought the Nazis' occupation of their homeland. In an unbelievable display of bravery, he allowed himself to be taken into custody by the Germans (most of the time, resistance members were immediately shot upon capture). He was imprisoned in Auschwitz for two and a half years, and collected information on the death camp, and later escaped. Witold took part in the Warsaw uprising and was captured by the Germans again and escaped, yet again. In 1945, the Soviets arrested Witold on bogus charges, convicted him in a rigged trial and executed this courageous freedom fighter. Laughably, he was accused of collaborating with the Nazis. In anyone's book, Witold was a hero, many times over, and he was murdered by the Soviets. His story deserves to be told, yet it is unlikely in today's American education system because it shines an unflattering light upon communism.

Nikolai Petkov.

Nikolai Petkov, of Bulgaria, was a dedicated government minister who resigned his post when communist violence spread across his country after WWII. He was arrested on false charges and hanged in 1947.

His family life was as tragic as his death. His brother had been assassinated in 1924, and his father had been murdered in 1907. Living in exile, he returned to Bulgaria in 1940. Once the Soviets occupied Bulgaria, a wave of communist violence swept the country, and moderate socialists and others were killed. During this time, Petkov suffered a torrent of threats, but when the violence and assassinations became too intense, he resigned from his ministerial job. He was later arrested on the laughable charges of supporting the fascists, and on August 16, 1947, he was sentenced to death. As the communist judge read out the verdict, "In the name of the people of Bulgaria," ... [at this point] ... Nikolai Petkov... [jumped up and]... cried out loudly: "No! Not in the name of the people of Bulgaria! I am being sent to my death by your foreign masters from the Kremlin...The people of Bulgaria, crushed by this bloody tyranny that passes for justice, will never believe your lies."

Petkov was executed on September 23, 1947. He was another innocent person "judicially murdered" on the orders of Moscow. There is a photograph of Nikolia protesting the verdict. A miscarriage of justice preserved for the ages.

Points to ponder: the murderers are murdered.

Ironically, two of the Bulgarian communist authorities who orchestrated Petkov's arrest and his "execution" were later executed themselves. The Bulgarian Party leaders took a page out of Stalin's playbook. Eliminate all those who possess awful knowledge about their bosses. Stalin had several of his secret police chiefs killed off, along with thousands of their murderous underlings; so was the fate of Petkov's killers.

Milada Horakova.

Milada Horakova was a Czechoslovakian patriot who resisted the tyranny of the Nazis and the Soviets. After the German occupation of her country, Milada joined the Czech resistance movement. In 1940, she was arrested by the Nazis. She endured torture and a sham trial in which she was convicted and sentenced to death. Unbelievably, her sentenced was later commuted to an eight-prison term, but as the Third Reich collapsed, and Milada was released.

Czechoslovakia's freedom was short-lived. After the Soviets captured the country, Nazi tyranny was replaced by totalitarianism directed from Moscow. Although she had the chance to flee the country, Milada chose to stay behind and speak out against the communist assault on the civil liberties of Czechoslovakians. Unfortunately for her, the Soviets and their loyal communist toadies would never accept any challenges to their political authority. Anyone who dared to question their rule was to be brutally eliminated. In mid-1950, the communist authorities arrested Milada and several others. The trial was a joke; she and three others were sentenced to death. Every aspect of Milada's trial had been choreographed down to the role of the lawyers, the judge, and the predetermined guilty verdict. Given her reputation as a staunch defender of democracy and women's rights, her death sentence prompted an international outcry for mercy. Winston Churchill, Eleanor Roosevelt, and Albert Einstein all wrote letters pleading for clemency, but these pleas fell upon deaf ears. Subsequently, she and the others were "judicially murdered..." She had been sentenced to the gallows, but the executioner added a wicked twist by designing the hangman's noose to slowly strangle Milada. She suffered a slow, gruesome death, which took roughly fifteen minutes. Her remains were cremated and disposed of in an undisclosed location. In 2000, a symbolic grave was created for the Czechoslovakian patriot. Milada received many posthumously awards, and a movie was made of her life in 2017.

General Heliodor Pika and Josef Podsednik.

General Heliodor Pika and Josef Podsednik were two Slovakian leaders who were arrested on false charges. The general had resisted the Germans during the war and was supportive of communist activities after the war. *The Black Book of Communism* noted that his devotion to Czechoslovakia was "uncontestable." After the war, he served in the Czechoslovakian armed forces until he was forced to resign. He was arrested on false charges of being a British spy and hung in 1949.

Points to Ponder: once again, the murderers are murdered.

The head of Czechoslovakian military intelligence, Bedrich Reicin, had been responsible for the arrest and execution of General Pika. He convinced the Czech communist authorities that Pika knew too much about Soviet intelligence activities. Several years later, Bedrich Reicin was executed. It was theorized that *he* probably knew too much about Soviet intelligence activities. Just like the movie, *Goodfellas*, gangsters whose hands were just as bloody as their crime bosses never lived long enough to talk.

Josef Podsednik.

Josef Podsednik was an admired Slovakian mayor in Czechoslovakia. Popularity and possessing democratic-socialist leanings were attributes not shared by hardcore communists. He sincerely wanted to work with the communists but was still arrested for plotting against the government. By now, it was a familiar pattern of eliminating political opponents within a communist regime. Stalin laid the foundation with his show trials of the 1930s, and the Eastern communist authorities copied his methods of killing or imprisoning potential political rivals. To survive in this type of totalitarian system, you had to be ruthless. This was a trait that Podsednik probably did not possess. As *The Black Book of Communism* pointed out, "All the witnesses in his trial were themselves political prisoners awaiting trial." One could theorize that these prisoners had every incentive to bear false witness against the former mayor. Podsednik was still lucky. He was convicted on false charges, but only served roughly 14 years in prison and was released in 1963. Dozens of others were also arrested around the same time as Podsednik; all received prison sentences.

These are just a few examples of the notable Eastern Europeans who were falsely arrested, tried in rigged show trials, which either ended with their execution or long prison sentences. Tragically, there were many more, thousands of victims, unknown to the public, who suffered the same fate. It bears repeating, these trials were meant to showcase the power of the communist world, as directed by Moscow.

Ironically, many of the communist authorities that participated in these fraudulent miscarriages of justice were themselves arrested when a wave of communist paranoia swept Eastern Europe in 1948. It is difficult to have pity for a gangster who meets a brutal end. This is a truism; communists and wild-eyed revolutionaries always seem to eat their own.

Stalin's dead, things calm down.

In 1953, Stalin died, and Nikita Khrushchev eventually assumed the reins of power within the Soviet Union. There were still arrests, executions, and the Gulags still existed, but none were near the level of mass murder demanded by the "Boss." The Soviet Union became reluctant to use overt military action to expand communism, but it used utter ruthlessness to maintain its empire. In 1955, the USSR spearheaded the creation of the Warsaw Pact, which was a political and military alliance foisted upon the Eastern European nations. It was dominated by the Soviet Union and was seen as a counterbalance to the North Atlantic Treaty Organization (NATO). NATO was created to counter Soviet aggression in 1949. [36]

---

36 Kissinger, Henry. Diplomacy. pp. 442-443, 447-448 Courtois, Stephane, et. al. The Black Book on Communism. Pp.379, 382, 384, 398-400, 407-438. Davies, Norman. No Simple Victory. P. 274, 334-5. Davies, N. Europe. Pp. 1092-3, 1095. Medvedev, Roy. Let History Judge. Pp. 499. Gieseke, Jens. The History of the Stasi. Pp. 184, 186. White, Mathew. The Great Big Book of Horrible Things. Pp. 424. Burns, Tracy. "Milada

Post WWII: the Baltics and Eastern Europe.

The Baltic states of Lithuania, Latvia, and Estonia.

Estonia: 1919-1945.

The Baltic nations of Latvia, Lithuania, and Estonia became independent of the Russian Empire at the end of WWI. Independence was almost short-lived. Before the end of the First World War, Estonian communists attempted to take over the small Baltic country, only to be driven out by the German Imperial Army before the end of the war. The Soviets then attacked Estonia (1919-1920) and occupied a portion of the country. They carried out massacres, which included killing a Christian bishop. Many victims were "clubbed to death with axes and rifle butts— ... [and]... one officer was found with his insignia nailed to his body." Before the Bolsheviks retreated, close to 2,000 Estonians were murdered. It would be this Baltic nation's first bloody brush with communism. Twenty years later, after the outbreak of WWII, the Soviets not only annexed Estonia, but also Lithuania and Latvia. Soviet domination was short lived. In the summer of 1941, the Germans pushed the Soviets out of Estonia during Operation Barbarossa and occupied the Baltic States. By the end of the Second World War, the Baltic States were reoccupied by the Soviet Army and forcefully annexed into the USSR in 1945. (See deportations and Waffen SS)

Horakova, Executed by the Communists." Private Prague Blog. Undated. Doering, Detmar. "Milada Horakova – A Victim of Two Dictatorships." Friedrich Naumann Foundation (For Freedom). June 27, 2020.

An old Resistance fighter chooses death over arrest.

August Sabbe chose suicide rather than being arrested by the Soviet secret police the KGB. Sabbe was the last member of the Forest Brothers, a small Estonian resistance group. This partisan group refused to submit to Soviet rule, and this put August Sabbe and his comrades on the communist most-wanted list. Although the resistance group ceased its activities years earlier, the KGB still sought the arrest of the members of the Forest Brothers. By 1978, the Soviet secret police were able to locate him, and they laid a trap to arrest him. August was spotted fishing at a river, and KGB agents, posing as anglers, approached him. They were friendly at first, and one of them even photographed August with the other agent. In the photograph, Sabbe was smiling; he was enjoying himself. He had no idea he would be dead within the hour. Suddenly, the secret policemen tried to arrest him, but the old resistance fighter fought back. He and one of the agents tumbled into the river. Sabbe broke loose from his grip, and that's when he wedged himself under a submerged log, preferring to drown rather than go to a Soviet prison. This final act of August Sabbe speaks volumes about the Soviet system and its empire of totalitarianism and injustice. Just like the Soviet POWs, over thirty years earlier, who chose suicide, the old freedom fighter decided it would be better to drown himself rather than fall into the KGB's murderous hands. (See Soviet POWs)

In 1945, the Baltic States lost their independence and were annexed into the USSR. The people of these regions suffered the same brutality as other countries taken over by the USSR. They would experience the loss of freedom, a communistic economic nightmare, arrests, imprisonments, and state-sanctioned executions. The Baltic States also suffered massive deportations. (See Deportations) As the

Soviet communist system started to fall apart, Lithuania, Latvia, and Estonia declared independence in 1990. As the USSR died, so did its grip on the Baltic nations.

Eastern Europe.

Poland and Oppression: 1919 to 1990.

From the eighteenth through the end of the twentieth century, Poland experienced more than its fair share of oppression, and communism was the last link in the chain of repression the Poles would eventually break. In Winston Churchill's book, *The Hinge of Fate*, the wartime prime minister of Great Britain described the early dark days of WWII. England stood alone against the Axis forces, but as the war progressed, the "hinge" swung back in favor of the British and the Allies. Almost six years (1939-1945) elapsed before the Nazis were vanquished. Poland's "hinge of fate," which started in 1939, would not swing back in its favor for over half a century.

A kingdom in need of a fortress.

Some countries have natural barriers that deter aggressors. Great Britain is surrounded by water, and the Alps are a natural mountain fortification that encircles most of Switzerland. In contrast, Poland is devoid of geographical barriers; just open range, making the former kingdom vulnerable to attack. Furthermore, the Polish tradition of electing kings put them at a disadvantage against empires with ruthless absolutist monarchs. The kingdom would fall prey to the large empires of Prussia, Russia, and Austria, which were able to diplomatically coerce Poland out of existence. The Three Partitions of Poland (1772, 1793, and 1795) saw these three empires pressure the kingdom into ceding all its land to these aggressor nations. Poland would not gain their independence until the end of the First World War in 1918. Poland's independence was almost short-lived. The world's first communist country, the future Soviet Union, attacked Poland at the beginning of 1919. In a life-and-death struggle, the heroic Poles defeated the Bolshevik menace in 1921. Less than two decades later, Poland's independence would be snuffed out for well over half a century.

Occupation, dual, single, and final repression.

The 1939 Nazi-Soviet Non-Aggression Pact, with its secret protocols of territorial ambition, spelled doom for Poland. The Germans attacked on September 1, 1939, and the Soviets on 17th of September, which caused Poland to surrender before the end of the month. The Poles would suffer a brutal dual occupation, which became a single occupation after the Germans attacked their former Non-Aggression Pact partner. Roughly three years later, the Soviets drove the Germans from the USSR and reoccupied Poland. Fighting decimated the country and the population; now a prolonged, unremitting misery of communism was just beginning for the Poles.

The Poles' resistance against the Germans and the Soviets.

Polish resistance heroically fought against both occupying forces. Polish partisans battled the Germans from 1939 until the Nazis were driven from their country by the Soviets. In the late 1940s, the Poles carried out guerrilla warfare against the Soviet occupiers. Organized resistance to the Soviets lasted until the 1950s, and the last active partisan was killed in 1963. One of the last Polish underground soldiers died from natural causes in 1982. He had evaded capture by the Germans and the Soviets for close to 43 years.

A national sentiment of identity courses through the veins of the Poles. They had been defeated and their government had surrendered, but the Polish spirit was not broken. The historian Norman Davies wrote that Polish resistance had:

"The longest... [history]... the greatest determination, the worst press, and the least success. It traced its origins to the anti-Russian... [groups]... of the eighteenth century; and it bred an armed uprising in every generation between the Partitions of Poland and the Second World War."

Poland's "phenomenal" underground government.

Although Poland's government officially surrendered to the Nazis and the Soviets, the Poles refused to give up resisting the occupiers. Polish leaders were able to set up what has been described as a "phenomenal underground government," right under the noses of the Germans and later the Soviets. No other European resistance government approached the "level of sophistication" and "organizational complexity." This underground movement had a functioning government, laws, and courts, with an organizational structure dedicated to fighting the occupiers and aiding the populace. They supplied the numerous Polish armed resistance groups during WWII. They lived in constant fear of arrest and execution, but still carried out their mission of serving the resistance. Although they were never able to free their homeland, their persistence and bravery would inspire the likes of Lech Walesa and the Solidarity Movement, which finally achieved Poland's freedom decades later.

William Johnson

After WWII, Poland's future looked bleak.

In early May 1945, the Second World War had ended, but the cessation of hostilities brought no relief to Poland. Since Poland's independence after WWI, it has been threatened by the Soviets. The Poles were staunchly anti-communist, and they had suppressed communist groups during the interwar years. After WWII, Stalin had the Soviet secret police, with the backing of the Soviet Army, set up a Polish version of the KGB. By the end of 1945, the Polish "Minister of Public Security" (the MBP) had tens of thousands of officers and policemen, along with thousands of informers. With KGB support, the MBP, and a newly formed internal security force (KBW), fought anti-communists from 1947 through the 1950s. The fighting was lopsided, and the resistance fighters and other "opponents" of the communist government suffered, with over 10,000 killed. By the 1950s, organized resistance was snuffed out; only periodic partisan activity occurred.

Before the Polish elections of 1947, the communists used every means to seize power. The newly created Polish secret police, along with other internal security agencies, arrested close to 100,000 people. Taking their orders from Moscow, the Polish communists ramped up a massive propaganda campaign smearing political opponents of the regime. To maximize the impact of propaganda, show trials were held just before the elections. To add insult to injury, resistance fighters, who had resisted the Nazis, were put on trial on the ludicrous charges of being German collaborators. These show trials consisted of fraudulent testimony, predetermined guilty verdicts, which usually ended with lengthy sentences that were decided by party bosses.

Mass arrests, outlandish propaganda, and bogus show trials worked; the communists did well in the elections, and they achieved a lock on single-party power. (See Kill: the non-communist heroes; show the people that gallantry is futile, Eastern European Show Trials, Witold Pilecki)

Polish hero jailed with a SS General, a wartime criminal.

Kazimierz Moczarski was a Polish resistance fighter who fought the Nazis occupation. In 1945, he was imprisoned by the Soviets on fraudulent charges. In a bid to demoralize him, he was incarcerated in the same prison cell with Nazi SS General, Jurgen Stroop, who had been responsible for destroying "the Warsaw ghetto in 1943." Miraculously, he survived years of confinement and wrote a book about his experiences. He recorded 49 different torture methods used against him, which included confining him for over six years in a cell so small that he could neither walk, nor could he stand up. Kazimierz was also kept in solitary confinement for over 4 years and was not allowed to bathe for almost 3 years. He endured torture, such as beatings with a variety of objects, burns, the ripping out of his hair, and sleep deprivation. Kazimierz said the sleep deprivation was the most nightmarish of all the tortures he endured. It entailed forcing him to stand for several days, and if he dozed off, he would be struck in the face. He was lucky to have survived.

1948, the "generalized terror."

In 1948, Poland and other Eastern European nations behind the "Iron Curtain" experienced another wave of persecution, after Yugoslavia broke diplomatic relations with the Soviets. Stalin ordered a "generalized terror" that was carried out throughout the Eastern Bloc. This "intensification of the class struggle..." entailed the arrest of thousands of innocent Polish citizens. Furthermore, communist officials who were deemed unworthy were also imprisoned or executed. By 1954, well over 100,000 had been arrested, and over

84,000 were sent to forced labor camps. The Polish "Security Services had also developed files on 5.2 million individuals, one-third of the adult population." Any mundane action could land you in prison, let alone an actual act of defiance against the state. "Freedom of action" was forbidden. *The Black Book of Communism* noted "the main function... of generalized terror was the diffusion throughout society of a feeling of permanent fear..."

Points to Ponder: What happened to Poland's history?

The movie, *National Treasure*, starring Nicolas Cage, involved thieves stealing the Declaration of Independence, so they could find clues from this historic American document. From these hidden clues, the thieves would try and retrieve a treasure trove of precious artifacts, hidden by the American founding fathers. Aside from the discovery of legendary antiquities, the movie illustrates the extensive level of security used by the National Archives to safeguard the Declaration of Independence. The movie was fiction, but the central idea of protecting a country's history is valid. If a nation loses its historical and cultural documentation, it could possibly lose its national identity. Historical primary sources serve as a bedrock that bridges the past to the present.

In ancient times, when an empire was toppled, the first thing the conquerors did was loot the treasury. The Soviets understood this fact all too well. After the Third Partition of Poland, the Russian army carted away much of the kingdom's historical documents and papers. After a century and a half, history would repeat itself when the Soviets plundered Poland's archives once again. After the fall of the Soviet Union, Poland was able to recover part of their recorded history. Fortunately, the Soviets' dastardly act of destroying Polish identity failed. It should be noted that in the United States, some educational institutions are still active pushing CRT (Critical Race Theory), which radically distorts American history. Liberal professors at universities and some teachers malign U.S. history. It could be argued that America is losing its historical heritage from within. (Please see the foreword of this book.)

Solidarity and Lech Walesa.

Norman Davies pointed out that the communist authorities were never able to completely break the Polish people. Authorities were reluctant to use overt force, such as mass arrests, torture, and lengthy prison sentences. Although the Polish communists dominated the country, many different groups, including the Catholic Church, small landholders, intellectuals, and many others, refused to knuckle under. The Poles remained non-compliant, and many did not embrace Marxism. Large protests and strikes did occur in 1956, 1970, and 1976, which would have been unthinkable in 1948. After the mid-1950s, Poland's large-scale, skilled industrialized labor force would evolve into a political force to be reckoned with.

By the 1980s, the trade union, *Solidarity,* was pushing for more economic compensation and political freedoms for Polish workers. Ironically, the trade union movement started in the **Lenin Shipyards** in Gdansk, Poland. Solidarity became an autonomous organization, which would have been forbidden by most communist governments. Lech Walesa was an unemployed electrician who led the noncommunist group. Solidarity's ranks swelled to ten million members, which was "more than four times the rolls of the Polish Communist Party." The trade union also had the support of the Polish Pope John Paul II. The support from the leader of the Catholic Church provided extra weight of moral authority. The Polish people chose faith over Marxism.

Although the communist authorities negotiated with *Solidarity*, they still infiltrated informers into the trade union. The movement, with its millions of members, alarmed the communist authorities within the Warsaw Pact. East Germany, Czechoslovakia, and the USSR contemplated mobilizing their own security forces to intervene in Poland. Polish authorities did crack down on *Solidarity* in 1981. Dozens were killed, and there were mass arrests, and over ten thousand people were imprisoned, but the independence movement was not broken. The days of communist domination of Poland were numbered.

Former Secretary of State Henry Kissinger noted the economic failures of communism and peoples' yearning for freedom were powerful forces within Poland (and the rest of Eastern Europe). Martial law that had been implemented in 1981 was lifted the next year. Sporadic attempts at quashing members of *Solidarity* failed, and in 1989, authorities began negotiations with the trade union. Elections were held, and the communists lost. By 1991, the last vestiges of communism were pushed out of the Polish government by democratic means.

Points to Ponder: The Miracle at Fatima and John Paul II.

At times, history is linked by the most tenuous of threads. It would be one of these tenuous historical threads which connected a miracle that occurred during WWI, the rise of Soviet Russia, and the eventual fall of Communism.

Fatima.

In the spring of 1917, three illiterate peasant children claimed to have witnessed on several different occasions a miracle at Fatima, Portugal. The children professed to have seen an apparition of the

Virgin Mary in the sky outside the town. Over the next several months, thousands of people made a pilgrimage to Fatima. There are photographs of crowds of people, many of whom are pointing to the sky. They seem to be looking at something extraordinary. The miracle at Fatima seemed providential; the Central Powers and the Allies were still slaughtering each other during WWI. Lucia dos Santos, the eldest child, maintained that the apparition told her that she was "the Lady of the Rosary." The vision warned of the coming of the Antichrist, and the threat would come from Russia, but if consecrated **"to my Immaculate Heart...there will be peace." The vision cautioned that if Russia was not consecrated, the country's transgressions would engulf the world, "provoking wars and persecution of the Church... But in the end, My Immaculate Heart will triumph."** The Bolshevik coup in Russia occurred in November of 1917, and they were able to successfully take over the former Czarist Empire.

Over twenty years later, WWII was raging when the Allies gathered at the Yalta Conference in the Soviet Union. Stalin was asked a question about the Papacy. The "Boss" could not conceal his contempt for the Vatican and religion when he quipped, "How many divisions has the Pope?" Indeed, the atheistic Soviets spent a considerable amount of time and energy trying to destroy people's faith in God. Ironically, approximately four decades later, the USSR's greatest challenge would stem in part from religion, and the faith and tenacity of a Polish Pope, **"provoking wars and persecution of the Church."**

John Paul II.

On October 16, 1978, Poland's Cardinal Karol Wojtyla became Pope John Paul II. He was an ardent anti-communist and a foe of the Soviet Union. This new Pope was a public supporter of *Solidarity*, and he was wildly popular with the Polish people. When he visited Poland in the summer of 1979, millions of people lined the streets to cheer him. Soviet authorities were so concerned with the pontiff's popularity that they tried to infiltrate spies into his entourage and disrupt his papal visits to other countries. The KGB even tried planting false stories (active measures) about John Paul II, but none of these dirty tricks worked. Papal support for *Solidarity*, even after the crackdown, did not diminish this movement.

The attempted assassination of John Paul II.

On May 13th, 1981, a Turk, Mehmet Ali Agca, shot John Paul II in Rome. The bullet came close to hitting a major artery, and it was considered a small miracle that the Pope did not succumb to his wound. John Paul credited his full recovery to the medical doctors and his prayers to "Our Lady of the Rosary." John Paul II would later make a pilgrimage to Fatima. The Polish pontiff prayed in the church that had been built on the site, in which the three peasant children had witnessed the miracle. The would-be assassin, Ali Agca, was said to have ties with "the Bulgarian secret services…" Furthermore, the Mitrokhin files have documentation that Bulgarians agents have, at times, carried out covert operations with the Soviet KGB. Ultimately, there is no definitive proof that the Bulgarians and the Soviets orchestrated the assassination attempt on John Paul II. Less than a decade later, the Soviet Union collapsed, and the "Iron Curtain" separating Eastern Europe from the West was torn down. **"But in the end, my Immaculate Heart will triumph."** Sometimes history is bound by the most tenuous of threads. You decide. [37]

---

[37] National Geographic, Vol. 178, No. 5. "The Baltic Nations". November 1990. P. 10-11. Courtois, Stephane, et. al. The Black Book on Communism. pp. 363-391. Wolek, Karol. "Post-war. The Years of 1944-1963 in Poland." The Warsaw Institute Review. Oct. 1, 2018. Online Ret. Kissinger, Henry. Diplomacy. Pp. 447, 793,794. During the 1830s,

The German Democratic Republic, or communist East Germany.

The German Democratic Republic (GDR) or communist East Germany lasted from 1949 to 1990. After the defeat of the Nazis, the victorious Allies created four occupation zones in Germany: French, British, American, and Soviet. As friction developed between the Soviets and the Allies over the future of post-war Germany, the Americans, British, and the French consolidated their respective zones of occupation. The Soviets retained their occupation zone, the eastern part of Germany, which included part of Berlin. Within their zone, the Soviets began to immediately set up a German version of the USSR. East Germany went from a fascist to a communist surrogate of the Soviet Union. The transition was quick; the Soviets set up a communist government, with a communist version of the Gestapo (Nazi secret police), the Stasi.

Europe was rocked by the outbreak of multiple revolutionary uprisings and the Poles were part of this continental independence movement. In 1830, the Russian Empire controlled part of what is considered part of modern Poland. These two Polish freedom fighters are examples of heroic individuals, who were part of this resistance. In 1831, Jozef Sowinski, a one-legged Polish general, was killed fighting the Russians. In keeping with his wishes, his compatriots placed "his wooden leg'...[upright]...in the Polish soil, so as not to bow to tyrants.'" In the same year, a patriotic noblewoman, "(Emilia Plater, 1806-1831)" donned a military uniform and was killed in action against the Russians. Davies, Norman. Europe. pp. 660, 661, 663, 679, 701, 732, **826**, **917**,1107, 1108, 1122, 1123. For looting treasuries during antiquity see this text, Wickham, Chris. The Inheritance of Rome. P.380-381. Jennings, Peter and Brewster, Todd. The Century. Pp.471. Utracka, Katarzyna. "The Phenomenon of the Polish Underground State." The Warsaw Institute Review. December 4th, 2019. Retrieved May 26th, 2023. Andrew, C. & Mitrokhin, V. The Sword and the Shield. 508-523. Andrew, C. & Mitrokhin, V. The World was Going our Way: The KGB And the Third World. Pp. 126, 242-3, 487. Moore, Charles. Margaret Thatcher the Authorized Biography. Pp. 633. Davies, N. No Simple Victory. Pp.13, 32, 53, 57, 78-79, 137, 138, 272, 480.

The East German communist Gestapo: the Stasi.

The *Black Book of Communism* noted that "in 1939 the Gestapo employed 7,500 people," while the communist East German Stasi had 90,000 security personnel. At its peak, East Germany had a population of a little over 18 million. It is estimated that one out of every seven persons was an informer. When the GDR collapsed in 1990, the Stasi archives were opened to the public. People were shocked to discover the vast network of informers employed by the East German security apparatus. One newspaper noted that the GDR was a "nation of traitors."

One must contemplate the corrosive effect of communism on the human spirit, which drove people to inform on others. Furthermore, anybody nursing a grudge against another could fabricate lies that could destroy an individual's life and land them in prison on baseless charges.

Some Stasi officials wanted to institute "blanket surveillance," which would include formal and informal informers. This also included a variety of different electronic surveillance options, along with actual security personnel spying on the populace. The amount of documentation accumulated by the Stasi was astronomical. One source indicated that if all the communist files were laid out, it would cover almost 70 square miles. Warehouses were crammed with note cards, audio and video recordings, and reports. They were literally drowning in data. Such was the level of communist mistrust of the populace.

East Germany communists; loyal minions to the USSR.

In Soviet-controlled countries, there were always those who were willing participants in totalitarian coercion, and the East Germans communist authorities did the bidding of their Soviet overlords. They contributed soldiers who helped crush the Hungarian uprising in 1956, the Czech uprising in 1968, and had contemplated sending troops into Poland in 1980.

East Germany also exported the Stasi's technical expertise in secret policing to other communist regimes in Africa and Nicaragua. They gave instruction in surveillance, torture, interrogation techniques, and a myriad of other aspects involving secret policing. East German spies were active throughout Europe, the Western Hemisphere, and Africa.

The GDR aided and abetted terrorist gangs such as the Baader Meinhof, various Middle Eastern terrorist groups, and Carlos (Ilyich Ramirez Sanchez), the Jackal. In one case, the East Germans provided technical expertise to Libyan terrorists who bombed a German disco, killing US military personal.

East German authorities directed their athletes to use performance-enhancing drugs so they could excel and win awards in international sporting events. The GDR bragged about the superiority of their athletic programs, when the reality was that their success was linked to a state-sponsored doping campaign. The doping campaign allowed the communist regime to rack up an impressive number of medals in several Olympics, only to have these victories declared invalid in later years, and this does not take into consideration the lives of athletes ruined by the communist drug doping program.

Living on the barest of essentials.

In the final days of Ethiopia's Marxist regime in 1990, Soviet envoys met with the African leader, Mengistu Haile Mariam. As they were driving through the capital of Addis Ababa, they passed a half-finished building that would have become the headquarters for Ethiopia's version of the East German Stasi. When the GDR collapsed, so did construction of the secret police headquarters. One must contemplate the amount of money and resources poured into this half-finished building and all the other East German endeavors in Africa and other parts of the world. How long did East Germans have to labor to create the funds that were squandered by the communist regime? It begs the question, why weren't these resources spent in East Germany? Note. US overseas involvement should contemplate East German folly.

The communists provided the bare necessities for life: food, shelter, and rudimentary health care, but discontent in the GDR ran deep. In June of 1953, Soviet troops and tanks crushed a small revolt led by East German workers, who rebelled against working and living conditions. It is estimated that approximately 100 East Germans were killed. With no political outlet and being simultaneously subjected to totalitarian rule from Moscow, East Germans sought their own solution: escape to Western Germany.

The Berlin Wall.

One of the few enduring historical icons of communist East Germany was the Berlin Wall. It was built in the summer of 1961 and epitomized the notion of the Iron Curtain. Since the inception of the GDR, Germans living in the communist sector tried to flee to West Germany. The communists claimed the wall was to thwart an invasion by the West, but this claim was ludicrous. The wall was to keep people in East Germany. Eventually, the wall obstacles included barbed wire, ditches, landmines, towers, and armed guards with orders to shoot to kill. Over seven hundred men, women, and children were killed while trying to escape. After the fall of East Germany, guards who killed people fleeing were put on trial. Several were convicted and given prison sentences. A 2007 Wall Street Journal article reported on a tremendous number of secret East German documents that proved that communist authorities had officially sanctioned shoot-to-kill orders. In the past, communist authorities had insisted that "shoot to kill" had never been the East German policy. In one document, the authorities wrote, "Do not hesitate to use your firearm, not even when the border is breached in the company of women, and children, which the traitors have often used to their advantage..." East Germans, yearning to be free, risked their lives to gain their freedom. It begs the question. If communism was so wonderful, why would anyone want to run from the workers' paradise?

The end of East Germany.

After East and West Germany were split, the fortunes of the two areas diverged. West Germany emerged from the ashes of the Second World War. It became economically powerful, while East Germany (DDR) became an appendage of the USSR, a vassal state of the Soviet Union. As communism began to crumble at the end of the 1980s, the East Germans were not zealously guarding the Berlin Wall. In 1989, miscommunication between East German officials, concerning the comings and goings through the Berlin Wall entrance, coupled with a guard's interpretation or misinterpretation of an order, threw the border open to east-west crossings. By 1990, East Germany was gone, and this area was reunited with the western part of Germany. The final irony, it would take capitalistic West German money to pay for the failed communist East German state to be reunited into one nation.

The final numbers.

After the fall of the DDR, the archives were opened to historians, who examined the records, and the butcher bill was clear. *The Black*

Book of Communism noted that after WWII, the "Soviets... [imprisoned]... 122,000 in their zone in between 1945-1950, 43,000 ... died ... and 736 were executed." The East German communists imprisoned between "40,000 to 60,000..." In East Germany, people were executed and imprisoned, but never came close to the mass murder that occurred in the USSR.[38]

Hungary: 1940 through 1990.

After the outbreak of the Second World War, Hungary diplomatically aligned itself with Germany, but by 1944, the fortunes of war had turned against the Axis. The Soviet Armies had pushed the Nazis out of the USSR; captured Poland, Romania, Bulgaria, and Hungary was next. Hitler had other ideas. Before the Soviets could attack Hungary, the Germans staged a coup, overthrowing the Hungarian government.

By the end of 1944, the Soviet Army attacked Hungary, and the capture of the country hinged on taking the capital of Budapest. Axis resistance was fierce, and the fighting brutal. After a four-month siege of the capital, Budapest was captured by the end of February 1945. Parts of the capital were destroyed, and the death toll for civilians and soldiers on both sides was high. Some 100,000 German soldiers

---

38 Courtois, Stephane, et. al. The Black Book of Communism. Pp. 357-358, 359, 388, 389, 400, 408, 446, Assisting with secret police training. 670, 685,690. "Shoot to Kill." Wall Street Journal. August 17, 2007. Pp. A # 12. Williams, Laura. "Ten terrifying facts about the East German Secret Police." FEE Stories. Nov. 14, 2019. Ungerleider, Steven. Faust's Gold. Inside the East German Doping Machine. Pp. 1-250. Andrew, C. & Mitrokhin, V. The World was Going Our Way. international terrorism. Pp. 256, 257, Stasi building project in Ethiopia, 478. Davies, N. Europe. Pp. 1123. Gieseke, Jens. The History of the Stasi. Pp. 48-122. Kennedy, Paul. Rise and Fall of the Great Powers. Pp. 379, 509. White, Mathew. The Great Big Book of Horrible Things. Pp. 390.

Murderous Marxism

surrendered, and the Soviets summarily executed 16,000 Axis troops on the streets of Budapest. Soon, all of Hungary was in Soviet hands.

Once the Soviets captured Hungary, a wave of communist instigated violence and repression swept the country. Since the Hungarian had aligned with Germany and fiercely resisted the Soviets during the war, the USSR enacted draconian reprisals against the Eastern European country. A Moscow-backed leader, Laszlo Rajk, moved quickly to set up the Hungarian version of the secret police, the State Protection Authority, which was known by the acronym AVH. The new Hungarian version of the "Gestapo" began immediately harassing and arresting non-communists. The Soviets carried out a massive deportation campaign and forcibly removed 600,000 Hungarians to labor and prison camps. It was not until after the fall of the USSR, and the opening of their archives, did the true magnitude of the Soviet deportations was revealed. Probably close to one out of three never returned. More history down the memory black hole. (See Soviet Deportations).

Even with the chaos, the mass arrests, and deportations, the Moscow-backed communists did not gain a majority within the Hungarian government after an election in 1945. The Smallholders' Party was able to garner almost 60% of the votes, but their political victory was short-lived. The local communists utilized the Soviet playbook of creating a fictitious enemy when none existed. Given the results of the 1945 elections, the Smallholders' Party became the new fictitious enemy for the communists. By the beginning of 1947, Laszlo Rajk had declared that the Smallholders' Party had been plotting against the government. State propaganda condemned the political group, and the newly created Hungarian secret police (AVH) started arresting Smallholders' Party leaders. Show trials were held, and many of the party's top leadership was falsely convicted and executed. Lower-level party members received lengthy prison terms. After crushing the Smallholders' Party, the communists forcibly shut down the Independence Party and the People's Democratic Party. This overt show of force achieved its goal of cowing the populace. Fearing arrests, democratic leaders either fled Hungary or were imprisoned.

Blind obedience to Moscow was no assurance of a long political career in a communist regime. Although Laszlo Rajk was a loyal minion, he still suffered the same fate as other communist leaders; he was marked for elimination. Although he organized the creation of the AVH and destroyed the Smallholders' Party, he was still purged. Rajk was arrested on false charges, convicted in a bogus trial, and executed in 1949. Communists always eat their own.

Communist Control starts to falter.

Their economic policies of the communists began to fail in Eastern Europe, and by 1953, East German workers had engaged in a small revolt that was quickly put down. A month later, Hungarian communist leaders were "summoned" to the USSR. Soviet authorities questioned the Hungarians' strict adherence to "Stalinist economic policy…" The Soviets warned that such policies could damage Hungary's economy, making it impossible to provide a good living standard for the people while undermining their faith in communism. Over three years later, Moscow's warnings would come true.

Points to Ponder: Blood in the Pool.

During the 1956 Olympics in Melbourne, Australia, a water polo match between the Soviets and Hungarians clearly demonstrated the deep-seated animosity between the two communist countries. The

Hungarians handily won the match, 4-0. Both sides exchanged punches, kicks, and curses. The match culminated with a Soviet player sucker punching a Hungarian player, opening a bloody gash over his eye. Spectators became so outraged at the Soviet polo player that authorities had to clear the arena. As the bloodied Hungarian polo player was led away to get medical attention, a photographer captured the image, which was seen around the world in magazines and newspapers. The Soviets lost twice that day.

Fast forward, twenty-four years, the United States, Communist China, Canada, West Germany, and a host of other nations boycotted the 1980 Olympics in Moscow, because of the Soviet invasion of Afghanistan in 1979.

The Hungarian Uprising of 1956.

On October 23, 1956, Hungarians revolted against Soviet control. They were fed up with communist repression and a state-controlled economy. Hundreds of thousands of people took to the streets, expressing their rage against the Soviet-backed communism in Hungary. A rising national sentiment was rippling through Eastern Europe, and Hungarians were clamoring for independence and free elections. What started as a college student protest in Budapest snowballed into an uprising when Hungarian secret police fired upon protesters. The next day, Soviet soldiers and tanks moved into Budapest and other areas of Hungary to crush a popular uprising. Initially, the Soviet Army stationed in Hungary was not successful in quelling the Hungarian protests.

Towards the end of October, Moscow became so alarmed at the escalation of protests, the Soviet leadership dispatched KGB Chairman Ivan Serov to take charge of the situation in Hungary. The KGB chief had quite the reputation. During WWII, Serov demonstrated his brutal effectiveness when he supervised the deportations of 100,000s of people. Most of the deportees never returned to their homes.

When Serov met with Hungarians authorities, he berated them for not shooting the protesters. The KGB head screamed that they had let "fascists and imperialists... bring... in their shock troops..." Budapest Police Chief, Sandor Kopacsi, was present at the meeting, and he bristled at the accusations hurled by the Soviet KGB chief. Kopacsi responded to Serov, saying, "these are not 'fascist' or... 'imperialists'" they come from the universities, the handpicked sons and daughters of the peasants and workers... demanding... rights." Kopacsi was later arrested and put on trial with the former Premier Imre Nagy. He was given a life sentence in 1958 but was paroled under a general amnesty in 1963. He was lucky; other Hungarian communists who refused to support the brutal crack down on the protesters paid with their lives.

By the end of October, protesters became freedom fighters, but their bid for independence was short-lived. Hungarians attacked government authorities and Soviet forces, seizing weapons, killing soldiers, and knocking out tanks with petrol bombs. Photographers not only captured images of armed civilians and destroyed Soviet equipment, but also of the hated Hungarian secret policemen (AVH) being hunted down and killed on the streets. In one series of photographs, close to half a dozen secret policemen were herded against a wall and shot. The images clearly show AVH policemen flinching as the bullets slammed into them; other photographs show lynched secret policemen.

In 1956, Hungary was still occupied by the Soviets, and their military units were stationed throughout the country. While most of the Hungarian Army "sat on the sidelines," protesters battled AVH units and the Soviet military. By November 3, 1956, the Soviets sent multiple divisions of infantry and armor into Hungary. The freedom fighters were blasted with heavy artillery and tank fire, and the infantry mopped up the rest. By the 6th of November, most of the intense fighting had died down. The remaining small groups of resistance held out until mid-November.

Aftermath.

The rebelling Hungarians killed dozens of Hungarian secret police and several hundred Soviet soldiers. Hungarian rebels suffered approximately 3000 killed, and almost 15,000 wounded. Several hundred were summarily executed without trial. Although Hungarian leadership promised leniency for the protesters, they lied. With the help of Soviet military police, the AVH rounded up tens of thousands of people, of whom 35,000 were tried and 22,000 were given prison terms. Some 229 Hungarians were sentenced to death, and thousands more were sent to the Soviet Union; 200,000 fled the country.

Imre Nagy.

Imre Nagy was an influential communist politician who held several important posts within post-war Hungary. Nagy had quite the communist pedigree. He had been in the Austrian Army during WWI and was captured by the Russian Army. He was still in Russia when the revolution broke out, and he joined the Bolsheviks. After the revolution, Nagy returned to Hungary, and after several years, he returned to the USSR. After the Soviet forces captured Hungary in 1945, Nagy returned to Hungary and held several positions, including speaker of the parliament and later Prime Minister of Hungary under the new Communist government in 1953.

Nagy and the uprising.

By the time of the Hungarian Uprising, Imre Nagy had been pushed out of politics by Soviet authorities. He was ousted for publishing a treatise suggesting that Hungary could find a new path in the socialist-Marxist world. Nagy was once a hardcore communist, but he became disillusioned with Soviet rule. As the uprising unfolded, protesters called for Nagy to become the premier, and he assumed the mantle of power and the communist government was shoved aside. Nagy's assumption of power was complicated. For the moment, he was premier, but members of the Hungarian government were engaged in back-channel communications amongst themselves and the Soviet authorities. There were still communists within Hungary that did not want to see democratic rule, and the USSR was eager to preserve the Soviet backed communist bloc.

Nagy's arrest and brutal execution.

After the uprising was crushed, Nagy sought asylum in the Yugoslavian embassy in Budapest. His support of the uprising and his refusal to recognize the Soviet hand-picked leadership in Hungary sealed his fate. Nagy and several other protest leaders had been offered safe passage from the Yugoslavian Embassy, but it was a ruse. They were snatched up by the Soviets and whisked away to Romania. The initial success of the uprising unnerved the Soviets, and they were taking no chances. From the end of 1956 to 1958, Nagy was imprisoned and held incommunicado, along with the other defendants. He was tortured and denied any legal counsel during his confinement. At the beginning of 1958, Nagy and the other defendants were returned to Hungary, and it was only then that they were informed of the charges against them. Hungarian authorities were reluctant to have a show trial for Nagy and the other defendants because it "might inflame the people in the wrong direction." To avoid negative publicity, a secret trial was held, and Nagy was convicted and hung. It was only then that the Hungarian public was informed of the trial and execution. There were nine other prominent Hungarians tried along with Nagy. Pal Maleter, Miklos Gimes were also executed, and the others received lengthy prison sentences.

Pal Maleter.

Pal Maleter had been a commander in the Hungarian Army at the time of the uprising. During WWII, he had fought with a small band of anti-fascist fighters against the Hungarian and German forces. He also backed the early communist regime after the country was captured by the Soviets in 1945. Over time, Pal had also become disheartened with Soviet repression. During the uprising, Maleter led military units against the protestors, but instead of using lethal force, he met with some of the protestors. A photographer captured the moment. Maleter, a tall man with chiseled features, can be seen intently listening to the protesters. From these images, one could infer that the military leader and the protestors had found some common ground. Instead of coercion, Maleter probably contemplated a political settlement that would be the best outcome for all concerned. This act of tolerance, captured on film, probably doomed the Hungarian military leader.

Betrayal; mock executions, then the real thing.

A month after KBG Chief Ivan Serov arrived in Budapest, the Soviet secret police planned to arrest several high-ranking Hungarian military officials, including Pal Maleter. In early November 1956, the Hungarians were lured to a meeting at the Tokol military base, on the pretense that they would be discussing the withdraw of the Soviet

Army. For several hours, both sides held cordial talks, when suddenly, KGB Chairman Serov burst into the room brandishing a pistol. The Hungarians were taken into custody at gunpoint. They were separated and subjected to mock executions. Each one of the Hungarian officials had been convinced that their colleagues had been executed. Maleter would remain in custody until his execution in 1958. One of the few remembrances of Pal Maleter is a statue in the city of Tokol.

Miklos Gimes.

From the end of WWII until 1955, Miklos Gimes had been a writer for the Hungarian Communist Party. He had been described as a "dedicated supporter of the regime… a fanatical, ruthless Stalinist." The system rewarded this wild-eyed supporter with luxuries and perks. Then something happened. This implacable supporter of communism changed. The temperamental journalist, who had used his writing talents to criticize capitalism and the West, now turned his ire against communism. Profound reflection upon events he witnessed behind the Iron Curtain and his travels to the West undermined his faith in this coercive system. He was an idealist whose opinions evolved. After the uprising, Gimes started a publication that dared to question communism and Soviet control. Gimes suffered the same fate as Nagy and Maleter.

Where were the bodies?

Some thirty years later, as the communist system across Eastern Europe was beginning to fall apart, a Hungarian civil rights lawyer pushed to reopen Nagy's case. In the process, he was able to discover information about the secret burial of Nagy, Maleter, and Gimes. After their execution in 1958, their bodies were buried in a Budapest prison. Pressure from the families to return the remains so unsettled the communist authorities that they had the bodies disinterred and secretly reburied in 1961. Authorities were so obsessed with concealing the location of the remains that they engaged in a clandestine operation, in which the bodies were moved in the dead of night. Without the knowledge of cemetery personnel, communist goons passed the bodies over a wall of the cemetery and buried them under false names. Family members were able to discover the new burial site, and they erected gravestones in a part of the cemetery they believed contained the bodies. Several times, the police ran off the family members and "knocked down the stones... trampling them with horses." As communism died in Hungary, so did the ability of the officials to conceal Nagy, Maleter, and Gimes's unmarked graves. By 1989, the bodies were finally located and reburied.

Points to Ponder: Why weren't the bodies destroyed?

Final footnote: It was quite common in the Stalin era to cremate the bodies of executed political rivals and dump the ashes in unmarked pits. The Hungarians authorities did not do that. They chose to bury the three and keep track of their unmarked graves. Communist officials probably understood that destroying the remains of these three men would be extremely unpopular.

The final analysis of Nagy, Maleter, and Gimes.

Nagy, Maleter, and Games had been ardent communists. Nagy had a long history of being a leading communist official. Maleter was an anti-fascist fighter who initially supported the Soviet backed government after the war. Gimes was a wild-eyed idealist drawn to the concept of communism. The abject repression and treachery of the Soviet Union stripped away their blinders. They saw the USSR for what it was, an "Evil Empire." The 1956 uprising brought all these frustrations to a head when these former communists rejected the very system they initially supported. It would have been easy to toe the line and survive. They chose otherwise, and in the process, they sealed their own fate. It is said that some are born to greatness, and some have greatness thrust upon them. For Nagy, Maleter, and Gimes, it was the latter. They should be remembered.

The end of Hungarian communism.

In 1956, Soviet firepower and treachery maintained their control over Hungary, but the rot persisted. The USSR was not interested in winning over the hearts and minds of the people it ruled. Over three decades after the revolt, the "Hungarian People's Republic was abolished." Once communist officials allowed other parties into the government and submitted to popular elections, they were no longer the rulers. In 1989, Hungarian courts reviewed the case against Nagy and the others; all were exonerated. On June 16, 1989, on the thirty-first anniversary of their execution, a long-overdue funeral was held, and some 200,000 people attended. Marxism and communism were dead in Hungary.

Points to Ponder: Rehabilitation.

Rehabilitation was a strange official political declaration used in the former Soviet Union and other communist states. It usually entailed an official admission that the communist state had made an error by condemning an innocent victim to death, imprisonment, or having their government status diminished. Not all people who were rehabilitated were innocent; some were outright savages. Communist authorities would issue a declaration stating that the victim was not guilty or rehabilitated. A stroke of a pen would restore a person's reputation and rank. Of course, the dead cannot come back to life, and

Murderous Marxism

a prisoner cannot have back the years they served in the GULAG. No communist official was put on trial for judicial misconduct, let alone imprisoned. Nobody was allowed to sue the state, just accept an empty, meaningless gesture, which ironically embodies communism.

After the death of Stalin, hundreds of thousands of these empty statements were issued. There were some tragic stories connected to those who were officially rehabilitated in the USSR. In two separate incidents, KGB interrogators dropped dead when they encountered rehabilitated prisoners, they had brutalized. In another incident, a rehabilitated victim had a heart attack and died when he encountered his torturer. In yet another case, a rehabilitated military officer shot and killed a KGB agent who had tortured him. Then there was the sad story of a widow of one of Stalin's victims. When a Soviet official called and informed the woman that her husband had been rehabilitated, she dropped dead from a heart attack. When authorities discovered her, she still had the phone receiver in her hand. [39]

---

39 Davies, N. No Simple Victory. Pp. 17, 121, 166, 288-9, 304, Courtois, Stephane, et. al. The Black Book of Communism. p. 217, 394-5, 397, 398-400, 413, 414-5, 417, 418, 423, 426, 428, 435, 438, 441, 449. Historically, the Russians Empire had victimized Hungary. Over a century earlier, the Russian Army had marched in and crushed the Hungarian revolution against the Austrian Empire in 1848. Kissinger, Henry. Diplomacy. Pp. 550, 551, 555, 557, 556, 558, 561, 562, 566, 567. Kennedy, Paul. The Rise and Fall of the Great Power. Pp. 160, 172, 379. Acheson, Dean. Present at the Creation. pp. 727. Andrew, C. Mitrokhin. The Sword and the Shield. 248-249, 251. Hollander, Paul. The End of Commitment. pp. 69, 70, 80, 81, 83-90. Davies, N. Europe. 1123. Schecter, Jerrold & Luchkov, Vyacheslav. Khrushchev Remembers: The Glasnost Tapes. Pp.121-127. Sandor Kopacsi was the Hungarian Police Chief threatened by KBG Chairman Serov at the beginning of the uprising for voicing his opinion. He was tried along with Nagy, and sentenced to life, but was later released under a general amnesty in 1963. Dornbach, Alajos. The Secret Trial of Imre Nagy. pp. 6,7, 14,15, 19, 24, 67, 68, 69,78-81,103,104,105,121, 148, 150,151, 119-160, 161,164,166, 176, 185-190. Roos, Dave. "'Blood in the Water': The Cold War Olympic Showdown Between Hungary and the USSR." The History Channel. June 4th, 2021. Medvedev, Roy, Zhores. The Unknown Stalin: His Life, Death, and Legacy. Pp. 114-118. Medvedev, Roy. Let History Judge. Pp.

Czechoslovakia

The state of Czechoslovakia, like Hungary, had been part of the Austrian Empire, and gained its independence after the First World War. As mentioned before, Hitler demanded the annexation of eastern Czechoslovakia, and Britain and France knuckled under and allowed Germany to take the Sudetenland in 1938. Later, the Germans would occupy most of Czechoslovakia. During the war, the Czech resistance was active during the German occupation. Probably the most dramatic action taken by the Czech resistance was the assassination of one of Hitler's main thugs, SS Obergruppenführer Reinhard Heydrich. In contrast, Slovakia aligned itself with the Nazis.

Czechoslovakia was one of the last Eastern European countries captured by the Soviets. Before the Soviets occupied the capital of Prague, Czech resistance fighters revolted against the German forces. A division of Soviet POWs that had fought for the German Army turned on the Nazis and helped liberate Prague. Helping liberate Prague curried no favor with the Soviet military authorities. Almost all the former Soviet POWs were immediately dispatched to the GULAG, and most of the officers were executed.

Post-War: the Communist Coup.

Unlike other Eastern European countries, Czechoslovakia did not suppress communist participation in politics. In 1946, the communists won the elections in the Czech part of the country but lost in Slovakia. The communists were not interested in democratically sharing power. In February of 1948, the communists staged a coup and toppled the

---

377, 387, 466-469. Vronskaya, Jeanne, Chuguev, Vladimir. A Biographical Dictionary of the Soviet Union 1917-1988. Pp. 375.

Czechoslovakian government. The communist takeover was punctuated by the mysterious demise of the "noncommunist Foreign Minister Jan Masaryk," who plunged to his death from an office window. Former U.S. Secretary of State Henry Kissinger concluded that Masaryk was "almost certainly pushed by communist thugs."

Czechoslovakia, the arsenal of repression.

Czechoslovakia was a coveted land for its natural resources, industrialization, and highly skilled labor force. These factors were a primary reason the Nazis annexed Czechoslovakia in the late 1930s, and the Soviets probably realized the value of snatching up the country. By the beginning of 1948, the Soviets prioritized armaments production in Czechoslovakia, and weapon manufacturing skyrocketed between 1948 through 1953. Furthermore, the Czech defense budget grew by a factor of ten, and Moscow's dictates also doubled the size of the Czechoslovakian armed forces to almost 300,000 military personnel for the 'inevitable war' with the West. Soviet mandates transformed Czechoslovakia into an arsenal for repression, which supplied the other Warsaw Pact countries.

Repression in Czechoslovakia.

The Czech communists used the same brutal tactics, which were utilized throughout the rest of Eastern Europe. Terrorizing the populace, rigged courts, executions, and imprisonments. The KGB facilitated the creation of the Czechoslovakian State Security, the StB. By the mid-1950s, the StB had recruited almost 200,000 informers to spy on the populace. There were also the high-profile show trials of Milada Horakova, General Heliodor Pika, and Josef Podsenik, along with numerous other non-communist politicians and government officials. Milada Horakova's case was especially tragic because she posed absolutely no threat. She was arrested, convicted and "judicially murdered" by the communists. (See Kill: the non-communist heroes; show the people that gallantry is futile, Eastern European Show Trials)

Once again, the communists began eating their own. One of those marked for elimination was the Secretary General of the Communist Party, Rudolf Slansky. The Secretary General was set up by a party official, who was supposedly a friend. He was arrested by the StB, along with other local party members. All were tortured and put on trial. It should be noted that during the trial, a discernable undercurrent of anti-Semitism was espoused by court officials, especially the judge who kept noting that Slansky was Jewish. He was convicted and later executed in 1952. In the wake of the Secretary General's trial, there were more arrests of communist loyalists; executions and long prison terms were the usual outcomes.

The people want freedom?? We better spy on them!

From the late 1950s through the early 1960s, Soviet authorities became obsessed with the influence of westernization on the peoples behind the Iron Curtain. During the 1930s, the Soviets had complete control of the media in the USSR. There was no television, radio broadcasts were limited, and publications were strictly censored by the state. Before the Second World War, the Soviets could still pump out negative propaganda about the Western democracies, and no one was the wiser. Once the Soviets gained control of Eastern Europe, propaganda was used to keep the populace in the dark. By the 1950s, it was difficult for the Soviets to censor the flow of information that made its way into Eastern Europe. Improved radio transmissions and technology allowed Eastern Europeans access to broadcasts from the West. The monopoly on information behind the Iron Curtain was broken. Furthermore, travel between East and West also undermined the false Soviet narrative about the West. People saw firsthand the material wealth and the freedom of Western Europeans, and they began to realize that authorities had misled them.

As Soviet paranoia grew, authorities dispatched KGB agents, known by the euphemism "illegals," to Soviet Bloc countries. They masqueraded as Western tourists and journalists and gathered intelligence on public opinion. The KGB was trying to gauge anti-Soviet sentiment and how much westernization had influenced people behind the Iron Curtain. They churned out reports saying that "Western-sponsored ideological subversion" was undermining communism within the Soviet Bloc, especially in Czechoslovakia. Instead of restructuring communism and granting some minor freedoms, the Soviets decided upon repression. False reports created by the KGB, gave the impression that Western democracy threatened communism, thus justifying the Soviet invasion of Czechoslovakia.

1968: the turbulent year.

1968 was a turbulent year across the globe. The year started with the North Vietnamese breaking a truce during the Vietnam War and launching the Tet Offensive. Bobby Kennedy and Dr. Martin Luther King were assassinated in the United States. France experienced riots, and Chicago erupted with political violence at the Democratic Party National Convention over the Vietnam War. Social unrest was widespread across the United States and the rest of the world, but discontent was also brewing behind the Iron Curtain.

The flashpoint would be Czechoslovakia, which resisted pressure from Moscow to adhere to strict totalitarian control of its people and economy. Moscow was adamantly opposed to any attempt to institute liberal policies, lest it infect the rest of the Soviet Bloc states. In 1968, the Czechoslovakian leader, Alexander Dubcek, the First Secretary of the Central Committee of the Communist Party, sought to loosen authoritative controls. Dubcek was not advocating democracy, nor a capitalistic system, but he wanted to dial back the political repression and modify the command economy. Leonid Brezhnev, the leader of the USSR, objected because it deviated from Soviet policy.

Prague Spring.

On August 20-21, 1968, Soviet military forces, along with Bulgarian, Hungarian, Polish, and East German soldiers, invaded Czechoslovakia to crush popular protests and head off the possibility of reforms being enact. Which might give the average Czech more political rights. The assault was months in the planning. The Soviet led Warsaw Pact invasion force was larger than the German invasion force during Operation Barbarossa in the summer of 1941. At the time, Czechoslovakia was a sovereign nation of 14 million people; a member country of the Warsaw Pact and presented no military threat to any nation.

Furthermore, there was no world war raging with millions of people dying. Nor was life and death hanging in the balance for the Soviet Union. The goal of the Soviet leadership was clear: they would do anything to keep their rotten empire together, so military overkill goes without saying.

The Prague Spring was not comparable to Budapest in 1956. Although there were many demonstrators, the Czech protests had minimal violence. Protesters mostly screamed at Warsaw Pact soldiers and tried to block the path of tanks. Less than 100 Czechs were killed, and another 800 were wounded; communist casualties were almost nil.

A famous photograph showed a Czech civilian mocking Soviet soldiers with a Nazi salute.

Thousands of tanks and soldiers had carried the day, but they certainly did not win the hearts and minds of the Czechs. There were arrests, but most Czech leaders were later freed. The Soviets used brute force to remain in control. History was repeating itself: the Soviets used military force to suppress the East Germans in 1953, the Hungarians in 1956, and the Czech protests in 1968.

Havel and the end of communism in Czechoslovakia.

By 1989, communism was falling apart in Eastern Europe, and there were protests in Czechoslovakia. After a student was killed during a demonstration, the former leader of Czechoslovakia, Alexander Dubcek, appeared with Vaclav Havel, who would become the first democratically elected president of Czechoslovakia. Vaclav Havel was a poet, a writer, a dissident, and the recipient of numerous awards from countries across the globe. By the end of the year, communism was gone in Czechoslovakia. Havel would be the first and last President of Czechoslovakia, and he facilitated the Velvet Revolution, which saw the peaceful splitting of the Czech Republic and Slovakia on January 1, 1993.[40]

---

40 Shire, William. The Rise and Fall of the Third Reich. Pp. 485-569. Courtois, Stephane, et. al. The Black Book of Communism. p. 401-6, 408, 409, 410, 411, 414, 415, 416, 428, 430, 431, 433, 434, 441, 442, 443,444, 446. Acheson, Dean. Present at the Creation. pp. 77, 727. Andrew, C. Mitrokhin. The Sword and the Shield. 252-269. Davies, N. Europe. 921, 927, 990-1, 1105-6, 1123. Nichols, C.S. Power, A Political History of the 20th Century. Pp. 182-3.

Bulgaria Post-war 1945-1990: a country purged in blood.

During the Second World War, Bulgaria was a client state of Nazi Germany, but not a formal ally like the Empire of Japan or Italy. This Eastern European country was a reluctant ally at best. After Germany steamrolled Yugoslavia in 1940, the Bulgarians filled the role of an occupation force. Bulgaria resisted German pressure to declare war on the USSR and would not turn over Jewish Bulgarians to the Nazis. The only action the Bulgarians took to support the Germans was to declare war on the United States, but they took no direct military action against the Americans.

Bulgarian neutrality and keeping Nazi Germany at bay did not deter the USSR. Although the Bulgarian government had never taken an aggressive action against the USSR, the Soviet Army marched into the Eastern European country in 1944 and occupied it. The Soviets aided the communist takeover of the country, and their army was forcibly incorporated into the Soviet Army. Stalin had their society purged. *The Black Book of Communism* pointed out that by early 1945, Soviet sponsored show trials numbered well over a hundred and resulted in over 10,000 convictions. Although the Bulgarians did not take part in Operation Barbarossa, the communists still handed out roughly 2,200 death sentences. After the fall of the communist regime in 1989, the nation's archives were opened. Sources indicated that the wave of violence that eclipsed the country probably claimed "30,000 to 40,000 people" who were either killed or vanished. Bulgarians, who showed the same dedication to their country as did Nikola Petkov, were tried in rigged court trials and executed. Well over eighty prison camps were established in Bulgaria after the communist takeover, and almost 200,000 people were imprisoned between the end of the war and the early 1960s.

A mysterious death and more show trials of communists.

One leading Bulgarian communist leader, Georgi Dimitrov, returned to Bulgaria and publicly floated the idea of a union of Balkan states. In 1949, Soviet authorities ordered him to Moscow, and shortly after his arrival, he died under mysterious circumstances. Historians believe that Stalin probably objected to the idea of an association of Eastern European states, which might chart a course that undermined Soviet control of the Balkans. Although Soviet authorities gave no conclusive cause of death, Stalin's track record of having potential rivals killed off presents the distinct possibility that the "Boss" had him eliminated.

Another Bulgarian communist, Traicho Kostov, was arrested and put on trial, along with others at the end of 1949. During the trial, Kostov deviated from the prewritten Moscow script, in which he was supposed to confess his guilt. Instead, Kostov surprised the authorities by "proclaiming that he was a friend" of the USSR. Although no evidence was produced, Kostov and others were found guilty in 1949. Kostov was sentenced to death and hung. Others received lengthy prison sentences.

Points to Ponder: A poison pellet and a murder on a London bridge.

In September of 1978, Georgi Markov, a Bulgarian writer who lived in exile in Great Britain, was assassinated. Markov worked at the British Broadcast Corporation (BBC) and was a vocal critic of the communist regime in his former country. The bizarre assassination was believed to have been carried out by Bulgarian agent[s] on the Waterloo Bridge in London. The assassin jabbed the writer in the leg with an umbrella, which discharged a poisonous ricin-soaked pellet.

Unbeknownst to the dissident, he had been dosed with a lethal amount of poison. Markov died several days later in agony. Only an autopsy revealed that he had been poisoned, and the assassin[s] were never arrested.

This was not a single incident. Another Bulgarian dissident, Vladimir Kostov, was assaulted several weeks earlier in Paris, but survived. The same type of weapon was used, and a pellet was recovered. Around the same time, another Bulgarian dissident working for the BBC, Vladimir Simeonov, was discovered dead at the bottom of the staircase in his house in London. The mysterious death of Simeonov was initially written off as an accident until Scotland Yard started looking into the murder of Markov and the attempted murder of Vladimir Kostov in Paris.

The Mitrokhin Files indicated that the Bulgarians had approached the Soviet KGB about obtaining a clandestine weapon to carry out assassinations of dissidents residing in the West. The KGB supplied the Bulgarians with the poison umbrella gun and trained their operatives to carry out the assassinations. The Bulgarian authorities had been very busy neutralizing opponents during the 1970s. In 1974, the Bulgarian agents successfully kidnapped Boris Arsov from Denmark and transported him back to the capital of Sophia for trial. Arsov was convicted and sentenced to fifteen years in prison but was said to have been found dead in his cell the next year. In 1975, three other Bulgarian dissidents were gunned down in Vienna. The Mitrokhin Files indicated that the Austrian authorities had identified the assassins as being Bulgarian agent[s], who escaped back to eastern Europe.

In the end, just more empty communist slogans.

In Bulgaria, communism collapsed just like it did in the rest of Eastern Europe. It just fell apart. *The Black Book of Communism* noted that the party failed to live up to one of the mottoes of the Bulgarian elites: "We took power with bloodshed, we won't give it up without bloodshed." Shakespeare's Macbeth best describes this empty communist slogan, "And then is heard no more: it is a tale told by an idiot, full of sound and fury and signifying nothing."

Romania: 1945-1990.

Romania, like Poland, was doomed by geography. Romania shared a border with the USSR, which loomed like a threatening totalitarian storm over the Eastern European country. In 1940, Stalin had already forced the country to cede a slice of their territory; so, it had firsthand experience of the imperialist intentions of the Soviets. The Romanians were a client state of the Nazis, diplomatically aligning themselves with Germany. As one historian noted, the Romanians were more "anti-Soviet than pro-German." The Romanians backed the Germans by contributing infantry divisions to the invasion of the USSR in 1941.

By the fall of 1944, the military situation had reversed for the Axis, and the Soviets were marching to the west. Romania fell quickly to the USSR. With the backing of the Soviet armed forces and secret police, the communists seized control of the parliament and forced the Romanian monarch to abdicate. Because Romania had been aligned with Germany, the Soviets brutally purged the country. The communists arrested tens of thousands of people, held rigged trials, and executed anyone who could possibly pose a threat. When peasants protested peacefully about the forced collectivization of their land, they were fired upon by authorities.

When it came to the destruction of civil society and organized religion, the Romanians were some of the most brutal. (See "The destruction of civil society" and "Religion destroyed in Eastern Europe.") By the end of 1948, the communists had outright banned the Greek Catholic Church and imprisoned 1,400 clergy, resulting in the deaths of several hundred individuals. Close to 2500 buildings, along with other church possessions, were confiscated by the state. Communist goons also destroyed religious archives and historical documents.

Nicolae Ceausescu takes over.

In 1965, the Romanian leader Gheorghe Gheorghiu-Dej died, and after a short power struggle, Nicolae Ceaușescu was able to assume power. Although part of the Soviet Bloc, the Romanians did not contribute military forces to Warsaw Pact operations in Eastern Europe. Ceaușescu chose to focus his energies on consolidating power within Romania. He lived like a king, with a luxurious home and exquisite furnishings, and in the process, he alienated the masses. As with the other Eastern European nations in the later 1980s, economic malaise led to social unrest in Romania. A wave of strikes involving tens of thousands of miners and factory workers occurred in 1977, 1980 and 1981. Violent crackdowns were used to deal with demonstrations.

More Repression.

By the 1980s, Ceaușescu had a tenuous control over Romania, and he was reluctant to use overt force to remain in power. At this point, authorities became imaginative, and they added new methods of repression; people were committed to insane asylums, lost their jobs, or killings were disguised to look like accidents.

Any action, no matter how trivial, could result in years of imprisonment. Handing out anti-government leaflets, printing unauthorized publications, or even throwing firecrackers during a government function could land a person in prison. One doctor was jailed for not falsifying a death certificate "for a political prisoner who had died under torture." In one instance, Ceaușescu's goons killed a government critic and staged a car wreck to make it seem as if the victim had died in an automobile accident.

The Romanian strongman was able to quell discontent for only so long, but as the 1980s came to an end, authorities could not stop the masses from protesting political repression and the stagnant economy. From 1987 through 1988, massive protests broke out, and the Romanian security forces used lethal force to kill hundreds, while thousands more were arrested. By 1989, Ceaușescu was hesitant to use force to stop the demonstrations, and when another protest broke out that same year, most of the Romanian military sided with the demonstrators. When Ceaușescu tried to address the demonstrators, the crowd became so unruly that he fled the city in a helicopter.

Points to Ponder: Vlad the Impaler and Ceaușescu

It is said that some leaders are reminiscent of rulers from the past. Stalin fancied himself as a twentieth-century version of Ivan the Terrible. Parallels could be drawn between Ceaușescu and Vlad III, or Vlad the Impaler. Both were known for cruelty, which undermined their ability to remain in political control. Vlad ruled an area that was in modern-day Romania. He ruled with an iron fist, and much has been written about his fiendishness and tendency to use violence. His cruelty and sadism became legendary, especially his use of impalement as a weapon of terror. Sources indicate that tens of thousands suffered this agonizing fate. In the later part of the fifteenth century, Vlad was killed, but the circumstances surrounding his death are shrouded in mystery.

Unlike Vlad, Ceaușescu's demise is well documented. He and his wife were arrested just before Christmas in 1989. Ironically, on Christmas Eve day, they were subjected to the same type of rigged trial that many thousands of innocent victims experienced behind the Iron Curtain. The Ceaușescu[s] were found guilty and sentenced to death. A short while later, soldiers shot the couple dead. A videotape showed their crumpled, bloody bodies. Communism was officially dead in Romania.

After the death of "Vlad the Impaler," German publications from the late Middle Ages sensationalized his bloody reputation. These books became the basis for Bram Stoker's novel on Dracula, which later became a staple in the modern horror movie industry. It is unlikely that the Ceaușescu[s] will inspire a movie genie like Dracula, but the Romanian strongman's house has become a tourist destination. [41]

Yugoslavia, not a Soviet satellite.

Yugoslavia shared the same fate as other Eastern European countries after WWII, communist domination. Josip Broz, known by the

---

41 Courtois, Stephane, et. al. The Black Book of Communism. citations cover Bulgaria and Romania. pp. 279-280, 398, 399, 401, 402, 414-421, 425, 427, 447, 448, 449, 453-4. Andrew, C. Mitrokhin. The Sword and the Shield. 388-9. Davies, N. Europe. pp. 449, 1,011, 1123. Nelsson, Richard. "The poison-tipped umbrella; the death of Georgi Markov in 1978" The Guardian. -From the Bulgarian Archive. Sept. 9, 2020. Britain: The Poisonous Umbrella." Time. 1978. Salisbury, Daniel & Dewey, Karl. "Murder on the Waterloo Bridge: placing the assassination of Georgi Markov in the past and present context, 1970-2018." CONTEMPORARY BRITISH HISTORY; 2023, VOL. 37, NO. 1. Pp. 128–156. Davies, N. No Simple Victory. 17, 18, 58, 62, 88,89, 117, 120, 156, 199-200, 289, 292, 320, 380-381. Shakespeare, William. The Complete Works of Shakespeare. "Macbeth": Act 5, Scene 5. Pp. 882. Source for Bram Stoker. Bridgewater, William, ED., et. al. The Columbia Encyclopedia. 3rd Ed. Pp. 2047.

Murderous Marxism

name Tito, led communist forces to victory in Yugoslavia. After victory, Tito ordered bloody reprisals against opposition forces, but by 1950, repression and brutal killings had lessened significantly. Furthermore, Tito broke with Stalin in 1948, and he kept Yugoslavia from becoming embroiled in the Cold War. Yugoslavia was communist, but Tito was not taking orders from Moscow. This Eastern European country would chart its own course in international relations.

This Eastern European country was short-lived; it lasted less than 75 years (1918-1992). Historical factors played a dominant role in the development of Yugoslavia. Centuries earlier, the Turkish Ottoman Empire conquered parts of the regions that would become the future Yugoslavia, but by the nineteenth century, this empire was in decline and losing control of the region. The rise of nationalist sentiments among the Serbians and Bulgarians fueled unrest, which led to several but bloody revolts. After the turn of the century, the region experienced two brutal Balkan wars between 1912-13. It involved the Turks, Bulgarians, Serbians, and other regional groups. By 1914, the Austrian Empire attempted to annex Bosnia, which lies in the center of what would become the future Yugoslavia. This attempt to grab territory only served to provoke the populace, which was already simmering with ethic and religious strife. On June 28, 1914, Archduke Ferdinand of Austria and his wife were assassinated in Sarajevo by a Serbian nationalist or anarchist (you pick). Europe was already a simmering continental powder keg, given the adversarial European diplomatic alliances. The assassination was the catalyst that sparked the outbreak of the First World War. Four years later, in 1918, with the defeat of the Central Powers and the collapse of the Austrian Empire, Yugoslavia emerged as an independent country.

After the outbreak of WWII, Yugoslavia was able to stay out of the fighting for roughly 20 months, although Germany eventually pressured it to allow soldiers to be stationed in the country. Fascist Italy's disastrous invasion of Greece in late August 1940 sealed Yugoslavia's fate. When the Italian Army invaded the small Mediterranean country, the Greek Army mauled the invasion force and drove them out of their country. To save their Italian ally, the Germans launched an invasion of Yugoslavia and Greece at the beginning of April 1941, and in several weeks, both countries were subjugated.

It was at this point that the real bloodshed began in Yugoslavia. The fighting in Yugoslavia had several aspects to it. It was a war of resistance against the Axis, a civil war between communists versus non-communists, but fighting also had a religious and ethnic component thrown into the fray. By the end of WWII, roughly four years later, 1.7 million had died. Yugoslavians were the main culprits, and they slaughtered well over a million of their own countrymen, which was not directly connected to fighting the Nazis. It can be said that German aggression set these murderous killings into motion.

Historian Norman Davies described these burning hatreds that consumed Bosnia and other parts of Yugoslavia.

"Bosnia is a country of hatred and fear. And the fatal characteristic is that the Bosnian is unaware of the hatred which lives within, shrinks from analyzing it, and hates anyone who tries to do so. Yet there are more people ready in fits of subconscious hatred to kill and be killed than in other much bigger lands… it is hatred acting as an independent force: hatred like a cancer consuming everything around it."

During the war, numerous groups fought in Yugoslavia, but cooperation against the Axis was elusive. The Axis occupation forces

Murderous Marxism

consisted primarily of Germans, with Italian assistance. Bulgarians and Hungarians soldiers also served the role of an occupation force in parts of Yugoslavia. One of the larger resistance groups, the Chetniks, was primarily Serbian, and they generally supported the monarchy. This resistance group was comprised of different groups throughout the country. The other larger resistance group was the communists led by Tito, who set up most of his bases of operation in Bosnia. He accepted fighters from different ethnic groups and played down the communist rhetoric. Tito gained victories against the Germans, which won him support from the British and the hatred of Stalin. His methods were cold-blooded and left no choice for the local populace but to join the communist ranks. When partisan groups, either communist or Chetnik, attacked the Germans, the reprisals against local villages and towns were ferocious. Dozens of people could be shot for every German soldier killed or wounded, and the number increased for the death of officers. In some villages, the numbers killed by the Germans were far greater. A military historian opined that Tito counted on German barbarism to swell the ranks of his partisan fighting force. After a partisan attack, they either joined the communists or were shot. What choice did they have?

As one historian noted, fighting in Yugoslavia was "murderous chaos." Chetniks fought Tito's communists, while regional groups, such as the Slovenes and the Croatians, aligned themselves with the Axis camp. Both groups fought the communists. One faction of Chetniks switched sides and aligned itself with the Germans. Bosnian Muslims and Croatians were also recruited into two German Waffen SS divisions. In Croatia, an independent regional paramilitary group, the Ustaše, allied itself with the Germans. The Ustaše considered Serbians, Bosnian Muslims, communists, and Jews to be foreigners who needed to be purged from Croatia. Their actions would foreshadow the savage ethnic cleansing (mass killings) which would be seen in Yugoslavia during the 1990s. Besides killing with military weapons, they also used knives, saws, sledgehammers, and farm tools. They were so brutal that even some of the German officers were shocked by their actions. There was one constant factor during this period: none of these different groups ever shied away from killing each other.

Fighting was constant, but primarily small-scale in comparison to fighting in Stalingrad or the Normandy Invasion. Ambushes were numerous, and guerrilla warfare was the norm; and massacres of whole villages were not uncommon. Prisoners, wounded combatants, and innocent villagers were routinely killed, and many times, their deaths were horrific. In Yugoslavia during the Second World War, mercy was an asset in short supply. All sides, to different degrees, were guilty.

"Woe to the Vanquished"

By the middle of 1944, the tide was turning against the Germans. Primarily, Tito's communists were successfully battling the Germans, and the British recognized his victories. He was winning on two fronts; the Germans were pulling out of the country, and they were defeating the anti-communists. With the German defeat in 1945, the pro-Axis Slovenes surrendered to the British, who turned them over to Tito's communist forces. Tito was pitiless to his enemies. One historian described Tito's retribution against this group as "diabolical." The Slovenes were slaughtered; the number of those killed probably approached 30,000. The Chetniks also suffered the same fate. They were turned over to the communists, marched miles, and then butchered. The few that did survive "brought the full story of the horror they had seen." All sides contributed to the horror; all share the blame, but in the end, it was Tito's communist forces that came out on top.

Tito breaks with Stalin.

After WWII, Tito did have one advantage over other Eastern European countries; the Soviets were never able to exercise direct control over Yugoslavia. Tito was able to chart his own course for Yugoslavia. The economy was state-controlled, but not to the extent of the USSR. It was a police state in which the communist party exercised total political control, and opponents could be brutally dealt with, but it never reached the level of depravity seen in Stalin's Soviet Union. After the war, Tito carried out political repression, executing or imprisoning Croatians, Slovenes, Chetniks and other opponents. This lasted until the late 1950s, when overt oppression ebbed. When analyzing communist conduct during the war, it was no different than the other groups fighting in Yugoslavia. During WWII, the Yugoslav communists were murderous, but so were the fascist Croatians and Slovenes. In the end, Tito was able to attract more to the communist side. He was flexible, working with the Allies, while his enemies collaborated with the Axis forces, which probably sealed their fate.

After the war, he aided other communist groups during the Greek Civil War. Tito allowed material and men to flow through Yugoslavia until 1948, when he broke with the Soviet Union. Stalin wanted other communist countries in Eastern Europe to take direction from the Soviet Union, but Tito was not about to take orders from the "Boss." A communist leader courted disaster if they publicly spoke about a potential future for Eastern Europe, which ran contrary to the wishes of the Soviet leader. When the Bulgarian leader, Georgi Dimitrov, talked about a Balkan League, he was summoned to the Soviet Union, and he mysteriously died after arriving.

Tito knew of Stalin's reputation for killing off rivals; it would be safe to assume that the Yugoslavian leader never trusted the "Boss."

Indeed, Stalin did try to have the Yugoslav leader assassinated, but all attempts failed. In 1950, Tito sent a letter to Stalin. It read, "Stop sending assassins to murder me... We have already caught five... If this doesn't stop, I will send one man to Moscow, and there will be no need to send another." Three years later, Stalin was dead, and the other Soviet leaders had little appetite for confronting Tito. Under Tito, Yugoslavia adopted a foreign policy of nonalignment. He would not let Yugoslavia get pulled communist confrontation with the Western democracies during the Cold War.

Yugoslavia breaks up after Tito dies.

Tito ruled Yugoslavia for three and a half decades, and he took a different tack when it came to the economy, but in the end, the state-controlled economy still faltered. Four years after Tito's death, the 1984 Winter Olympics were held in Sarajevo. This international gathering of goodwill did little to keep Yugoslavia from falling back into the same type of racial and regional hatreds, which gripped the country during WWII. In 1991, the same type of murderous killing broke out again. Bosnia was once again the flashpoint. It has been estimated that 100,000 to 250,000 died in the fighting, conservatively. By 2006, Yugoslavia had broken into individual states. In the past, true believers in Marxism have claimed that communism was the cure for what ails a society: poverty, corruption, and ethnic strife. It was all snake oil; it cured nothing. It certainly did not cure the ethnic and religious strife in Yugoslavia. [42]

---

42 Davies, Norman. Europe. p.834, 869, 870, 874, 980-981, 1,010, 1,033, 1,124, 1,319. Davies. Norman. No Simple Victory. Pp.18, 24, 57, 61, 64, 91,120-121, 179-180, 200, 276, 312, 317, 318, 319, 362, 379, 449. Albania suffered the same fate as other Eastern European nations after the Second World War, communism. By 1941, Albania, Greece, and Yugoslavia were occupied by Axis forces and became embroiled in fighting

Murderous Marxism

Greece: The Greek Civil War 1943-1949.

While the Second World War was still raging, the Greek Civil War broke out in this Mediterranean country in 1943. It was only two years earlier, in April 1941, that the Nazis attacked Greece, and the government surrendered several weeks later. Almost immediately, different partisan resistance groups began carrying out guerrilla military operations against the German Army. Different partisan groups individually attacked German forces. A united front against the Axis never really happened. One of the primary resistant groups was the communist 'People's Army of National Liberation' (ELAS), which waged hit-and-run raids against the German Army. The Nazis weren't the only targets; ELAS also attacked other anti-communist resistance groups, trying to force them to submit to their control. A German military offensive at the end of 1943 created such chaos amongst the partisan groups, that they began battling each other again, causing what one historian called a "civil war within a main war..." After another short truce, ELAS once again turned on one of the other non-communist Greek resistance groups. In one instance, ELAS guerrilla

---

during the war. Enver Hoxha, a communist guerrilla leader, led the resistance movement in Albania. With the defeat of the Axis forces, he became the supreme leader of the country. Hoxha consolidated power by killing off potential rivals. He attempted to eradicate all religion within Albania. So intent, in wiping out opponents, communist authorities established almost 20 prison camps in a country that is slightly larger than the US state of Vermont. An official communist publication "proudly" noted that authorities had "destroyed or closed" almost 2,200 Christian, and Muslim places of religious worship. The Black Book of Communism wrote that "in 1967, Enver Hoha declare [d] that Albania...[was]...the first officially atheist state in the world." It would remain a communist atheist state until 1990, when communism collapsed. After the collapse, Albania has remained an undeveloped country. No one's life had been dramatically improved by communism, yet history books rarely note that fact. Courtois, Stephane, et.al. The Black Book of Communism. p. 310, 311, 324-6, 330, 380, 397-398, 418, 424, 425, 438, 449. Keegan, John. A History of Warfare. Pp. 51-55. Medvedev, Roy & Zhores. The Unknown Stalin: His Life, Death, and Legacy. Pp. 70.

249

fighters surrounded the opposing partisan group, massacring most of the fighters when they tried to surrender. In a final act of ruthlessness, ELAS guerrillas cut the partisan commander's head off. Terror was the central pillar of the communist strategy to win control of Greece, and ELAS never shrank from using it.

The Germans pull out of Greece, and the fighting becomes more savage.

As the Third Reich started to crumble in 1944, the Germans began to pull their forces from Greece. It was at this point, the fighting between the resistance groups intensified. ELAS stepped up its attacks against the remaining partisan groups. Brutality was commonplace, and ELAS was especially savage. They routinely killed prisoners and massacred all the inhabitants of villages, which undermined their ability to win the hearts and minds of the populace. An ELAS military leader put it bluntly: "*We did not kill enough people... Everyone described me as a killer—that's the way we were. Revolutions only succeed when the river runs red with blood... for... the perfectibility of the human race.*" The communist leader who made these comments was later killed during the Civil War.

The anti-communist forces fought fire with fire, carrying out reprisal killings of communists. By the end of 1947, communist brutality still had the edge, and ELAS was getting the upper hand during the Greek Civil War.

Points to Ponder: Crossroad of the World.

Why was Greece so important? Geography. Greece lies at the crossroads of the world, making it a strategic location which had been fought over for thousands of years. Greeks, Persians, Romans, Turks, and a host of other powers sought to control the waterways, which allowed ships from the Black Sea to access the Mediterranean Sea. Greece was also strategic because it was the doorway from Europe to Asia and vice versa. To the east of Greece lay Asia Minor (Turkey), the steppingstone to Asia, which leads to modern-day Iraq and Iran, which have vast petroleum reserves. Any empire that controlled the land routes and the waterways associated with the "crossroads of the world" could become fabulously wealthy through trade, while dominating a worldwide strategic location. In 1948, the Soviet Navy could be bottled up in the Black Sea. A communist dominated Greece could potentially allow Soviet warships from Ukrainian ports, unfettered access from the Black Sea to the Mediterranean Sea. A communist victory at the "crossroads of the world" would bring the possibility of global domination well within Soviet grasp, and Greece was the key. Americans and British officials understood the looming potential disaster if the communists gained control of Greece. Not only did the US supply aid to Greece, but also to Turkey. Turkey (formally known as the Ottoman Empire) was important because it controlled Asia Minor, the geographical steppingstone between Europe and Asia.

Tito and Stalin split, American and British support stop the Greek Communists.

The Greek Civil War marked the breaking point for British influence in the region. The British could no longer economically sustain their military involvement in Greece, and they diplomatically reached out to the United States for support. The US, seeing the imperialistic intentions of the Soviet Union, stepped in, and US President Harry Truman and Secretary of State Dean Acheson succeeded in getting aid for the Greek democratic forces. US and British aid tipped the scales in favor of the Greek anti-communist forces.

At the same time, the geopolitical split between Yugoslavian leader, Tito and Stalin doomed support for the Greek communists. Tito closed off bases and stopped supplies from flowing through Yugoslavia, and shortly afterward, Albania followed suit and cut off bases within their country. By 1949, the Greek government forces, bolstered by US and British aid, defeated the Greek communists. After the victory, Greece joined the recently created North Atlantic Treaty Organization (NATO). During the Civil War, fighting had been intense, and casualties heavy; the Greek Army suffered over "17,000 killed in action, and almost 38,000 wounded... [the]... communists... [lost]... 38,000 killed... 40,000 captured." Tens of thousands of non-combatants had also perished during the fighting.

Where did the Greek Children Go??

The Soviets and other communist regimes have a fixation on keeping records of all their despicable deeds. When the Soviet Union and other communist regimes collapsed, their secret archives became public knowledge, and all their savage history was exposed. Captured documentation revealed that the Greek communists would massacre the adults in a village, then abduct the children. Records indicated that well over twenty thousand children were kidnapped. The International Red Cross, a relief agency, attempted to find out what happened to the missing children, but they were stonewalled by the communist regimes of Eastern Europe. The Red Cross was still able to compile a report that indicated that over 28,000 children were forcibly taken. Initially, several thousand Greek children were moved into Albania, Yugoslavia, and Bulgaria. After the split between Tito and Stalin in 1948, the Yugoslavian leader sent roughly 12,000 abducted children to other communist countries behind the Iron Curtain. The UN passed resolutions demanding that the abducted children be returned to

Greece, but the communists ignored the international organization's proclamation. The abductees were kept in squalid "children's villages," and were moved from location to location. Many died from disease and neglect. When they were old enough, the children, who were now young adults were forced to do manual labor under appalling conditions. In short, they became slaves. The communists tried indoctrination, but it was unsuccessful, and most of the Greek children resisted. Some children were able to escape to West Germany. By the mid-1960s, approximately 4,600 kidnapped children, who were now adults, were able to return to Greece. With the collapse of communism, several thousand Greeks children, who had been sent to Poland, returned to their homeland in 1989. These kidnappings produced nothing but misery and separated families, and yet few history books note these terrible actions. More History down the memory blackhole. (Please see the notes)

Points to Ponder: Eleni: A mother makes the ultimate sacrifice.

The movie, *Eleni,* is a true story, based on the personal family tragedy of the writer, Nicholas Gage. The book was a tribute to his mother, Eleni Gatzoyiannis, and was adapted into a film. She made the ultimate sacrifice and was killed while trying to protect her family during the Greek Civil War. When the Second World War ended, the writer's mother wanted to stay out of the brutal civil war, which engulfed Greece. The odds were against Eleni because she was alone. Her husband had gone to the United States to work, and her son, Nicholas, had been sent to America to live with relatives after the war.

Furthermore, the central government of Greece barely functioned, so there was no protection from the communist partisans that showed up in her village in 1948. The communists wanted to take some of her remaining children and force them to serve with their forces. Besides the distinct possibly of dying in the civil war, there was also the other possibility that her children would be sent to countries behind the Iron Curtain. Unarmed, Eleni bravely tried to find different ways to prevent the kidnapping of her children, but in the end, the communists "tortured and murdered" her. *Eleni* was a tragic story of a mother's love and communist brutality. Her son's book was a testimony to her devotion. Watch the movie.

After the fall of communism in the USSR and Eastern Europe, where were the trials?

After the fall of communism in the USSR and Eastern Europe, there were some trials of communist officials for crimes committed by their totalitarian regimes. The trials were few, and sentences were quite lenient compared to the death sentences and long prison terms that were routinely handed down under communist courts. Trials of former communists never approached the scope of the Nuremberg trials of the Nazis, although the number of people killed over the decades certainly rivals what the Nazis had committed during WWII. The former communists benefitted from the proper application of the rule of law, something they denied others in their rigged communist courts. Talk about getting away with murder.

Conclusions.

What did the collapse of communism in Eastern Europe signify? It must be remembered that the Soviets forced their system upon them, and millions paid the ultimate price. With the death of Stalin, the ever-present threat of death or imprisonment lessened, but life behind the Iron Curtain was still repressive. Over the decades, people mustered the courage to refuse to comply with totalitarian mandates, which meant that communism's days were numbered. They rejected secret police, concentration camps, and a command economy that rewarded the communist elites, while the populace suffered. They rejected baseless arrests and imprisonment. What remained was the trauma inflicted on generations of Eastern Europeans. No one is clamoring to bring back communism. [43]

---

43 Laffin John. Brassey's Dictionary of Battles. p. 186. Courtois, Stephane, et.al. The Black Book of Communism. Pp. 310, 326-331. Acheson, Dean. Present at the Creation. Pp. 67,217-219, 226, 310. LeFeber, Walter. The American Age. 452-455. Darnton, Nina. "'Eleni' Enshrines on Film a Mother's Legacy of Love." New York Times. Oct. 27, 1985. The Marxist Internet Archive has an article, by an anonymous author, that adamantly denies the Greek children were abducted, but relocated for humanitarian reasons. Anonymous. "The Abducted Greek Children." World News and Views, Vol. 29, No. 44. Marxist Internet Archive. January 2, 1950. I believe this article to be patently untrue. The abducted children were never adopted by caring families but were more slaves for the communist counties in which they were sent. As stated before, they were kept in squalid conditions, and forced to perform manual labor, while authorities tried to indoctrinate them. Nor was there any attempt to return them to Greece after the war. Please see the above source, The Black Book on Communism. For personal account of the terrible fate of these child victims; please read Niki Karavasilis book, The Abducted Greek Children of the Communists: "Paidomazoma." She was held against her will in Yugoslavia for thirty-three years under deplorable conditions until she able to leave. Elini (movie) 1985.

Chapter 4
If Communism is not that Frightening, Why did so Many People Flee Marxist Regimes?

The Vietnamese Boat People.

After South Vietnam fell to the communist North Vietnamese in 1975, it has been estimated that "almost two million fled Vietnam," many on small, flimsy ships. These refugees became known as the Vietnamese "boat people," and they suffered every type of calamity when they fled by sea. Many of the boats were not seaworthy and sank, drowning all on board. Refugees were denied entry into other countries, and many died from hunger and thirst. Others fell prey to pirates who robbed the refugees of all their possessions. These sea marauders raped refugee women and, on other occasions, killed all those aboard the small boats. It is estimated that maybe 200,000 or more Vietnamese refugees died at sea.

It must be repeated. If communism was not threatening, why did people go to such great lengths to flee? Vietnam is hardly the exception. The southeast Asian nation of Laos had close to 300,000 or 10% of its population flee the communist takeover, while 100,000s of Cambodians became refugees. After the Soviet invasion of Afghanistan in 1979, millions fled this central Asian country by the end of the 1980s. Before the outbreak of the Korean War, thousands left the northern part of the peninsula controlled by the communists. Since the demilitarized zone (DMZ) at the 38 Parallel is so heavily guarded, it is almost impossible to cross. Some North Koreans go to the extreme of crossing into, of all places, communist China. East Germany built the Berlin Wall to keep people from leaving, and guards shot people trying to get to West Germany. After the Hungarian uprising in 1956, it is estimated that 200,000 people were able to get out of this Eastern European country.

Points to Ponder: Fleeing Vietnam and ANTIFA.

The parents of investigative journalist Andy Ngo have experience with communist tyranny. Both his mother and father resided in South Vietnam when it fell to North Vietnam in 1975. The journalist's parents met when they fled Vietnam in a rickety boat in 1979. Prior to their escape, Ngo's father had been imprisoned for being a police officer and was forced to do slave labor in agricultural fields. His mother's family had owned a small jewelry shop, that was stolen away by the state. Most of her family members, including children, were imprisoned under deplorable conditions. The future parents of Andy Ngo, along with hundreds of thousands of other Vietnamese, decided on their own course of action: make a run to freedom. After fleeing communist Vietnam, they were able to settle in the United States and they married in 1980.

Decades later, their son's investigation into the domestic terrorist activities of ANTIFA has made him a target of this anarchist-communist group. Andy Ngo has been attacked and beaten up twice and has experienced several close calls. The journalist has been threatened on numerous occasions, and ANTIFA thugs have harassed Andy and his family members at their residences. He has filed numerous police reports, yet law enforcement has been useless in combating these extremists. To ensure his safety, Andy Ngo used safe houses, and on two separate occasions, he temporarily fled to England.

One family, two generations victimized by communism.

Cubans risking death for freedom.

Many Cubans have fled Castro's regime, especially in the early days of the communist takeover. Later, Cubans with very few resources started voting "with their oars," by making home-made rafts known as "*balsas*." They took their chances with the 90-mile sea journey to Florida.

The Mariel Boatlift: Castro empties his prisons and his asylums.

In 1980, unrest stemming from communist misrule and economic failure saw over 100,00 people leave Cuba, in what became known as the "Mariel boatlift." The whole affair started when several Cubans, desperate to flee, crashed a small bus through the gates of the Peruvian Embassy. Castro demanded their return, but the Peruvian diplomats refused, so the authorities pulled the Cuban security detail. From this point, things snowballed. Thousands mobbed the embassy, seeking visas to leave. So many Cubans sought asylum that the embassy was practically overrun. It was quickly becoming a small humanitarian nightmare due to the lack of food, water, and restroom facilities.

As events unfolded, the situation started to become a political nightmare for Castro. If outside news agencies had found out the true magnitude of events, it could have possibly tarnished his reputation. Furthermore, people have speculated that Castro saw a chance to rid

Cuba of people who wanted to leave. He also saw it as an opportunity to empty Cuba's prisons and asylums. Juan Sanchez, Castro's former bodyguard, noted that Castro was able to dump 2,000 hardened criminals on the USA, and they ended up on the "streets of Miami."

Castro's sandbag bombs.

In 1994, more unrest led to another wave of people fleeing Cuba on rafts. This new exodus put such a negative light on Castro's regime, the dictator sent out helicopters to either machine gun or bombard the "*balsas*" with sandbags. Thousands of people died from exposure, thirst, and drowning when Castro's "sandbag" bombs sank their rafts. It should also be noted that some desperate Cubans stowed away in the wheel wells of jets leaving the island. Some survived the flights; others died.

As the *Black Book of Communism* points out, in over three decades, well over 100,000 tried to flee and approximately 30,000 died, and "two million... [Cubans]... now live in exile." There are two contradictions that need to be acknowledged. First, Castro preached that the revolution would benefit the lower classes, but it was the poorest who suffered the most and sought to flee the economic stagnation created by communism. Second, the media and celebrities refuse to acknowledge these failures. (See Media Bias) They try to perpetuate the myth that Marxism/communism is somehow succeeding. Yes, things like infant mortality are down, and more people have access to education, but it begs the question. Why are people still trying to flee Cuba? (Please read notes)

Points to ponder: The Elian Gonzales Story.

In 1999, Elian Gonzales was only five years old when his mother and several others decided to leave Cuba on a *"balsa."* The perilous journey to the United States ended in tragedy when the makeshift boat capsized. A fishing boat found the child floating in an inner tube, miles off the Florida coast. All perished except Elain. His parents had separated, and the boy became a pawn in the geopolitical rift between the United States and communist Cuba. Elian's father still lived in Cuba, and the communist government demanded the child's return. Relatives of Elian's mother lived in Miami, and they petitioned to keep the child. The US Justice Department sided with the father and ordered the child returned to Cuba. Elain's relatives were under the impression that they could negotiate a peaceful turnover of the child, but the US Attorney General, Janet Reno, ordered a raid on the home of the child's relatives. US federal agents, clad in military gear, breached the home with automatic weapons. None of the relatives were armed, nor offered any resistance. There is a famous photograph of a federal agent ripping open a closet door and pointing an automatic weapon in the direction of one of the relatives holding the frightened child. The five-year-old can be seen screaming in terror of the armed US agent. The child was seized and sent back to Cuba. Sadly, Elian Gonzales' mother sacrificed her life to seek freedom, only to have her son sent back to Cuba. (On a personal note. Castro must have viewed the photograph. The dictator must have found it amusing and quite ironic that the USA, a country that champions civil rights, resorted to tactics that he would of no doubt approved of using himself.) Others, in individual acts, have fled communist countries for freedom. Defectors from communist countries are too numerous to note in this text. So why do they flee? You decide. [44]

---

[44] White, Matthew. The Great Book of Horrible Things. p. 473, 491. Courtois, Stephane, et. al. The Black Book of Communism. pp. boat people; 574, Laos, people fleeing; 575, Cambodia; 635; fleeing Cuba; 663. This online article provides numbers on the amount of people fleeing. Bui, Grace. "The Resettlement of Vietnamese and Montagnard Refugees Residing in Thailand" The National Bureau of Asian Research (NBR). Sept. 10, 2022. Online. Maclear, Michael. The Ten Thousand Day War: Vietnam: 1945-1975. Pp. 353. Luscombe, Richard. "Elian Gonzalez poised to be top Cuban lawmaker decades after Florida deportation" The Guardian. Feb. 7th, 2023. Fontova, Humberto. "Desperately Fleeing Cuba's Free and Fabulous Healthcare." Breitbart.com. July 17, 2011. Another online article by the same author; Fontova points out ludicrous articles praising Cuba as a wonderful place to live. His article also noted that thousands of Cubans died making the crossing from the island to Florida, while roughly 200 to 300 East Germans died trying to cross the Berlin Wall into West Germany. Fontova, Humberto. "Dying to Escape Socialism." Front Page Magazine. Feb. 8, 2023. Armando Ramirez tells of his harrowing gamble to escape Cuba in a jet wheel well. Fodor, Denis & Reddy, John. "How I escaped from Cuba in the wheel well of a jet." Reader's Digest Online. Revel, Jean. Last Exit to Utopia. Pp. 134. Sanchez, Juan. The Double Life of Fidel Castro. Pp. 161-163. Ngo, Andy. Unmasked: Inside Antifa's Radical Plan to Destroy Democracy. Pp.223-233, 257-8

William Johnson

Chapter 5
Fake News: Bias Reporting, and Censorship of Communist Brutality and Famines.

Since 2020, "fake news" has become a commonplace word. The media, and at times, historians have bent the truth and suppressed information that put communism in a bad light. At the beginning of this book, I made the argument that there has been a tendency to under-report the brutality of Marxist states in history books and classrooms. Notable writers have glossed over or covered up some of the worst deeds of communist dictators.

Edward Snow, an American journalist, traveled and wrote extensively about China. He was one of the first Western journalists to write about Chairman Mao Zedong, thus becoming an informal biographer of the Great Helmsmen. Edward Snow first met the Chairman in 1936 and interviewed him several times over the next thirty years. His tendency to praise the Chinese communist leader's actions, painted a less-than-accurate picture of Mao. As the Great Leap Forward failed and tens of millions of Chinese starved to death, the authorities lied about the terrible death toll. Edgar Snow toured the country and wrote that no famine existed.

Walter Duranty was another literary hack who suppressed Soviet brutality. He was a *New York Times* correspondent who reported on the former USSR, and in the process, won a Pulitzer Prize. Duranty adamantly denied that the "Ukrainian Terror Famine" ever happened. He wrote that the notion of an apocalyptic famine was absurd; Ukraine was the "land of milk and honey..." Stalin's 'Terror Famine' in the Ukraine claimed at least six million or more lives, just as many as the Holocaust. Privately, he spoke at length about the famine and acknowledged that it indeed occurred. With unscrupulous journalists like Duranty and Snow, it is small wonder that few people know of the Ukrainian Terror Famine or the Great Leap Forward.

Points to Ponder: Leonid Brezhnev and Joe Biden, zombie leaders.

In 1964, Leonid Brezhnev became the First Secretary of the Communist Party of the Soviet Union after ousting Nikita Khrushchev from his leadership position. By the 1970s, Brezhnev had consolidated power within the USSR, and he would lead the Soviet Union until his death in 1982. Under his leadership, the Soviet state was beset by massive corruption and bureaucratic incompetence, which marked the eventual collapse of the USSR. Ironically, there is a strange symbolic correlation between the fall of the USSR and the physical decline of Leonid Brezhnev.

It should be reiterated that the Soviets prohibited freedom of the press, and authorities strictly enforced censorship. *Pravda* is the Russian word for truth, and it was also the name of the state-controlled newspaper, which was the official mouthpiece for the Soviet communist party. It could be argued that *Pravda* never candidly reported on the bloody legacy of the USSR; its crumbling economy in the 1980s, nor did this periodical investigate the apparent physical and mental decline of Brezhnev in his later years.

While the Soviet people were officially kept in the dark about Leonid Brezhnev's problems, the US intelligence became aware of the Soviet leader's health issues through a high-level American spy, Morris Childs. This well-placed US spy had access to the Soviet elites, which included the ailing Soviet leader. Morris and his wife, Eva, made numerous trips to the USSR, and they gathered information by simply observing. On two separate occasions, the Childs's met the Soviet leader, and they were shocked at his appearance. Morris and Eva noted that Brezhnev appeared to be zombie-like, with "glazed eyes … " Two attendants, who were probably KGB agents, had to help the ailing leader stay on his feet.

Ironically, it would be the KGB that tried to expose Leonid Brezhnev's frail health. The Mitrokhin Files indicated that at the time, the head of the KGB, Yuri Andropov, devised an "unprecedented decision to embark on an… active measure against… [the]… Soviet leader…" Andropov's devious plan was to expose Brezhnev's decrepit health by having him make televised appearances on Soviet state television. The KGB chief hoped that this "active measure" would force the Politburo, the ruling Soviet governmental body, to replace the ailing Soviet leader. For his part, Andropov wanted to become Secretary General, making him the first head of the KGB to assume the highest political leadership in the USSR. The public appearances did catch the attention of the Soviet people, but since criticizing Soviet leadership could land you in the GULAG or a psychiatric hospital, people made private jokes about Brezhnev. One hilarious version entailed the Secretary General's "daily schedule." At "9 a.m.: reanimation, 10 a.m.: breakfast, … 11 a.m.: awarding medals… noon: recharging his batteries, … [followed by] … lunch, 6 p.m.: signing… documents, 8 p.m.; clinical death, 9 p.m.: reanimation…"

Murderous Marxism

The "active measures" and the clandestine jokes did not work; Leonid Brezhnev hung onto the Soviet leadership until he died in 1982. Yuri Andropov did get his wish, and he became the first KGB head to become the Secretary General of the Soviet Union in 1982. His leadership did not last long. Andropov died in 1984 from a kidney ailment that had **_been kept secret from the public_**.

Fast-forward over forty years to 2025. Jay Tapper, a correspondent for CNN, coauthored a tell-all book, *Original Sin*. The book details the cognitive decline of the former 46th U.S President, Joe Biden, and the attempt by presidential staffers and others to cover up his diminished mental capacity. A reviewer of Tapper's book noted that, "a code of silence among Democratic elites and many in the media discouraged public talk of Joe Biden's decline, until it was too late..." Prior to the 2020 elections and throughout his presidency, one could readily see Biden's physical problems. On numerous occasions, he looked confused, uttered nonsensical sentences, and wandered off stage during official state functions. He either forgot people's names or did not recognize individuals he'd known for years. Videos show the aged president stumbling and falling, while yet another video has Biden claiming to have spoken to two different world leaders who had been dead for years.

Critics of the mainstream media point out that the "legacy media" refused to report on the painfully obvious cognitive problems suffered by the 46th president. For their part, the mainstream media ridiculed reporters who questioned Biden's fitness to be president. It would take a disastrous 2024 presidential debate with Donald Trump, which eventually forced Biden to bow out of the presidential race, and subsequently brought the scandal to the forefront of public awareness. Presently, the concealment of Joe Biden's mental infirmities is, in part, a blatant example of media bias. Yet, as with Walter Duranty and Edward Snow, the mainstream media will probably not endure any serious repercussions. Only lost viewership will be the most tangible penalty they will suffer.

Ironically, presidential staffers, Democratic political elites, mainstream media reporters and a host of other bad actors sought to keep secret Joe Biden's mental deficiencies, much in the same way the Soviets kept the lid on Leonid Brezhnev's physical decline. State censorship in the former Soviet Union was to be expected, while private sector censorship in a country that champions the First Amendment is intolerable. When the American main media decides what people should know, the potential to mislead, divert attention, and outright lie becomes a threat to a nation. This is how powerful fake news can be. [45]

My Lai Massacre, versus the Communists' massacre at Hue: Selective rage.

---

45 Pantsov, Alexander & Levine, Steven. Mao: The Real Story. P1,2, 474, 475. Hollander, Paul. The End of Commitment. Duranty: 31-32, Edward Snow; 119. Snow peddled the Mao fabrication that Chinese soldiers would not operate outside the borders of China. Then Mao sent troops into the Korean War in the fall of 1950. Kissinger, Henry. Diplomacy. Pp. 661. Davies, N. No Simple Victory. Pp. 49. Davies, N. Europe. P.965. Acton, Edward. The Past and the Present: Russia. Pp. 176. Vronskaya, Jeanne, and Chuguev, Viktor. (Editors). A Biographical Dictionary of the Soviet Union,1917-1988. pg. 15, 52-3. Andrews, C. Mitrokhin, V. The World was Going our way: The KGB and the Battle for the Third World. Pp. 472. Barron, John. Operation Solo: The FBI's Man in the Kremlin. pp.156, 288-290, 302. Hosking, Geoffrey. Russia and the Russians: A History. Pp. 17-18. 542. Varadarajan, Tunka. "'Original Sin" Review: A Conspiracy in Plain View." Wall Street Journal. May 19,2025. Freeman, James. "Jake Tapper Applauds." Wall Street Journal. May 22, 2025. Strassel, Kimberley. "Who is to Blame for the Biden coverup" Wall Street Journal. May 21, 2025.

Murderous Marxism

Warfare is terrible, and unfortunately, the massacre of innocent civilians happens during conflicts, and the Vietnam War was no different. It was a conflict that divided the United States, and journalists spilled a great deal of ink denouncing American war efforts.

In March of 1968, Americans soldiers opened fire upon unarmed South Vietnamese villagers, killing between 200 to 500 civilians. It would become known as the My Lai massacre. Yet, it was a year before the information on the killings was made public. Once the information was publicized, newspapers and television stations across the country covered every appalling detail. The actions of the American troops were widely condemned. Even today, the My Lai Massacre provokes anguish about America's involvement in Vietnam. Presently, Amazon has over a dozen books on My Lai. Pulitzer Prize winner Seymour Hersh's book, *Cover-Up*, certainly gives the reader an indication of the public's outrage at the U.S. military's concealment of the massacre.

Selective Outrage. Hue Massacres.

Yet it begs the question, where was the liberal outrage at the massacre of civilians by the communists during the Tet Offensive? In January 1968, the North Vietnamese Army (NVA) and the South Vietnamese communist insurgents, the Viet Cong launched a massive surprise attack against US and South Vietnamese forces, the Tet Offensive. The communists suffered heavy casualties, and the attack was beaten back. The initial success of the attack surprised the American public, who had been led to believe that the Americans and the South Vietnamese were turning the tide and winning the war. The negative publicity undermined the American public's commitment to involvement in Vietnam. Journalist focused on the initial success of the attack, and the lack of military progress by the Americans and their South Vietnamese counterparts. It must be pointed out that very little coverage was given to the massacre of civilians in the city of Hue by the Viet Cong and the NVA units. *The Black Book of Communism* noted that well over 3,000 were murdered. *The Great Big Book of Horrible Things* puts the death toll at 2,800, while "another 3,000… [disappeared and] … were never found." The communists targeted "government officials, teachers, doctors… students…" priests, nuns, and foreign international relief agency workers. There was an attempt to conceal the mass killing by the communists, but mass graves were discovered. Many of the victims had their hands tied behind their backs when they were killed, and some were even buried alive; almost all were noncombatants.

While the US media "underreported" the communist killings at Hue, the massacre was common knowledge throughout South Vietnam. It was probably the primary reason for the mass exodus of South Vietnamese fleeing the country after the fall of Saigon in 1975. People did not want to be murdered by the communists. Yet journalists and liberal historians rarely cover the Hue massacre. If the killing of 200 to 500 villagers at My Lai was bad, was not the murder of between 2,800 to 3,000 civilians, and the disappearance of another 3,000 significantly worse? This is a recurring theme in the American media and US history books. Communist atrocities are downplayed or not covered, and many refuse to acknowledge this awful truth. Selective outrage permeates this subject matter. More history down a memory black hole?

Points to Ponder: The photograph that undermined the war.

It could be debated that one of the most iconic photographs of the Vietnam War probably undermined, in part, the American will to keep fighting in the conflict. The photograph was the killing of a Viet Cong leader on the streets of Saigon by a South Vietnamese general, during the height of the Tet Offensive. The photo captures the split second the bullet struck him in the head. It clearly shows the Viet Cong leader's

Murderous Marxism

contorted face, the recoil of the pistol in the general's hand, and a nearby soldier wincing at hearing the shot. The executed man had been captured by a mass grave that contained the corpses of thirty civilians. He was also suspected of being responsible for the killing of an entire family that were friends of the general. As brutal as the actions of the general were, he was also credited for rallying the local forces and keeping Saigon from falling to the communists. The photo only brought home the brutality of the war and fanned antiwar sentiment.

The photographer, who captured the image, was Eddie Adams, and he would later have the chance to travel with the South Vietnamese General, Nguyen Ngoc Loan. Initially, Adams considered the general to be a "cold, callous killer," but after spending time with Loan, he concluded that, "He... [was]... a product of modern Vietnam at his time." After the fall of Saigon, the general fled to the United States. Loan moved to Washington, DC and opened a small restaurant, but the notorious image caught up with him once again, and he had to shutter his business. In contrast, Adams found fame and fortune, and he won a Pulitzer Prize in 1969. Years later, when Adams heard that Loan had passed away, he noted, 'Two people died in that photograph...' The General killed the Viet Cong; "I killed the general with my camera." Adams was correct; a photograph without context can be misleading. The Vietnam War had many incidences of brutality; Adams just happened to capture the split second the general shot the Viet Cong leader. Few people realize that the Viet Cong murdered between 5800 to 6000 people during the Tet Offensive. None of those split seconds was ever caught on film. Food for thought.[46]

---

46 Maclear devotes almost four pages to the My Lai Massacre, and just one paragraph to the communist massacre at Hue, and his analysis Tet Offensive slaughter was a joke. This is just one example of the bias reporting by journals and historians.

William Johnson

Liberals and other leftists romanticize the Cuban Communists.

The Cuban communist revolution has been highly romanticized over the decades. At the time of the revolution, groups in the United States and South America voiced support for Castro's revolutionaries. Newspapers, such as the *New York Times*, wrote favorably about Castro, and American intellectuals, such as Allen Ginsberg, supported Castro. Even after the revolution turned towards totalitarianism, and more Cubans fled communism, intellectuals, college professors and a host of other apologists could find no fault with Castro and his regime. In 2010, the great-grandson of Alexander Graham Bell, Kendall Myers, was convicted of spying for Cuba for years. Myers, an official in the US State Department, was unrepentant about his role in passing information to the Cubans. He received a life sentence without parole, and his wife, Gwendolyn, received 5 years in prison. Even today, with the multiple failures of this Marxist state, woke NFL player Colin Kaepernick has defended communism in Cuba. It seems that the world

---

Maclear, Michael. The Ten Thousand Day War. Tet Offensive; p. 204-6, 210, Only one paragraph on the killings in Hue; 211, My Lai; 272-276. Courtois, Stephane, et.al. The Black Book of Communism. Tet Offensive and the Massacre in Hue; pp. 572. White, Matthew. The Great Book of Horrible Things. Tet Offensive and Hue; pp. 469-471. "Eddie Adams' Iconic Vietnam War photo: What happened next," BBC News. Online. Jan. 29th, 2018. Kissinger, H. Diplomacy. 656, 670-3. Andrews, C. Mitrokhin, V. The World was Going our way: The KGB and the Battle for the Third World. American anti-war sentiment during the war. The Soviets were gleeful about the antiwar sentiment and the American press's insinuation that US intentions in Vietnam were imperialistic. p. 12-15, 52. Lefeber, Walter. The American Age. 583-585. This historian covers the cumulative negative press from the Vietnam war and its lasting effects. Critical press coverage, when combined with the later publications of mostly unfavorable books, documentaries would have a negative impact on the American psyche, for decades to come. Kennedy, Paul. The Rise and the Fall of the Great Powers. 404, 405,406.

has no shortage of what Lenin supposedly called "useful idiots." [47] (See notes).

CHE Guevara: wild-eyed revolutionary.

"Physician, do no harm," is a guiding principle of medicine. It was a principle, Ernesto "CHE" Guevara, a trained doctor, never embraced. He was tactless, ruthless, and a wild-eyed revolutionary. He was an ardent supporter of the USSR and wanted to replicate the Soviet communist system in Cuba. After the communist victory in Cuba, authorities clamped down on civil liberties. For instance, officials executed a young man for counterrevolutionary activities. He was handing out anti-government leaflets. Dissent could be a death sentence in Castro's new Cuba.

Unfortunately, for decades, less than honest historians have glorified this killer, and in the process, turned CHE into a cultural pop icon. The remarks of this university professor are just one example of delusional social elitists who have propagated this farcical narrative

---

[47]Anderson, Jon. Che Guevara, A Revolutionary Life. P. 292-298, 372, 389. The list of "so-called" intellectuals that detests the USA, and love Castro is quite long. Frances Fitzgerald, a leftist writer, asserted that "'many North American radicals who visit Cuba...have performed a kind of surgery on their critical faculties and reduced their conversation to a kind of baby talk...everything is wonderful, including the elevator that does not work and the rows of Soviet tanks on military parade that are in the "hands of the people."'...Similar examples of self-administered brain surgery have proliferated across. both the West and the Third World. Even Jean-Paul Sartre... [a 20th century philosopher, who had a] ...global reputation for rigorous philosophical analysis, became...incoherent in his hero worship...'" The philosopher wrote a gushing piece praising Castro, which amounted to complete gibberish, and I will not burden the reader. If you would like to read it, please see page 28-29. Andrew, C & Mitrokhin, Vasili. The World Was Going Our Way: The KGB And the Battle for the Third World. Pp. 28-29, 50-52. Aguila stressed that the New York Times article on Castro did more to establish him as a freedom fighter, rather than the ruthless communist dictator he would become. Aguila, Juan m. Del. Cuba: Dilemmas of a Revolution. Pp.35. Revel, Jean. Last Exit to Utopia. Pp. 131.

about CHE Guevara. In 2019, while speaking at a University of California seminar, the professor likened Guevara to Jesus Christ and "a quasi-divine cosmic force." One journalist, who was horrified at the comparison, noted, "It is a sad reflection of the warped moral mirror of our time that... Guevara, a squalid killer and totalitarian tyrant... remains, more than 40 years after his death, an iconic emblem of ignorant idealists the world over."

CHE Guevara, the romanticized version; the guy on the poster and T-shirts.

CHE Guevara is best known for his iconic photograph, the bearded revolutionary, with his slicked-back hair and beret. It conjures up a romantic image of a Cuban revolutionary, but nothing could be further from the truth. The myth that surrounds CHE stems, in part, from his prerevolutionary motorcycle road trip through Latin America, which became the basis for his memoirs, *The Motorcycle Diaries*. His book outlines his experiences during the road trip, which consists of a jumble of philosophical notions and his belief that many of the woes of the southern hemisphere stemmed from the geopolitical actions of the United States. His writings also reveal a racist side of this revolutionary. He disparages people of African descent for their lack of hygiene, and being "indolent," while contributing little to South America culture. If we apply the liberal Marxist WOKE litmus test of zero tolerance for racism, then clearly CHE Guevara should have his myth cancelled, and his historical legacy removed from history books. I doubt this will happen anytime soon.[48]

---

48 . The young man who was executed was part of a Catholic Organization and was philosophically opposed communism. The Motorcycle Diaries, was published, under said title, in the 1990s. Anderson, Jon. Che Guevara, A Revolutionary Life. P. 64, 92, 93, 95, 96-121, 364-365, 436, 415, 416, 722, 750, 784. Courtois, Stephane, et.al. The Black Book

Bias reporting: again.

Christopher Andrew, the historian, who collaborated with Vasily Mitrokhin's two books on the KGB, noted that the New York Times wrote 66 articles condemning civil rights violations in Chile in 1976. The United States had been involved in undermining a Marxist leader, who later died under mysterious circumstances. The Chilean rightest government probably killed thousands. In contrast, Pol Pot's Khmer Rouge committed mass murder, killing between 1.5 to 2 million Cambodians, and this genocide **only warranted four articles** by the New York Times. Bias reporting goes without saying. Probably explains

---

of Communism. p.647-654. Guevara, Ernesto. The Motorcycle Diaries. Ocean Press, Chapter, "His Strange 20th Century, page 2. Online version. Llorente, Elizabeth. "UCLA speaker compares Che Guevara to Jesus Christ" Fox News. April 8, 2019. Andrews, C & Mitrokhin, V. The World Was going our Way: The KGB and the Battle for the Third World. 50, 51. To call Aguila an apologist for Castro, and communism in general, would be an understatement. When commenting, on Castro going back on his word about holding elections, Aguila wrote, "Once Castro discarded the electoral option –on the grounds that such frivolities would divert the masses from greater tasks--…[but]…legitimate resistance could…severely curtail Nonidentification with the direction of the Revolution…" In short, election and democracy are bad, because no one will embrace communism. In another statement, he writes that, "Elections in a one-party state cannot be judged from a competitive democratic standpoint… Cuba's system is one of the most democratic in the world." Democracy usually entails plurality of political opponents from different parties, which are not excluded from running for office. Democracy usually involves compromise; a give and take within the political system. Castro's "give," was to ram communism down the throats of the people, while he took their rights. My head spins when I read the limitless, crazy excuses Aguila makes from Castro's despotism. Cuba is fine, if, you ignore all the civil rights violations and other acts of totalitarianism. Aguila, Juan m. Del. Cuba: Dilemmas of a Revolution. Pp. 13, 15-23, 52, 53. 166. Wright, Thomas. Latin America in the Era of the Cuban Revolution. 22, 23. Burns, Bradford. Latin American: A Concise Interpretive History. 6th ED. Pp. 220. Clayton, L. & Conniff, M. A History of Modern Latin America. Pp. 440, 441, 445, 447, 450-452. Graham, Richard. Independence in Latin America: A Comparative Approach, 2nd ed. p. 149.

why no one knows about the communist wars. More history down the memory black hole? [49]

---

[49] Andrews, C. Mitrokhin, V. The World was Going our Way: The KGB and the Battle for the Third World. p. 87-88.

Chapter 6
Communist countries wage war against each other.

Since 1950, the communist world has tried to promote the notion of Marxist solidarity. A Google search will show propaganda posters of Stalin and Mao shaking hands in harmonious agreement. Other posters show Russian, Asian, and African communists marching in lockstep, pumping their fists into the air in a display of unity. By the early 1960s, diplomatic relations between the two communist superpowers, Soviet Union and China, had begun to fray.

The deterioration of Soviet-Chinese relations had several factors. The primary reason was the Soviet led invasion of Czechoslovakia in 1968. The Chinese were appalled at the invasion of one communist country by another. There were other factors for the diplomatic split. Mao Zedong took exception to the USSR's Nikita Khrushchev's criticizing Stalin's murderous reign. Mao felt that Stalin had the right path for communism. Furthermore, Mao was upset that the Soviet Union had backed out of supplying technology for developing nuclear weaponry. Finally, the Chairman was displeased because he felt China was being treated as a junior partner within the worldwide communist community.

Prague Spring of 1968, the USSR and other Warsaw Pact countries attacked Czechoslovakia for contemplating the liberalizing of laws and the economy. (See Prague Spring Chapter 3: Czechoslovakia)

The undeclared Chinese-Soviet border war.

In 1969, tensions escalated between China and the USSR. Subsequently, these two communist superpowers fought a small, undeclared border war on the Amur River, which separates the two countries. There were numerous incidents of Soviet and Chinese soldiers exchanging gunfire. In one incident, the Soviets fired a limited barrage of small, short-range missiles into China. By 1972, Moscow became so alarmed at the intermittent clashes that it deployed 44 infantry divisions along the 4,500-mile-long border with China.

In contrast, the Soviets had only had 31 divisions facing NATO in Europe. The Soviets also transferred the bulk of their air force from west to east and even contemplated a nuclear attack on China. In one incident, a Soviet diplomat invited an American diplomatic specialist to dine with him. During the meeting, he casually asked how the United States would react to a preemptive nuclear strike against China. American authorities surmised that the Soviets wanted to gauge US reaction to such a drastic strike. The attack never occurred, but it illustrated the deterioration of solidarity between the two communist superpowers.

Communist Vietnam attacks communist Cambodia / Kampuchea.

By the end of 1975, North Vietnam had captured South Vietnam, and in short order, Cambodia, and Laos, both fell to communist forces. It should be noted that North Vietnamese aid had been critical for the communist victory in Cambodia. They had supplied Soviet weaponry to the Khmer Rouge and helped topple the Cambodian government. The Khmer Rouge renamed Cambodia, and it became officially known as

Kampuchea. Subsequently, the Khmer Rouge began slaughtering a large swath of their own population.

It should be noted, that from the 1950s through the late 1960s, North Vietnam had been supported by the Soviets and the Chinese. By 1968, the diplomatic relationship between the communist superpowers had deteriorated. The USSR entered into cooperation pacts with Vietnam, and Cambodia / Kampuchea became a communist satellite of China.

Ba Chuc, the final straw.

While the Khmer Rouge were slaughtering their own population, they started carrying out attacks against Vietnamese border villages, during the mid-1970s. They killed hundreds of unarmed civilians and soldiers. The final straw, which probably sparked the war between the two former communist allies, was the massacre at Ba Chuc. In 1978, the Khmer Rouge killed almost 3,200 civilians in this Vietnamese town located near the Cambodian border. For days, unarmed villagers were slaughtered. The Khmer Rouge killed indiscriminately, shooting, stabbing, slitting throats, and beating people to death. Although there was little to no resistance, they shot people trying to surrender. Women were raped and murdered; their corpses defiled. People who were able to initially evade the Khmer Rouge were hunted down with dogs and murdered. Others were forced to march into Cambodia. The Vietnamese forces were able to track the communist raiders, but the Vietnamese military mostly found piles of corpses. Sources indicate that only 2 or 3 villagers survived the slaughter. This bestial massacre by the Khmer Rouge would not go unanswered. In December of 1978, Vietnam attacked and quickly destroyed the Khmer Rouge forces and occupied Cambodia.

Note* Historians tend to view the swift defeat of the Khmer Rouge as a short war. Afterwards, both the newly liberated Cambodians and the Vietnamese fought a counterinsurgency war against the remnants of the Khmer Rouge.

The 1979 Sino-Vietnamese War.

Although the People's Republic of China (PRC) had supported the North Vietnamese's conquest of South Vietnam, the Chinese were angered by the Vietnamese attack and occupation of Cambodia/Kampuchea. China's leadership had the People's Liberation Army (PLA) attack Vietnam on February 17, 1979. Although the PLA captured Vietnamese territory, the offensive stalled, and the Chinese began retreating towards their own border. The Vietnamese forces battered the Chinese army during their retreat, inflicting numerous casualties on the PLA in roughly one month of fighting. The Vietnamese claimed to have killed and wounded well over 60,000 PLA soldiers, and "destroyed 300 tanks." The Chinese said that 20,000 of their soldiers had been killed or wounded, while they inflicted 50,000 casualties on the Vietnamese. Communist China's last war of aggression ended in failure.

Vietnam fights a Vietnam-like war in Cambodia.

After the Vietnamese drove the Khmer Rouge from power, they became a de facto occupying force in Cambodia. While seen as liberators in 1979, Vietnam began to be seen as occupiers by the 1980s. The Vietnamese found themselves fighting a protracted guerrilla war with small groups of Khmer Rouge fighters along the Cambodian-Thailand border. Ironically, the Khmer Rouge used Thailand as a sanctuary to conduct hit-and-run raids, much in the same way the NVA used Cambodia as a base against South Vietnam! These raids prompted

Vietnam (without consulting the Cambodians) to build a crude, 450-mile bamboo wall to seal off the jungle border between Cambodia and Thailand. The wall was ineffective, and throughout the 1980s, the Vietnamese became bogged down fighting an insurgency war, with no sight of victory over the Khmer Rouge. As the USSR began to economically crumble, the Soviets stopped subsidizing Vietnam's war in Cambodia. By 1989, Vietnam had withdrawn from Cambodia. The Vietnamese have never publicly acknowledged their losses, but casualties have been estimated to be between 25,000- 30,000 killed in action. (See notes below.)

Similarities? What goes around comes around.

The Vietnamese experience in Cambodia mirrored the American (and French) experience in Vietnam. American GIs and the Vietnamese both experienced post-traumatic stress disorder (PTSD), along with substance abuse. One Vietnamese soldier, traumatized by the combat, wrote a book about his experiences in Cambodia, only to have it suppressed by the communist authorities in Vietnam.

The Vietnamese found themselves fighting an elusive foe. Pol Pot's thugs used guerrilla tactics, terrorized Cambodian villages, and raided from bases in Thailand, which violated that country's sovereignty. Sound familiar?

Why have we not heard of these communist wars against each other?

To summarize, in less than half a year, from December 1978 through March of 1979, two wars, the Cambodian-Vietnamese War (or Third Indochina War) and the Sino-Vietnamese War, were both fought almost back-to-back, between three different Asian communist countries, which had been former allies. Yet this history is not common knowledge. As one writer noted, the collapse of Sino-Soviet cooperation resulted in warfare between two communist superpowers. The fallout from this violent split spilled into Indochina and, in part, spawned two more wars and a protracted counterinsurgency war. It was "the other Cold War the West never saw..." It could be argued that the Soviets saved face within the communist world when their surrogate, Vietnam, destroyed China's satellite, Cambodia/Kampuchea, then fought off the People's Liberation Army. In the end, it would be the Soviet Union that would lose. The cost of the Soviets' juggling so many communist insurgencies across the globe would be a primary factor behind the collapse of the USSR in 1991.

PostScript: North Vietnam attributes its victory over South Vietnam to Communist China.

Ironically, the North Vietnamese attributed their victory over South Vietnam, in part, to Communist China. China contributed in many ways, from Mao Zedong's political thought to his strategy on warfare, and to the 30,000 Chinese troops that fought with the North Vietnamese from 1965-1970. Brutal purges in China inspired the Vietnamese to carry out the same type of culling of their own cadres in the 1950s. The North Vietnamese acknowledged that Marx, Mao, Lenin, and Stalin were their role models, and the communist Chinese provided the blueprint to victory. Then the communist allies turned on each other. No honor among thieves. [50]

---

50 Nguyen Minh Quang, "The Bitter Legacy of the 1979 China-Vietnamese War." The Diplomat. February 23, 2017. Internet Ed. Kissinger, Henry. Diplomacy. P.721-722. Ginger, Charles & Madden, April. "The Sino-Soviet Split." History of Communism. pp.1, 112-117. Pantsov, Alexander & Levine, Steven. Mao: The Real Story. Pp. 535-539. Courtois, Stephane, et. al. The Black Book of Communism. p. Prague Spring, 1968, 442-

Murderous Marxism

Warfare between Soviet surrogates, Ethiopia, and Somalia.

The Ogaden War stemmed in part from Somalia's claim to territory within Ethiopia's borders. Historical rivalries over this disputed territory only fueled the animosity between the two African nations. The Soviet Union made the war possible by arming both countries to the teeth. Furthermore, the Soviets' geopolitical goal of trying to dominate the strategic Horn of Africa would be the primary factor in the outbreak of fighting.

Somalia's location on the Horn of Africa made it a strategic region. Whoever controlled this area could dominate trade along the Red Sea shipping lanes, which allowed passage into the Indian Ocean. Initially, in 1972, Somalia signed a treaty with the USSR, and within four years, Soviet weaponry deliveries made "Somalia... the fourth most heavily armed state in sub-Saharan Africa."

445, China- Cambodia, alliance. 465. Laffin, John. Brassey's Dictionary of Battles. pp.99, 118, 484-485. Doyle, Kevin. "Vietnam's forgotten Cambodian War." BBC News. Sept. 14, 2014. Internet. Brooke, James. "Why Did Vietnam Overthrow Khmer Rouge in 1978." Khmer Times. August 7, 2014. Internet. Freeman, Joe & Seangly, Phak. "The forgotten massacre Killing Fields in Vietnam recalled by few" The Phnom Penh Post. April 19, 2013. Pringle, James. "Meanwhile: When the Khmer Rouge came to kill in Vietnam" International Herald Tribune. Published by The New York Times. Jan. 7th, 2004. "Victory over Pol Pot Regime: They died for Cambodia to Revive" Vietnam plus. 2, March 2019. C. Mitrokhin, V. The World was Going our Way: The KGB and the Battle for the Third World. p. 264, 265, 476. Kennedy, Paul. The Rise and the Fall of the Great Powers. Pp. 398, 399, 400, 403, 404, 407. Barron, John. Operation Solo: The FBI's Man in the Kremlin. pp. 122-124, 130-131, 138-139, 170-171. The jungle terrain of Indochina favored protracted irregular-guerrilla warfare. Keegan, John. History of Warfare. Pp. 380. Historian Jean Revel noted that the wall was also supposed to stem the flow of Cambodians fleeing to Thailand. Several times a year, well over 100,000 '" volunteers'" were used to maintain the structure. Revel wrote that workers were "decimated by the working conditions, ... malaria, and undernourishment..." Revel, Jean. Last Exit to Utopia. Pp. 308-309. Morris, Stephen. Why Vietnam Invaded Cambodia. Pp. 5-6, 98-102, 103, 105, 106-108, 110-111, The influence of Soviet Invasion of Czechoslovakia. 143-4, Vietnam aligning with the USSR,152-163, 212, 215-223, 227-228.

Ever ready to seize an opportunity to dominate the Horn of Africa, the USSR hedged their bets. The Soviets had secretly supported the Ethiopian officers who staged a coup, overthrowing the aged Emperor Haile Selassie. One of the ringleaders, Mengistu Haile Mariam, a Marxist military officer, came to dominate Ethiopia through murder and intimidation. He readily accepted Soviet diplomatic missions. By 1977, Mengistu had formed an alliance with the USSR, which caused friction with the Soviets' other sub-Saharan ally, Somalia. The Soviet gamble of trying to build an alliance with Ethiopia and Somalia backfired. As military aid flowed into Ethiopia, it fueled the paranoia of the Somali leader, Siad Barre. As tensions intensified between Ethiopia and Somalia, the Soviets tried to mediate between the two African nations, but to no avail. (See notes.)

By the summer of 1977, the treaty between the USSR and Somalia had lapsed, and Soviet advisers left the African nation. Shortly afterward, Siad Barre led an invasion into Ethiopia. Historian Christopher Andrew and former KGB agent Vasili Mitrokhin concluded that Ethiopia would have been defeated without massive Soviet military aid. The military situation for the Ethiopians was so dire that the Soviets used a tremendous amount of military assets to defeat the Somali attack. From the end of 1977 through the beginning of 1978, the Soviet military delivered 17,000 Cuban soldiers, along with supplies. Soviet military aircraft landed "every twenty minutes over a period of three months..." Communist support clinched Ethiopian victory over Somalia, and Mengistu was now totally aligned with the Soviets and the Cubans. [51]

---

51 Andrew, Christopher, & Mitrokhin, Vasili. The World Was Going Our Way, The KGB and the Battle for The Third World. P.458-459. Courtois, Stephane, et.al. The Black Book of Communism. Pp. 689. White, Matthew. The Great Big Book of Horrible Things.

Murderous Marxism

pp.487-488. The geopolitical situation between the communist bloc and the western powers was complicated. The Soviets had been aligned with Egypt, but the Egyptians broke relations with the USSR in the 1970s. Kennedy, P. The Rise and Fall of the Great Powers. Pp. 394. Kissinger, Henry. Diplomacy. 763. This source covers Cuban intervention in Ethiopia. Aguila, Juan M. del. Cuba Dilemmas of a Revolution. 3rd Ed. Pg.129. The Soviets lavished military aid on Somalia, to pull the African country into the USSR's orbit of influence. The Soviets wanted vital access to critical Somali seaports. LaFeber, Walter. The American Age. Pg. 655. After Mengistu, seized control of Ethiopia, the Soviets aligned themselves with the new tyrant, and in the process, alienated the Somalis. The Somalis had always laid claim to the Ogaden border region, which was part of Ethiopia. Barre took the opportunity to use Soviet weaponry to attack the Ogaden region, and annex it from Ethiopia. By 1977, the USSR "provided Ethiopia with approximately $2.5 billion in arms and services out of $4 billion in signed contracts in return for air and naval access to Ethiopian facilities in support of Soviet operations in the Red Sea and Indian Ocean." "Ethiopia-Somalia: Continuing Military Imbalance in the Ogaden Region." Central Intelligence Agency Intelligent Assessment Paper. August 1983. Pp. iii, iv.

Chapter 7
Conclusions

Points to Ponder: If millions must die for the revolution to succeed, so be it.

Through deed and action, Lenin, Stalin, Mao, the Sung family, and Pol Pot were responsible for the deaths of tens of millions in the name of communism. Others expressed a willingness to murder millions to achieve their Marxist revolutionary goals. On numerous occasions, CHE Guevara stated that he was comfortable with the deaths of millions. During the Greek Civil War, a communist general, Aris Velouchiotes, complained, "We didn't kill enough people." He further noted that, "Revolutions succeed only when rivers run red with blood, and blood has to be spilled if what we are aiming for is the perfectibility of the human race." Ironically, he gave his own blood, when he was killed several months later after voicing his apocalyptic opinion. Finally, we have the leader of Sendero Luminoso, the philosophy professor, Abimael Guzmán. Guzman had been referred to as "the fourth sword of Marxism (after Marx, Lenin, and Mao) ... [and he asserted] ... that 'the triumph of... revolution... [would]... cost a million lives." It has always amazed me that these self-appointed guardians of the working class display a willingness to sacrifice millions of innocent people to achieve their Marxist utopia.[52]

---

52 Courtois, Stephane, et.al. The Black Book on Communism. Pp. 328, 675-681. Laffin, John. Brassey's Dictionary of Battles. Pp.496. Andrew, C. & Mitrokhin, V. The

The USSR: The Nexus of Evil.

During his presidency, Ronald Reagan called the Soviet Union the "Evil Empire." Reagan was derided by critics, who accused him of using confrontational language during the height of the Cold War. The 40th president never backed down from his critics.

From the moment the Bolsheviks gained controlled of the old Czarist Empire, they tried to export communism to every part of the world. Furthermore, apologists for the Soviet Union downplayed the brutal nature of this former totalitarian regime. Throughout this book, I have made the case that the former Soviet Union and other communist regimes had a blood-drenched history and were a threat to other democracies. One fact that is irrefutable, when the USSR's command economy started to falter in the late 1980s, it could no longer hold together their vast coercive system. The Soviets had invaded Afghanistan in 1979, but the lack of military progress and the economic decline of the USSR forced them to withdraw in 1989. Between 1989 and 1990, the "Iron Curtain" collapsed and Eastern European nations became free. As Soviet aid ceased to flow to other communist regimes across the globe, they too soon collapsed. In Africa, the murderous communist regime in Ethiopia collapsed, along with the Soviet backed regimes in Angola and Mozambique by 1991. In Central America, the communist Sandinistas had to submit to popular elections and lost. Although the communists in Cuba are still hanging on, the loss of Soviet aid has ended all their overseas attempts to export communism. Repeated raids by Pol Pot's Khmer Rouge guerrillas prompted the Vietnamese to attack and occupy Cambodia. Consequentially, Vietnam

---

World was Going our Way: The KGB and the Battle for the Third World. pp. 59, footnote 36, p. 513.

had to end its counterinsurgency war against the Khmer Rouge guerrillas, because Moscow could not foot the bill. How can so many Marxist regimes fall apart so quickly if the Soviets were not the nexus connecting these regimes? On Christmas Day, 1991, the former Soviet Union collapsed. The "Evil Empire" was no more. [53]

Marxism, as a political philosophy, and communism as a form of government, are complete failure on both accounts. Marxism might be fine to debate in a classroom, but it is an awful theory that encourages a "Cult of Resentment." It is the stock and trade of this bankrupt political philosophy to gin up hatred by invoking class warfare. Communists magnify the flaws of a nation, while they minimize the achievements of a country. If communism was so wonderful, why did they need censorship, secret police, and prison camps? Why did all the mass murders take place during times of peace? Why did people flee communist countries? Conversely, if the United States is such a rotten country, why do so many come to America? If WOKE people used the same critical lens to analyze communism, it is doubtful anyone would embrace this murderous system. Yet many of these WOKE warriors are still enamored by communism. When I taught at a community college, students would ask me, "If Marxism is so bad, why do you teach about it?" The answer is simple: You must know what wrong looks like.

---

53 Andrew, Christopher, Mitrokhin, Vasily. The World was going our Way: The KGB and the Battle for the Third World. Pp. 417-419, 475-481. White, Matthew. The Great Big Book of Horrible Things. pp.489. Kissinger, Henry. Diplomacy. Pp. 498, 507, 508, 773-774. Wright, Thomas. Latin America in the Era of the Cuban Revolution. Pp. 199. Kennedy, Paul. The Rise and the Fall of the Great Powers. Pp. 397.

Bibliography

-Acheson, Dean. Present at the Creation: My Years in the State Department. (W.W. Norton Co., New York, 1969).

-Acton, Edward. The Present and the Past Russia. (Longman, New York, 1986).

-Aguila, Juan M. Del. Cuba: Dilemmas of a Revolution. (Westview Press, Boulder, Co., 1994)

- Ambrose, Stephen & Sulzberger, C.L. American Heritage: World War II. (Tess Press, New York, 2009).

-Amis, Martin. Koba the Dread: Laughter and the Twenty Million. (Hyperion; New York, 2002).

-Anderson, Jon Lee. Che Guevara: A Revolutionary Life. Revised Edition. (New York, Grove Press, 2010).

-Andrew, Christopher & Mitrokhin Vasili. The Sword and The Shield: The Mitrokhin Archive and the Secret History of the KGB. (Basic Books, New York, 1999).

-Andrew, Christopher & Mitrokhin Vasili. The World Was Going Our Way: The KGB And the Battle for the Third World. (Basic Books, New York, 2005).

-Barron, John. Operation SOLO. (Regnery Publishing, Inc. Washington, DC, 1996).

-Barron, John. KGB: The Secret Work of Soviet Secret Agents. (Reader's Digest Press, New York, 1974).

-Beevor, Anthony. Stalingrad: The Fateful Siege: 1942-1943. (Penguin Books, New York, 1998).

-Beevor, Anthony. The Battle for Spain: The Spanish Civil War, 1936-1939. (Penguin Books, New York, 2006).

-Bridgewater, William, ED., et. al. The Columbia Encyclopedia. 3rd Ed. (Columbia University Press, New York, 1963).

-Burns, Bradford. Latin America: A Concise Interpretive History: 6th ed. (Prentice Hall, Englewood Cliffs, N.J., 1994).

-Conniff, Michael, Clayton, Lawrence. A History of Modern Latin America. (Thomson Wadsworth, Belmont, California, 2005).

-Courtois, Stéphane, et al. (Translated by Jonathan Murphy and Mark Kramer). The Black Book of Communism: Crimes, Terror, Repression. (Cambridge, Massachusetts, Harvard University Press, 1999). -Davies, Norman. Europe: A History. (Harper Perennial, Oxford University Press, 1996).

-Davies, N. No Simple Victory: World War Two in Europe, 1939-1945. (Viking, New York, 2006).

-Dornbach, Alajos. The Secret Trial of Imre Nagy. (Praeger, Westport Conn., 1994).

-Engerman, David. Know Your Enemy: The Rise and Fall of America's Soviet Experts. (Oxford University Press 2009)

-Fairbank, John King. The Great Chinese Revolution 1800-1985. (Harper Perennial, New York, 1987).

-Fleet, Xi Van. Mao's America: A Survivor's Warning. (Center Street, New York, 2023).

-Fugate, Bryan. Operation Barbarossa: Strategy and Tactics on the Eastern Front, 1941. (Presidio, Novato, California, 1984).

-Haynes, John Earl & Klehr, Harvey. In Denial: Historians, Communism & Espionage. (Encounter Books, San Francisco, 2003).

- Hosking, Geoffrey, Russia and the Russians: A History. (Cambridge, Massachusetts, The Belknap Press of Harvard University, 2003).

-Gieseke, Jens. The History of the Stasi. (Berghahn Books, New York, 2014)

-Glinsky, Albert. Theremin: Ether Music and Espionage. (University of Illinois Press, Urbana, 2005)

- Greene, Thomas. Comparative Revolutionary Movements. (Prentice Hall, Englewood Cliffs, New Jersey, 1990).

Haynes, John Earl & Klehr, Harvey. Venona: Decoding Soviet Espionage in America. (Yale University Press, 1999).

-Hingley, Ronald. Joseph Stalin: Man & Legend. (Konecky & Konecky, New York, 1974).

-Hollander, Paul. The End of Commitment: Intellectuals, Revolutionaries and Political Morality. (Chicago, Ivan R. Dee, 2006).

- Jennings, Peter and Brewster, Todd. The Century. (Doubleday, New York, 1998).

- Karavasilis, Niki. The Abducted Greek Children of the Communists: "Paidomazoma." (Rosedog, Jan. 1, 2006)

-Katamidze, Slava. Loyal Comrades, Ruthless Killers: The Secret Services of the USSR 1917-1991. (Lewis International, Inc. London, 2003).

-Keegan, John. A History of Warfare. (Vintage Books, New York, 1993).

- Keegan, John. The First World War. (Alfred Knopf, New York, 1999).

-Kempton, Nicole, Richardson, Nan, Andrew, Nathan, Wu, Henry. Laogai, The Machinery of Repression in China. (Umbrage Editions, 2009). PDF. Version.

-Kennedy, Paul. The Rise and Fall of the Great Powers. (Vintage Books, New York, 1989).

-Kissinger, Henry. Diplomacy. (Simon & Schuster, New York, 1994).

-Jones, Steve. In The Blood: God, Genes, and Destiny. (Harper Collins, London, 1996).

-LaFeber, Walter. United States Foreign Policy at Home and Abroad since 1750. (W&W Norton & Company, New York, 1989).

-Laffin, John. Brassey's Dictionary of Battles: 3,500 Years of Conflict, Campaigns, Wars. (Barnes & Noble Books, New York, 1995).

-Li, Dun. The Ageless Chinese: A History. 3rd Ed. (Charles Scribner's Sons, New York, 1978).

-Maclear, Michael. The Ten Thousand Day War: Vietnam: 1945-1975. (Avon Books, New York, 1981).

-Matanle, Ivor, World War II. (Military Press, New York, 1989).

-Marx, Karl & Engels, Friedrich. Manifesto of the Communist Party. (The University of Chicago, Chicago, 1952).

-Medvedev, Roy. Let History Judge. (Columbia University Press, New York, 1989).

- Medvedev, Roy & Zhores. The Unknown Stalin. (Overlook Press, New York, 2003).

- Merridale, Catherine. Lenin on the Train. (Penguin House, United Kingdom, 2016).

-Merridale, Catherine. Night of Stone. (Viking Adult, New York, 2001).

-Montefiore, Simon Sebag. Stalin: The Court of the Red Tsar. (Alfred A. Knopf, New York, 2003).

-Moore, Charles. Margaret Thatcher the Authorized Biography. (Vintage Books, New York, 2015).

-Moore, Jonathan. Hung, Drawn and Quartered. (Metro Books, New York, 2017).

-Morris, Stephen. Why Vietnam Invaded Cambodia. (Stanford University Press, Stanford, California, 1999).

-Nelson, Rebecca. Ed. The Handy History Answer Book. (Visible Ink Press, Detroit, 1999).

-Nicholls, C.S. (ed). Power: A Political History of The Twentieth Century. (New York: Oxford University Press. 1990).

-Ngo, Andy. Unmasked: Inside ANTIFA's Radical Plan to Destroy Democracy. (Center Street, New York, 2021).

-Orwell, George, (Eric Blair) 1984. (Books and Coffee Publications, Istanbul, 2021 ed.).

-Pantsov, Alexander & Levine, Steven. Mao: The Real Story. (Simon & Schuster, New York, 2012).

-Radzinsky, Edvard. Stalin: The First in Depth Biography Based on Explosive New Documents From Russia's Secret Archives. (Anchor Books, New York, 1997).

-Radzinsky, Edvard. The Last Tsar: The Life and Death of Nicholas II. (Doubleday, New York, 1992).

-Reader, John. Africa: A Biography of the Continent. ((Alfred A. Knopf, New York, 1998).

-Revel, Jean-François. Last Exit to Utopia. (New York, Encounter Books, 2000).

-Sánchez, Reinaldo Juan. The Double Life of Fidel Castro. My 17 Years As Personal Bodyguard To El Lider Maximo. (New York, St. Martin's Griffin, 2014).

-Schecter, Jerrold & Luchkov. Translated and Edited. Khrushchev Remembers: The Glasnost Tapes. (Little, Brown and Company, Boston, 1990).

-Shakespeare, William. The Complete Works of Shakespeare. (Grolier, Inc. New York, 1958).

-Shifrin, Avraham. First Guidebook to the Prisons and Concentration Camps of the Soviet Union. (Bantam Books, New York, 1982). PDF Version.

-Shirer, William. The Rise and Fall of the Third Reich. (Fawcett Books, Greenwich, Conn., 1959).

-Smith, Charles. Palestine and the Arab-Israeli Conflict: A History with Documents. (Boston, Bedford / St. Martin's, 2013).

-Solzhenitsyn, Alexander. The GULAG Archipelago, 1918-1956. (Westview Press, Boulder, Colorado, 1973).

-Spector, Ronald. In The Ruins of Empire. (Random House, New York, 2007).

-Stokesbury, James. A Short History of World War II. (William Morrow and Company, Inc., New York, 1980.)

-Sullivan, Rosemary. Stalin's Daughter. (Harper Perennial, New York, 2016).

- Toland, John. The Rising Sun: The Decline and Fall of the Japanese Empire. (Bantam Books, New York, 1971).

- Ungerleider, Steven. Faust's Gold. Inside the East German Doping Machine. (New York, St. Martin's Press, 2001).

- Vronskaya, Jeanne, and Chuguev, Viktor. (Editors). A Biographical Dictionary of the Soviet Union,1917-1988. (K.G. Saur: New York, 1989).

-Wickham, Chris. The Inheritance of Rome. (Viking, New York, 2009).

-Willmott, H.P. World War I. (Dorling Kindersley Publishing, Inc. New York, 2006).

-White, Matthew. The Great Big Book of Horrible Things. (W. W. Norton & Company LTD. New York, 2012).

-Wright, Thomas. Latin America in the Era of the Cuban Revolution. (Praeger, New York, 1991).

-Young, Peter Brigadier Editor. Atlas of the Second World War. (Berkley Publishing Corp., New York, 1974).

Printed Newspaper and Magazines.

-Associated Press. "Files shown on Stalin henchman," Reprinted in: The News & Observer. Jan. 18, 2003, p. 16A.

- "Shoot To Kill" Editorial. Wall Street Journal. August 17, 2007. A # 12.

-National Geographic, Vol. 178, No. 5. "The Baltic Nations". November 1990.

- Perez, Evan. "Spy for Cuba, Unrepentant, Gets Life." Wall Street Journal. July 17, 2010.

- Ginger, Charles & Madden, April, et. al. History of Communism. 3rd ED. (Future Publishing Limited, London, 2021.)

-Satter, David. "100 Years of Communism- and a 100 Million Dead." Wall Street Journal. 11/7/2017. Pp. A17.

VIDEOS

-China in Focus video channel. "How communism killed 80 million in China: Chinese Communist Party at 100 years. NTD. (New Tang Dynasty). I did not include this video, but it certainly casts doubt on the official death tolls in communist China. #EpochTV http://ept.ms/3enuN71

-Simon Whistler. "Lavrentiy Beria: Stalin's Architect of Terror." Biographics. Video: YouTube.

-Anastasia. Walt Disney; Movie. 1997.

-Goodfellas: Movie. 1990.

-Matt Walsh's video, *What is a Woman?* 2023.

-National Treasure 2004.

- Elini CBS Productions, 1985.

ONLINE EDITIONS

- Bartrop, Paul. Cambodian Genocide: The Essential Reference Guide. ISBN. 9781440876547. Retrieved Jan. 25, 2022.https://www.google.com/search?q=Bartrop%2C+Paul.+Cambodian+Genocide%3A+The+Essential+Reference+Guide.&rlz=1C1GCEU_enUS1074US1078&oq=Bartrop%2C+Paul.+Cambodian+Genocide%3A+The+Essential+Reference+Guide.&gs_lcrp=EgZjaHJvbWUyBggAEEUYOTIHCAEQIRiPAjIHCAIQIRiPAtIBCDI1NTBqMG0oqAIAsAIA&sourceid=chrome&ie=UTF-8

-Blauvelt, Timothy. Patronage and betrayal in the post-Stalin succession. The strange case of Krumlov and Serov. Communist and Post-Communist Studies,

-Brotherton-Bunch, Elizabeth. "Despite Accusations That It Benefits from Forced Labor in Xinjiang, Nike Remains Committed to China," Alliance For American Manufacturing. Aug. 9th, China Forbes

De Witte, Melissa. "China's Cultural Revolution was a power grab from within the government, not from without, Stanford sociologist finds," Stanford Report. Oct. 29th, 2019. Online https://news.stanford.edu/stories/2019/10/violence-unfolded-chinas-cultural-revolution

-Isakowitz, Mark. VP, Government Affairs & Public Policy, US., & Canada Google LLC. Letter to Senator Rodger Marshall. Aug. 12, 2024.
https://static.foxbusiness.com/foxbusiness.com/content/uploads/2024/08/Senator-Marshall-Response-Autocomplete-08-2024.pdf

-Lynn, Andrew. "Cultural Marxism." The Hedgehog Review. ONLINE Fall 2018. https://hedgehogreview.com/issues/the-evening-of-life/articles/cultural-marxism

- MCCA Report on the 2020 Protest and Civil Unrest. 2021. PDF. https://majorcitieschiefs.com/wp-content/uploads/2021/01/MCCA-Report-on-the-2020-Protest-and-Civil-Unrest.pdf

- Salisbury, Daniel & Dewey, Karl. "Murder on the Waterloo Bridge: placing the assassination of Georgi Markov in the past and present context, 1970-2018." CONTEMPORARY BRITISH HISTORY; 2023, VOL. 37, NO. 1, 128–156 https://doi.org/10.1080/13619462.2022.2160707© 2023 https://www.tandfonline.com/doi/full/10.1080/13619462.2022.2160707#abstract

- Shifrin, Avraham. The First Guidebook to Prisons and Concentration Camps of the Soviet Union. (Bantam Books, New York, 1982). PDF downloaded.

- Trotsky, Leon. "Publication of Secret Treaties," Izvestiia, No. 221, Nov. 23, 1917. https://archive.org/stream/russianrevolutio011007mbp/russianrevolutio011007mbp_djvu.txt

-Utracka, Katarzyna. "The Phenomenon of the Polish Underground State." The Warsaw Institute Review. December 4th, 2019. Retrieved May 26th, 2023. https://warsawinstitute.org/phenomenon-polish-underground-state/

- Wolek, Karol. "Post-war. The Years of 1944-1963 in Poland." The Warsaw Institute Review. Oct. 1, 2018. Online Ret. https://warsawinstitute.org/post-war-war-years-1944-1963-poland/

- Xiuzhong Xu, Vicky, et. al. "Uyghurs for Sale: 'Re-Education', Forced Labor, and Surveillance" Australian Strategic Policy Institute. March 1, 2020. https://www.aspi.org.au/report/uyghurs-sale

- Online Source Yale: Genocide Studies Program. Cambodia. https://macmillan.yale.edu/gsp

Online News
Sources and Articles

-Bowlby, Chris. "Fritz Haber: Jewish chemist whose work led to Zyklon B" BBC Online. April 12, 2011.

-Brooke, James. "Why Did Vietnam Overthrow the Khmer Rouge in 1978?" Khmer Times. August 7, 2014. Internet. https://www.khmertimeskh.com/50673/why-did-vietnam-overthrow-the-khmer-rouge-in-1978/

-Buck, Daniel. "Woke Education Is Going Strong, Even in Middle America." Wall Street Journal. May 23, 2025. http://www.wsj.com/opinion/woke-education-is-going-strong-even-in-middle-america-schools-sexuality-gender-5d1ccd11

-Bui, Grace. "The Resettlement of Vietnamese and Montagnard Refugees Residing in Thailand," The National Bureau of Asian Research (NBR). Sept. 10, 2022. https://www.nbr.org/publication/the-resettlement-of-vietnamese-and-montagnard-refugees-residing-in-thailand/

-Burns, Tracy. "Milada Horakova, Executed by the Communists." Private Prague Blog. Undated. https://www.private-prague-guide.com/article/milada-horakova/

-Cahill, Paul. "Interesting Histories: Vasily Blokhin-A True Monster." April 18, 2017. https://medium.com/interesting-histories/interesting-histories-vasily-blokhin-a-true-monster-c6180dc78d66.

- Campbell, Sean. "Black Lives Matter Secretly Bought a $6 Million House." New York Magazine: Money, Intelligencer. April 4th, 2022. https://nymag.com/intelligencer/2022/04/black-lives-matter-6-million-dollar-house.html

. Crossette Barbara. "Korean Famine Toll: More Than 2 million." New York Times. Aug. 20, 1999. Sec. A, pg. 6. "Korean+Famine+Toll%3A+More+Than+2+million."+New+York +Times.+Aug.+20%2C+1999.+Sec.+A%2C+pg.+6.+&gs_lcrp=EgZ jaHJvbWUyBggAEEUYOTIHCAEQIRiPAjIHCAIQIRiPAjIHCAMQIRiP AtIBCTYxNDFqMGoxNagCCLACAQ&sourceid=chrome&ie=UTF-8

Donahue, Deidre. "Cambodian Doctor Haing Ngor Turns Actor in the Killing Fields' and Relives His Grisly Past" People.com. Archived from the Original. On 2016-03-03. https://www.google.com/ search?q=donahue%2C+deidre.+%E2%80%9Ccambodian+docto r+haing+ngor+turns+actor+in+the+killing+fields%E2%80%99 +and+relives+his+grisly+past%E2%80%9D+people.com.com&rl z=1C1GCEU_enUS1074US1078&oq=Donahue%2C+Deidre.+%E2% 80%9CCambodian+Doctor+Haing+Ngor+Turns+Actor+in+the+K illing+Fields%E2%80%99+and+Relives+His+Grisly+Past%E2% 80%9D+People.com.&gs_lcrp=EgZjaHJvbWUqBwgDECEYjwIyBgg AEEUYOTIHCAEQIRiPAjIHCAIQIRiPAjIHCAMQIRiPAtIBCDczNTJq MGo5qAIAsAIB&sourceid=chrome&ie=UTF-8

-Central Intelligence Agency. "Motivations for the use of Chemical Weapons in Afghanistan and Southeast Asia" An Intelligence Assessment. (SECRET SOV 83-10005x, January 1983. COPY 484.) Approved For Release 2008/04/15.

-Darnton, Nina. "Eleni' Enshrines on Film a Mother's Legacy of Love." New York Times. Oct. 27, 1985. https://www.google.com/search?q=Darnton%2C+Nina.+%E2%80%9C%E2%80%99Eleni%E2%80%99+Enshrines+on+Film+a+Mother%E2%80%99s+Legacy+of+Love.%E2%80%9D+New+York+Times.+Oct.+27%2C+1985.&rlz=1C1GCEU_enUS1074US1078&oq=Darnton%2C+Nina.+%E2%80%9C%E2%80%99Eleni%E2%80%99+Enshrines+on+Film+a+Mother%E2%80%99s+Legacy+of+Love.%E2%80%9D+New+York+Times.+Oct.+27%2C+1985.&gs_lcrp=EgZjaHJvbWUyBggAEEUYOTIHCAEQIRiPAjIHCAIQIRiPAjIHCAMQIRiPAtIBCTQ1OTNqMGoxNagCCLACAQ&sourceid=chrome&ie=UTF-8

- Doering, Detmar. "Milada Horakova – A Victim of Two Dictatorships." Friedrich Naumann Foundation (For Freedom). June 27, 2020. https://www.freiheit.org/central-europe-and-baltic-states/milada-horakova-victim-two-dictatorships

-Doyle, Kevin. "Vietnam's forgotten Cambodian War." BBC News. Sept. 14, 2014. https://www.bbc.com/news/world-asia-29106034

- Dunn, Morgan. "How Josef Stalin's Favorite Executioner Personally Killed 7,000 Poles During the Katyn Massacre." All That's Interesting. ATI ATI. Dec. 14, 2020. https://allthatsinteresting.com/vasily-blokhin

- Ebert, Rodger (March 24, 1985). The Day Haing S. Ngor won the Oscar." RogerEbert.com.

- Everts, Sarah. "A Brief History of Chemical War." Science History Institute Museum & Library.

May 12, 2015. http://www.sciencehistory.org

-Flood, Brian. Parents Defending Education leader says Chinese Communist influence on American schools is deeply troubling," Fox News. Sept. 12, 2023. Flood%2C+Brian.+Parents+Defending+Education+leader+says+Chinese+Communist+influence+on+American+schools+is+deeply+troubling"+Fox+News.+Sept.+12%2C+2023.&rlz=1C1GCEU_enUS1074US1078&oq=Flood%2C+Brian.+Parents+Defending+Education+leader+says+Chinese+Communist+influence+on+American+schools+is+deeply+troubling"+Fox+News.+Sept.+12%2C+2023.&gs_lcrp=EgZjaHJvbWUyBggAEEUYOdIBCDE5NDBqMG0oqAIAsAIA&sourceid=chrome&ie=UTF-8

- Freeman, James. "Jake Tapper Applauds." Wall Street Journal. May 22, 2025. http://www.wsj.com/opinion/jake-tapper-applauds-8dac0212

-Friedrichs, Rebecca. "Why America's kids are hip to BLM and LGBT but are failing ABC and 123." Fox News. Feb. 12, 2024. https://www.foxnews.com/opinion/americas-kids-lgbt-failing

- Fodor, Denis & Reddy, John. "How I escaped from Cuba in the wheel well of a jet." Reader's Digest Online. Updated: Nov. 4th, 2022. https://www.rd.com/article/escape-from-cuba-dc-8/

-Fontova, Humberto. "Desperately Fleeing Cuba's Free and Fabulous Healthcare." Breitbart.com. July 17, 2001. https://www.google.com/search?q=Fontova%2C+Humberto.+%E2%80%9CDesperately+Fleeing+Cuba%E2%80%99s+Free+and+Fabulous+Healthcare.%E2%80%9D&rlz=1C1GCEU_enUS1074US1078&oq=Fontova%2C+Humberto.+%E2%80%9CDesperately+Fleeing+Cuba%E2%80%99s+Free+and+Fabulous+Healthcare.%E2%80%9D+

&gs_lcrp=EgZjaHJvbWUyBggAEEUYOdIBCTI5NTZqMG0xNagCCL
ACAQ&sourceid=chrome&ie=UTF-8

-Fontova, Humberto. "Dying to Escape Socialism." Front Page Magazine. Feb. 8, 2023. https://www.frontpagemag.com/dying-to-escape-socialism/

- Gallagher, Mike. "Time for Accountability on the Covid Lab-leak Coverup." Wall Street Journal. April 15, 2025. http://www.wsj.com/opinion/time-for-accountability-on-the-covid-lab-leak-coverup-fauci-gain-of-function-194730d4

- Gardener, Frank, et. al. "Wagner chief Yevgeny Prigozhin presumed dead after Russia plane crash." BBC News. Aug. 23, 2023. Sept. 15, 2023. https://www.bbc.com/news/world-europe-66599733

- Gaskins, Kayla. "BLM finances under fire: Only 33% of donations given to charities as execs paid millions" The National Desk. May 31, 2023. blm-finances-under-fire-only-33-of-donations-given-to-charities-as-execs-paid-millions-black-lives-matter-racism-bankruptcy-deficit-fundraising-fundraisers-george-floyd-breonna-taylor-patrisse-cullors-tamir-rice-fraud-scam

- Gordon, Michael, Strobel, Warren. "Behind Closed Doors: The Spy-World Scientists Who Argued Covid was a Lab Leak." Wall Street Journal. Dec. 26, 2024. http://www.wsj.com/politics/national-security/fbi-covid-19-pandemic-lab-leak-theory-dfbd8a51

- Grossman, Hannah. "Colorado teacher calls for 'FORCEFUL cultural revolution' targeted at 'whiteness': 'This is sacred'" Fox

News. May 18, 2023." https://www.foxnews.com/media/colorado-teacher-calls-for-forceful-cultural-revolution-targeted-at-whiteness-this-sacred

-Grossman, Hannah. Marxist teacher who called for 'forceful cultural revolution' lands seat on state legislature," Fox News. August 28, 2023. https://www.foxnews.com/media/marxist-who-called-for-forceful-cultural-revolution-lands-seat-on-state-legislature

-Hauser, Christine. "Christopher Columbus Statues Removed From 2 Chicago Parks." The New York Times. July 24, 2020. https://www.nytimes.com/2020/07/24/us/christopher-columbus-chicago.html

-Herlihy, Brianna. "Oklahoma schools chief to announce plan to ban DEI in Sooner State's public schools." Fox News. Dec. 21, 2023. https://www.foxnews.com/us/oklahoma-schools-chief-announce-plan-ban-dei-sooner-states-public-schools

-Hill, Bailee. "North Korean defector shocked at what she learned at 'woke' Ivy League school: Brainwashing" Fox News. Feb. 13, 2023. https://www.foxnews.com/media/north-korean-defector-shocked-learned-woke-ivy-league-school-brainwashing

- Hinshaw, Drew & Parkinson, Joe. "Could the U.S. Have Saved Navalny?" Wall Street Journal. August 7, 2025. https://www.wsj.com/world/russia/navalny-secret-plan-death-da19e811?gaa_at=eafs&gaa_n=ASWzDAioJI7_rHD7rO4ZZpidh9UAkLSaG2cdOQ-EGOolWHreYxkSN6sgCaIo&gaa_ts=68a13403&gaa_sig=Lo3NcAR6t89m2CuW1EpybFCThBiPxL4RRbMFokUskExaWoJC_hZhQqenEc-cOBJbabBFvgBHfQDP4WAm1GtUJA%3D%3D

- Hinshaw, Drew, et. al. "Russians Keep Turning Up Dead All Over the World." Wall Street Journal. March 3, 2024. Online. http://www.wsj.com/world/europe/russians-keep-turning-up-dead-all-over-the-world-6acc8990

-Johnson, Julia. "Google execs pressed to testify after admitting Trump assassination attempt search omissions were by design." Fox Business News. August 14, 2024. https://www.foxbusiness.com/politics/google-execs-pressed-testify-after-admitting-trump-assassination-attempt-search-omissions-were-design

- Katz, Brigit. "DNA Analysis Confirms Authenticity of Romanov's Remains," Smithsonian Magazine: Online. July 17, 2018. https://www.smithsonianmag.com/smart-news/dna-analysis-confirms-authenticity-remains-attributed-romanovs-180969674/

-Kennedy Philip. Project coordinator. "How Punch Magazine Changed Everything." Illustration Chronicles. 2016-2023. Partridge, Bernard-Interwar Cartoons Punch Magazine 1938, 12.21.21.687.tif.

-Kingson, Jennifer. "Exclusive: $1 billion-plus riot damage is most expensive in insurance history." AXIOS. Sept 16, 2020. https://www.axios.com/2020/09/16/riots-cost-property-damage

- Kokal, Mitch. BLM Dealing with Founder's Financial Fallout." John Locke Foundations. June 11, 2024. https://www.johnlocke.org/blm-dealing-with-founders-financial-fallout/

- Kole, William. "Statue of Slave kneeling before Lincoln is removed in Boston. Associated Press. Dec. 29, 2020. https://apnews.com/article/05086cb91f02ed4fb0991441f1417f87

-Liefer, Richard. (April 27, 1996). 3 Teens Are Charged with Murder of "Killing Fields' Actor Haing Ngor, Chicago Tribune. Retrieved Sept 15, 2016. https://www.chicagotribune.com/1996/04/27/3-teens-are-charged-with-murder-of-killing-fields-actor-haing-ngor/

-Luscombe, Richard. "Elian Gonzalez poised to be top Cuban lawmaker decades after Florida deportation" The Guardian. Feb. 7th, 2023. https://www.theguardian.com/world/2023/feb/07/elian-gonzalez-cuba-lawmaker

-Mackenzie, Jean. "North Korea: Residents tell BBC of neighbors starving to death." BBC. June 14, 2023. http://www.bbc.com/news/world-asia-65881803

-MacKinnon, Douglas. "Woke bullies rewrite 'Willie Wonka' book and will censor every bit of history and literature... if we let them," Fox News. Feb. 21, 2023. https://www.foxnews.com/opinion/woke-bullies-rewrite-willy-wonka-book-will-censor-every-bit-history-literature-if-we-let-them

-Marcus, David. Google's Gemini AI has a White people problem." Fox News. Feb. 24, 2024. https://www.foxnews.com/opinion/googles-gemini-ai-has-white-people-problem

Matthews, Christopher. "Trump Endorses Covid 'Lab Leak' Theory on Government About the Virus." Wall Street Journal. April 19, 2025. http://www.wsj.com/world/china/trump-endorses-covid-lab-leak-theory-on-goverment-websites-about-the-virus-8300dd3c

-Mistreanu, Simina. "Study Links Nike, Addias and Apple to Forced Uighur Labor. Editors' Pick. March 2, 2020. https://www.forbes.com/sites/siminamistreanu/2020/03/02/study-links-nike-adidas-and-apple-to-forced-uighur-labor/

-Natsios, Andrew. "The Politics of Famine in North Korea." United States Institute of Peace. Aug.2, 1999. https://www.usip.org/publications/1999/08/politics-famine-north-korea

-Nelsson, Richard. "The poison-tipped umbrella; the death of Georgi Markov in 1978" The Guardian. -From the Bulgarian Archive. Sept. 9, 2020. Retrieved 6/29/2023. https://www.theguardian.com/world/from-the-archive-blog/2020/sep/09/georgi-markov-killed-poisoned-umbrella-london-1978

- Noble, Kenneth B. "Cambodian Physician Who Won an Oscar for Killing Fields' is Slain". The New York Times. (27 February 1996). https://www.nytimes.com/1996/02/27/us/cambodian-physician-who-won-an-oscar-for-killing-fields-is-slain.html

- Norman, Greg. "Putin critic Alexei Navalny dead at 47, Russian officials say... " Fox News." Feb. 16, 2024. https://www.foxnews.com/world/putin-critic-alexei-navalny-dead-47-russian-officials-say

- Nguyen Minh Quang, "The Bitter Legacy of the 1979 China-Vietnamese War." The Diplomat. February 23, 2017. Internet Ed. https://thediplomat.com/2017/02/the-bitter-legacy-of-the-1979-china-vietnam-war/

- Ochab, Dr. Ewelina "U.N. Concerned about Organ Harvesting in China." Forbes. Downloaded Dec. 18, 2022 https://www.forbes.com/sites/ewelinaochab/2021/07/08/united-nations-concerned-about-organ-harvesting-in-china/

-Olivastro, Andrew, Gonzales, Mike. "Like the Soviets, Black Lives Matter Purges Its History" The American Heritage. Sept. 23, 2020. Retrieved Jan. 1st, 2023. https://www.heritage.org/progressivism/commentary/the-soviets-black-lives-matter-purges-its-history

-Parks, Kristine. Arizona Republican whose family fled communist regime says some Americans ignore ideology's atrocities." Fox News. Feb. 5th 2024. Parks, Kristine. Arizona Republican whose family fled communist regime says some Americans ignore ideology's atrocities." Fox News

-Pengelly, Martin. "Frederick Douglass statue torn down on anniversary of the great speech." The Guardian. July 6th, 2020. https://www.theguardian.com/us-news/2020/jul/06/frederick-douglass-statue-torn-down-rochester-new-york-anniversary-july-4-speech

- Pringle, James. "Meanwhile: When the Khmer Rouge came to kill in Vietnam" International Herald Tribune. Published by The New York Times. Jan. 7th, 2004. https://www.nytimes.com/2004/01/07/opinion/meanwhile-when-the-khmer-rouge-came-to-kill-in-vietnam.html

-Post, Colin. "15 more rescued from second Shining Path 'production camp'" Peru Reports. August 2, 2015. https://perureports.com/15-more-rescued-from-second-shining-path-production-camp/1869/

- Pogrebin, Robin. "Roosevelt Statue to Be Removed from Museum of Natural History." The New York Times. Jan. 19, 2022. https://www.nytimes.com/2020/06/21/arts/design/roosevelt-statue-to-be-removed-from-museum-of-natural-history.html

-Rengifo-Keller, Lucas. "Food Insecurity in North Korea is at its worst since the 1990s Famine." 38 North: Informed Analysis of North Korea. Jan. 19, 2023. http://www.38north.org/2023/01/food-insecurity-in-north-korea-is-at-its-worst-since-the-1990s-famine/

- Roos, Dave. "'Blood in the Water': The Cold War Olympic Showdown Between Hungary and the USSR." The History Channel. June 4th, 2021. Roos, Dave. "'Blood in the Water': The Cold War Olympic Showdown Between Hungary and the USSR.

- Roth, Andrew. "The Mysterious, violent and unsolved deaths of Putin's foes and critics." The Guardian. Feb. 16, 2024. https://www.theguardian.com/world/2024/feb/16/the-mysterious-violent-and-unsolved-deaths-of-putins-foes-and-critics-alexi-navalny

- Sang-Hun, Choe. "North Korea Executes People for Watching, Rights Group Says..." The New York Times. Dec. 15, 2021. https://www.nytimes.com/2021/12/15/world/asia/north-korea-kpop-executions.html

-Sedacca, Matthew. North Koreans dying of Starvation following COVID isolation measures. US. News. June 17, 2023. http://nypost.com/2023/06/17/north-koreans-are-dying-of-starvation-report/

- Smith, Gayle. "Ethiopia and the Politics of Famine Relief," *Middle East Report* 145 (March/April 1987). https://merip.org/1987/03/ethiopia-and-the-politics-of-famine-relief/

- Smith, Saphora. "China forcefully harvests organs from detainees, tribunal concludes." NBC, World. June 18th, 2019. https://www.google.com/search?q=Smith%2C+Saphora.+%E2%80%9CChina+forcefully+harvests+organs+from+detainees%2C+tribunal+concludes.%E2%80%9D+NBC%2C+World.+June+18th%2C+2019.&rlz=1C1GCEU_enUS1074US1078&oq=Smith%2C+Saphora.+%E2%80%9CChina+forcefully+harvests+organs+from+detainees%2C+tribunal+concludes.%E2%80%9D+NBC%2C+World.+June+18th%2C+2019.&gs_lcrp=EgZjaHJvbWUyBggAEEUYOTIHCAEQIRiPAjIHCAIQIRiPAjIHCAMQIRiPAtIBCDM5MjlqMG0oqAIAsAIA&sourceid=chrome&ie=UTF-8

- Soloman, Alex. "YCL in 2024: Fighting Fascism at Home and Abroad." Communist Party: USA, ONLINE. Dec. 3, 2024. https://www.google.com/search?q=Soloman%2C+Alex.+%E2%80%9CYCL+in+2024%3A+Fighting+Fascism+at+Home+and+Abroad.%E2%80%9D&rlz=1C1GCEU_enUS1074US1078&oq=Soloman%2C+Alex.+%E2%80%9CYCL+in+2024%3A+Fighting+Fascism+at+Home+and+Abroad.%E2%80%9D&gs_lcrp=EgZjaHJvbWUyBggAEEUYOTIHCAEQIRiPAjIHCAIQIRiPAtIBCDI4NjBqMG05qAIAsAIA&sourceid=chrome&ie=UTF-8

- Strassel, Kimberley. "Who is to blame for the Biden cover-up?" Wall Street Journal. May 21, 2025. http://www.wsj.com/opinion/ who-to-blame-for-the-biden-coverup-ec8307a8

-Tiedemann, Garrett. "A History of the Theremin in Movie Music." Your Classical Radio. July 15, 2016. http://www.yourclassical.org/story/2016/07/15/theremin-movie-music

- Varadarajan, Tunka. "Original Sin" Review: A Conspiracy in Plain View." Wall Street Journal. May 19, 2025. http://www.wsj.com/arts-culture/books/original-sin-review-a-conspiracy-in-plain-view-855e7729

- Villasanta, Arthur. "Kim Jong Un Net Worth: How Is North Korea's Leader Spending His Billions?" International Business Times, World. May 23, 2019. https://www.ibtimes.com/kim-jong-un-net-worth-how-north-koreas-leader-spending-his-billions-2794221

-Volodzko, David. "Dear Fremont: We need to talk about Lenin and your statue of the genocidal tyrant." The Seattle Times. July 7, 2023. https://www.seattletimes.com/opinion/dear-fremont-we-need-to-talk-about-lenin-and-your-statue-of-the-genocidal-tyrant/

- Watson, Michelle. "Black Lives Matter executive accused of 'syphoning' $10M from BLM donors, suit says" CNN. Sept. 5th, 2022. https://www.cnn.com/2022/09/04/us/black-lives-matter-executive-lawsuit/index.html

- Werleman, CJ. "Death is Everywhere' Millions More Uyghurs Missing" Byline Times. Aug. 24, 2020. https://bylinetimes.com/2020/08/24/death-is-everywhere-millions-more-uyghurs-missing/

- Williams, Laura. "Ten terrifying facts about the East German Secret Police." FEE Stories. Nov. 14, 2019. https://fee.org/articles/10-terrifying-facts-about-the-east-german-secret-police/

- Yi, Daniel, Krikorian, Greg. "Three Men Convicted of Killing Ngor", Los Angeles Times. April 17, 1998. https://www.latimes.com/archives/la-xpm-1998-apr-17-me-40165-story.html

Online Articles, Without an Author's Name.

-Anonymous. "The Abducted Greek Children." World News and Views, Vol. 29, No. 44. Marxist Internet Archive. January 2, 1950. https://www.marxists.org/subject/greek-civil-war/1950/01/21a.htm

-African Union. AUHRM Project Focus Area: Ethiopian Red Terror. ONLINE 2024. https://au.int/en/auhrm-project-focus-area-ethiopian-red-terror

-Britain: The Poisonous Umbrella." Time. 1978. Retrieved 6/29/2023. https://time.com/archive/6850185/britain-the-poisonous-umbrella/

- "Cult of Resentment." Prager University.

-Eddie Adams' Iconic Vietnam War photo: What happened next," BBC News. Online. Jan. 29th, 2018. https://www.bbc.com/news/world-us-canada-42864421

-Ethiopia-Somalia: Continuing Military Imbalance in the Ogaden Region." Central Intelligence Agency Intelligent Assessment Paper. August 1983. Released 9/2/2011. Online. https://www.cia.gov/readingroom/docs/CIA-RDP84S00552R000300100003-4.pdf

-Evil Days. *30 Years of War and Famine in Ethiopia*. "An Africa Watch Report". Sept. 1991. https://ia601601.us.archive.org/35/items/bub_gb_RcVFXUwraxsC/bub_gb_RcVFXUwraxsC.pdf

- Heroes: Kosmodemyanskaya. Times: Online. March 2, 1942. https://time.com/archive/6770664/heroes-kosmodemyanskaya/

- Ngor, Haing S. Encyclopedia Britannica from The original 2012-07-20. https://www.britannica.com/biography/Haing-S-Ngor

-PBS. The American Experience. The Man behind Hitler: Heinrich Himmler 1900-1945. Article. https://www.pbs.org/wgbh/americanexperience/features/goebbels-himmler/

-Peru rescues 39 'slaves-workers' from Shining Path farm" BBC News. July 28th, 2015. https://www.bbc.com/news/world-latin-america-33697753

- "Stop arming the fascist Netanyahu Regime!" Communist Party USA: http://www.cpusa.org. https://www.cpusa.org/article/stop-arming-the-fascist-netanyahu-regime/

-Vasily Blokhin, history's most prolific executioner. Rare Historical photos. Nov. 23, 2021. Online. https://rarehistoricalphotos.com/vasily-blokhin-executioner/

-"Victory over Pol Pot Regime: They died for Cambodia to Revive" Vietnam plus. 2, March 2019., Retrieved Jan. 28th, 2022. https://en.vietnamplus.vn/victory-over-pol-pot-regime-they-died-for-cambodia-to-revive-post154573.vnp

- "Vietnam's forgotten Cambodian War." BBC News. Sept. 14, 2014. Internet. https://www.bbc.com/news/world-asia-29106034

-United Nations Human Rights: Office of The High Commissioner; Media Center. China: "UN human rights experts alarmed by 'organ harvesting' allegations." June 14th, 2021. United Nations. https://www.ohchr.org/en/press-releases/2021/06/china-un-human-rights-experts-alarmed-organ-harvesting-allegations

-U.S Department of Labor. Bureau of International Labor Affairs; Against Their Will, The Situation in Xinjiang. Sept. 4th, 2018. https://www.dol.gov/agencies/ilab/against-their-will-the-situation-in-xinjiang

- "Who are the Uighurs and why is China being accused of Genocide?" BBC, May 24th, 2020. https://www.bbc.com/news/world-asia-china-22278037

www.ingramcontent.com/pod-product-compliance
Lightning Source LLC
Chambersburg PA
CBHW032033150426
43194CB00006B/264